Workers and Automation

Workers and Automation

The Impact of New Technology in the Newspaper Industry

Ranabir Samaddar

SAGE PUBLICATIONS
New Delhi/Thousand Oaks/London

To Krishna

First published in 1994 by

Sage Publications India Pvt Ltd
M-32, Greater Kailash Market-I
New Delhi 110 048

Sage Publications Inc
2455 Teller Road
Thousand Oaks, California 91320

Sage Publications Ltd
6 Bonhill Street
London EC2A 4PU

Published by Tejeshwar Singh for Sage Publications India Pvt Ltd, phototypeset by Pagewell Photosetters, Pondicherry, and printed at **Print Perfect, New Delhi.**

Library of Congress Cataloging-in-Publication Data

Samāddāra, Ranabīra.
    Workers and automation: the impact of new technology in the newspaper industry / Ranabir Samaddar.
        p.   cm.
    Includes bibliographical references and index.
    1. Newspaper publishing—Automation. 2. Newspaper publishing—India. 3. Newspaper employees—India. I. Title.
    PN4784.E5S26   331.25—dc20   1994   94–7772

ISBN: 0–8039–9174–6 (US-hb)
        81–7036–401–9 (India-hb)

Contents

List of Tables

Preface

Today, one more Wage Board for the newspaper industry is being appointed. The forms and issues of the new trade union movement, which I have discussed in this book, sometimes speculatively, are becoming clearer with movements like that of the Kanoria Jute Mill situated a few miles away from the metropolis of Calcutta. Yet, I increasingly realise, as I look again at the pages of the manuscript lying before me, that this book has remained a halfway one. I intended to write on technology, and its impact on labour in the Indian newspaper industry. I discern a shift somewhere in the middle of the book. I felt I should discuss at length the impact of technology on the wage settlement process, the relevance of the structure of industrial relations and how management, by developing and maintaining hierarchical work arrangements and an organisation of work that dominates the worker, successfully introduces a new technology. I find my concluding note remains unresolved: should I have emphasised more the structure of relations between capital and labour, or should I have delved more into the subjectivity of labour in its response to technology? I could probably have shown, had I opted for the second course, how labour has an impact on technology, and in some cases decisively. The circle would then have been complete. Beginning with an exploration of the impact of technology on labour, the study could have ended with an examination of the impact of labour on the latter!

Definitely, in a way the strikes, resistances and wage board arguments dictated how the bosses in the newspaper industry should proceed with the drive for efficiency, for profitability and for labour control: in short, with modernisation. This, I feel now, has remained underemphasised. It is the same old problem of being much too concerned with capital and not paying adequate attention to exploring the world of labour.

Stephen Marglin's by now classic note 'What do Bosses do? The Origins and Function of Hierarchy in Capitalist Production' emphasised the eminent role of consciousness in the evolution of the division of labour and the factory system. We can stand this forcefully upon its head and ask, 'What Do Workers Do? The Specific Designs and Introduction of New

Technology by the Bosses'. This has been my central enquiry, though I am not sure of the outcome.

I shall explain my feeling of unease with one example. When talking of labour, I talk of unionised labour. And when talking of unionised labour, I talk of the most formalised statements and actions of unionised labour. How could I take one to be the other? The hiatus between the individual worker and the shop floor collectivity of workers, between the shop floor existence of workers and the unionised existence of workers, between the plant level existence of a collectivity and industry level unionisation, and so on, is a phenomenon which labour historians and analysts have to always take into account when reconstructing the world of labour. The labour organisers, of course, know this only too well. Yet, I could do justice to one part of the phenomenon only, namely, the hiatus between the plant level collectivity and industry level unionisation.

There is no doubt that there was a definite emphasis on efficiency when the bosses introduced modernisation. But the thrust for efficiency was an ideological one too. It disarmed the union, which could not deny that the company could and should be more efficient. However, the individual worker in newspaper plants showed more gut reaction. The arguments based on rationality often defeated the unions. Unions would become confused and would be hard put to convince the rank and file workers of the intrinsic rationality in the thrust for efficiency. The particulars of the Taylorist strategy may be long extinct. Workers may not be likened any more to 'more or less of the type of the ox, heavy both mentally and physically,' as Taylor had described his ideal worker. But the thrust for efficiency remains. The ideological thrust and the ideology of thrust have often caught the unions in a pincer-attack. They succumb to its rationality. But they cannot convince the workers.

Thus robbed of its existential ground by the offensive in the form of a campaign for efficiency, at the same time stripped of its legitimacy in the eyes of shop floor level workers because of its capitulation to that ideological thrust, the union in the newspaper industry is neither here, nor there. I am sure unions in other industries, too, face such a predicament. This could have been better studied if the task of examining the subjectivity of labour had gone deep down to the level of the workers. Hiatus and hierarchy remain among the dominant features of capital, even in its contra-realisation.

Yet, if part of my enquiry remains unfulfilled, the rest of this structuralist account certainly deserves a few introductory remarks. In discussing new technology, the enquiry is imperative: how do social power and political authority remain connected in the context of a factory, plant or company? If political authority processes and transforms power relations in a modern factory, I have shown that power relations aided and abetted by modernisation can define political authority too. It can announce, in most emphatic terms, the political victory of bosses over the workers. This political victory dispels the 'pluralist' and 'dispersed' notions of power inherent in ideas of company unionism, new syndicalism, and so on. However, the older currency of monolithic political trade unionism that never took into account the dynamics of the labour process is also of no use today.

For a study like this, I could not but be indebted to many people. My foremost debt is to Jayanta Dasgupta, the most dogged organiser of workers and employees of the *Statesman*. I gained from interminable rounds of discussions with him. Pickets and strikes, processions and sit-ins—our relationship has been beyond intellectual comradeship. In a sense I owe this book to him. To K.L. Kapur, the General Secretary of the All India Newspaper Employees' Federation, I also remain heavily indebted. Without him I could not have had access to Federation literature, as well as an idea of how the Federation's mind was working in those days. Similarly, to the late S.Y. Kolhatkar, the Federation's President, I remain grateful. Amulya Bhattacharya, ex-President of the Statesman Employees' Union who was thrown out of work, never had much faith in academic research on modernisation. He was convinced of the ultimate power of modernisation. With almost benign care, he would speak his mind to me. Yet, with his dismissal, I have been rudely awakened as never before to the reality of power in a modern plant. There are others too who helped me with utmost cooperation. S. Franswah, Chenna Basappa Bapuri, K. Rammurthi, N. Sawant and Deben Ganguly—to all these persons I remain indebted. And to nameless others, who would throng the union offices where I would be sitting and talking, volunteering information for my perusal, I am forever grateful. They are all workers and union militants.

I cannot resist reporting a small incident. I had concluded my visit to a newspaper plant in south India. The union activists had spent much of their time on me. After two days, as I was leaving, a printing worker came forward. He was a union leader. Along with warm words of farewell, he suddenly took out a small packet from his pocket. I sensed from his embarrassment that it must be money. 'Please take it,' he exhorted. 'You are doing this for our sake. You must be requiring money.' Ignorant as he was of the modern ways of social research, where one can be funded for such a study, he would not believe that I had money. 'It is a union decision,' he said, and refused to take the packet back. I did not have the strength to hurt him. On my return to Calcutta, I sent the money to the Federation's office at Delhi with a request that the amount be accepted as their contribution to the fund. Now, at the end of my narrative on modernisation, the managerial thrust for efficiency and workers' resistance in the industry, I feel like asking, in the words of another labour historian of another country, shall this be all?

I could not have undertaken this study without a three year fellowship at the Centre for Studies in Social Sciences, Calcutta. To the Centre and its staff I am deeply grateful. Amiya Bagchi, Nirmala Banerjee, Anjan Ghosh, Partha Chatterjee, Pradip Basu, Debdas Banerjee, Asok Sen, and others at the Centre helped with comments on various chapters. Partha Chatterjee helped me revise the entire manuscript at a difficult time. Pradip Basu went through some chapters and helped me similarly. To them I remain especially grateful. Partha Sarathi Banerjee of the National Institute for Science, Technology and Development Studies, New Delhi, and Ranajit Dasguta of the Indian Institute of Management, Calcutta, helped me with their comments. Michael Swartz, Gerry Rodgers and Laurids Lauridsen provided me with certain insights in their comments and discussions. I am also grateful to the participants at the various seminars, including the staff seminars where I had occasion to present my views.

An earlier version of a chapter of this book has been published in *The Indian Labour Market and Economic Structural Change* (Delhi: B.R. Publishing Corporation, 1994); another will come out in *New Technology and the Workers' Response* (New Delhi: Sage). The publishers and editors of these books are gratefully acknowledged. I am also grateful to the libraries of the Research Institute for Newspaper Development, Madras, and the Institute of Mass Communications, New Delhi.

To Prof. Bagdendu Ganguly, who came forward ten or twelve years ago to gently guide my work on technology along formalised lines of research, I remain eternally indebted.

To Krishna, however, I cannot express my gratitude fully. At her cost this book came to be undertaken and finished. I remain beholden to her in every way.

February 1994   **Ranabir Samaddar**

1

The Story of the Federation Foretold

This work begins with the unionisation of the Indian newspaper workers on an all-India scale. I shall briefly outline the birth and growth of the All India Newspaper Employees' Federation (AINEF). The Federation has also written its own story (AINEF, 1986b). Yet, as we go through it, we shall see that the official story of the Federation, which it has written itself, is an unreal account. The reader is not able to make out from the account that the Federation has written the story of newspaper workers at a *particular* time—the time of technical change. In a way, the story of Indian newspaper workers, as officially narrated, runs parallel to the story of the worker who has been caught in the throes of technological change. However, this official story is a real account also, for it shows how its author—the workers' all India leadership—thought, and in what measure these technological changes influenced the unionised workers' perceptions, decisions and actions. Thus, in order to understand this parallel account, it is imperative that while traversing along the official path, we transgress as well.

However, in making such a start, we are faced with another situation. It is common knowledge, almost a stereotype, in fact, that a union is born of some struggle. Hence the biographer of a union, while narrating the story of the union, feels that it is correct and proper that the account should begin by depicting struggle so that he/she can show how unionisation comes about. There are certainly reasons for such a belief. One is that the primitiveness of the work system forces the workers to get unionised. This idea is probably true, but it is reinforced by half true, strange and almost mythical accounts of the behaviour of 'angry' and 'riotous' workers. For example, one very early account of the birth of trade unions in Bombay states:

> The Union seems to have arisen out of the riotous scenes at the mills on the occasion of the trial and condemnation of Tilak, when mill windows were smashed . . . . The prevailing idea of the coolies was that a Trade Union was a combination for the purpose of fighting and terrorising the masters . . . . The Indian operative is no more fit for Trade Unions than he is for scientific education or even reading and writing . . . .
>
> [But] it is useless today to talk of Trade Unions in India. A workman in this country, when he chooses not to work, does not starve even if he likes to take a three month holiday.[1]

Or

> The millhand is not an easy man to help: he is notoriously unpunctual, careless and destructive in his method of work, and he seems incapable of concentrating his attention for any length of time on his duties . . . . A meeting of Bombay millhands recently expressed their approval of Mr. Gokhale's Education Bill although their ideas on education must have been no clearer than those of the bulk of the Indian people, who believe that the purpose of education is not to make the recipient an honest, capable and intelligent workman, but to raise him above the degradation of manual labour.[2]

There is no reason to dismiss these as merely colonial accounts, for sympathetic accounts also portray unionisation as a process emanating from struggle. But, evidently, the all-India unionisation of printers did not originate from such struggles or riotous scenes at Bombay, Delhi or Calcutta (the major centres of organisation of newspaper workers). Wage bargaining at the industry level and the decision of the Government of India to treat the wage revision issue in the industry as a serious matter meriting its attention through the Journalists Act (1955) provided the impetus for such

[1] *Indian Textile Journal,* Vol. XXI, No. 246: 190–91, quoted in S.D. Punekar and R. Varickayil (1990): 337–38
[2] ibid.: 339.

an organisation. It can be viewed as an uneventful birth which certainly led to an eventful history over three successive decades. Contrary then to the stereotype, we can view this process of unionisation differently: in the context of the labour process and the interaction between the labour process and the process of surplus value production, (that is, the process of valorisation). Considering the process of unionisation as part of the process of labour amounts to viewing the response of labour to the valorisation process as an integral part of the labour process. The Federation's story, then, is not a story of unionisation *per se*, but a story of labour as the active subject in the labour process. This story of the Federation will thus proceed along the lines of an enquiry into the structure of industrial relations. This enquiry may, then, be described as an enquiry into the elementary structures of industrial relations, marked by three processes—the process of valorisation, the process of labour and the process of unionisation. It is, thus, less a human story—though certainly a story of labour, it is most emphatically a story of *collective labour*. As I analyse industrial relations in the newspaper industry and assess the impact of technical change, the Federation's account will spill into it. The entire book thus chronicles the response of the Federation in the critical epoch of modernisation, and the account of the Federation thus goes well beyond this chapter.

Yet, there is a reason why, in this discussion on technical change in the newspaper industry, I start by narrating the biography of the Federation. It is as if the story has been foretold even before the account has properly begun. It serves no purpose denying that many of the things to be narrated later are anticipated by starting with the rise and decline of the Federation. But having foretold the story here like the promoted ending of a chronicle, we shall see that the decline of the Federation in the late eighties had a sense of déjà vu. Personalities, the style of organisation, the state of intra-organisational democracy—all these factors certainly mattered and affected the fate of the Federation.[3] But, given the structure of industrial relations, the might of technological change, and the structured relationships between the labour process and the valorisation process, the near collapse of the Federation was almost a

---

[3] This is how Lipset analysed American newspaper workers; see Lipset, Trow and Coleman (1956).

fait accompli. Why not thus begin this story with the end, pull down the curtains and then see what was enacted before it was over?

According to the official chronicle, the AINEF was founded in 1960. It initially consisted of 16 trade unions of newspaper employees representing 10,000 employees, which included both working journalists and non-journalists. From the very beginning it was ready to identify itself with the broad struggles of the workers and all-India industrial action. In its founding year itself, it joined all-India action in various parts of the country in support of 22 lakh Central Government employees. The Bombay AINEF leader, S.Y. Kolhatkar, then president of the AINEF, was arrested under the Preventive Detention Act, in connection with the strike of newspaper employees in the Times of India and allied publications. It is surprising how the initially strong bastion of the AINEF, Bombay, subsequently turned out to be a weak spot in the AINEF organisation—perhaps because the Bombay unions could not tackle the onslaught of technological modernisation since late seventies (a story to which we shall come later). Nor could the AINEF successfully chalk out an effective tactic in view of the increasing tendency of the unions to strike productivity deals and accept modernisation in all the industries in general and the newspaper industry in particular under the patronage of R.J. Mehta and Datta Samant. Probably this was also because of the fact that the AINEF leadership was partially based at Bombay, and Bombay proved to be a collapsing bed of old-style Left trade unionism of the fifties and sixties which had so far been a curious mixture of demand for wages, bonus, dearness allowance, union recognition, and a little bit of parliamentary politics of the Left.

From 1961 to 1967, the AINEF conducted innumerable struggles for a wage board. In 1961, 11 April was observed as demand day. AINEF delegations and morchas to the President of India and Chief Ministers were conducted throughout 1962–63. Wage boards for journalists and non-journalists were ultimately formed in 1967. Even then their recommendations were not implemented by various employers on the plea that these were of a non-statutory nature. Thus the first all-India token strike of all the newspapers along with news agencies came about on 24 January 1968. This token strike was followed by a continuous strike from 23 July 1968 covering about 65 newspapers. The recommendations of the wage board were implemented to a great extent as a result of the strike, with the aid of arbitration by the government. The AINEF again went on a token strike on 21 March 1973 for wage revision, and this agitation lasted up to 1975, till the government appointed a wage board for both journalists and non-journalists under the chairmanship of a retired judge of the Supreme Court, Justice D.G. Palekar. Thus, the Palekar Wage Boards were the immediate precursors to the wave of computerisation in the newspaper industry. The employers objected in various ways to the functioning of the Board and Tribunal. There were repeated all-India token strikes (for instance, on 9 March 1977, 16 June 1977 and 24 January 1978). Due to stay orders of the Court on the recommendations and functioning of the Boards due to petitions of the employers of the *Indian Express* (which had closed its Delhi establishment) and Bennett and Coleman, the government was forced to change the status of the board to tribunal, which subsequently handed the Palekar Award.

The Palekar verdict, by awarding various benefits to the employees, hastened automation by the employers. A previously under-capitalised industry now resorted to heavy mechanisation and automation. As we shall now see, while throughout these long years, from 1960 to 1978, the AINEF was engaged in protecting and fighting for economic benefits for the workers, it had not prepared itself for the new issues of the post-Palekar phase.

The post-Palekar change in the production process of the newspaper industry came as a surprise to the AINEF leadership. This was not merely due to the sudden introduction of new technology, but due to its old thought process and ideas as well as a total involvement with old style economic demands which left it intellectually defenceless against a completely new technology. Even its association with broad trade union struggles was of the old type and nature, that is, episodic, oriented towards a commonality of economic demands and mainly on the basis of old issues like increased wages. The general picture of anti-automation struggles in other industries in the country after the defeat of the LIC strike was not encouraging. In fact, it was only in 1981–82, when the National Campaign Committee (NCC) was formed as a broad platform of the non-Congress central trade unions and other independent federations, that the AINEF's association with the central trade unions was organised on a regular structured basis, however weak that basis may have been. As the various circulars of the NCC, sent by the AINEF General Secretary K.L. Kapoor to its different units showed, the formation of the NCC encouraged the AINEF in its subsequent anti-rationalisation slogans. This point however does not come out in the official history of the AINEF, brought out by itself (AINEF, 1986b, Chapter 12). Indeed, with Kolhatkar belonging to the CPI(M) and K.L. Kapur, the General Secretary, belonging to the CPI, the political reason for the confusion in the AINEF leadership as to how to cope with the introduction of new technology has to be located in the confusion among the Left groups regarding the issues thrown up by new technology. In the course of the narration of the issues involved in the introduction of new technology, I shall return again and again to this question of political confusion of the AINEF leadership.

However, before dealing with the problem of confusion, let us look at the identity pattern of the AINEF with other trade unions briefly so that we can locate our discussion properly. On 15 May 1974, the all-India newspaper employees went on a token strike in support of the railway workers. In 1982, when the National Campaign Committee of trade unions gave a call for a *Bharat Bandh* on 19 January against price rise, unemployment and the curb on civil and trade union rights, the strike engulfed the newspaper industry as well. On 3 September 1982, there was an all-India token strike against the Bihar Press Bill. Apart from this token strike, numerous rallies and *dharnas* were held in different state capitals against the bill. Against the Essential Services Maintenance Ordinance the newspaper employees observed 17 August 1981 as 'Black Day'. In fact, after the formation of the National Campaign Committee, the AINEF started taking a joint stand on the demands of need-based minimum wage, full neutralisation in the rise of cost of living, ban on retrenchment owing to modernisation, withdrawal of the Essential Services Maintenance Act and National Security Act and reduction in the price of essential commodities. These were the demands raised in the 4 June 1981 National Campaign Committee national convention in Bombay, where the AINEF also actively participated, as well as in the massive Workers' March to Parliament on 23 November 1981. The newspaper workers participated in state level marches too (AINEF, 1986b, Chapter 12).

The way in which the All India Newspaper Employees Federation identified itself with the general struggle of the workers showed that it was mainly at the top where the AINEF made common cause with other sections of the working class, hastened by the formation of the NCC. But at the ground level, at the state and city level, this unity was not evident. One reason could be the structural weakness of the AINEF organisation, as newspaper unions were directly affiliated to the AINEF (the all-India body) and not through state level federations which, in any case, were lacking in most states. Moreover, the Confederation of Working Journalist Unions and News Agency Employees Organisations was also confined to the top. Coordination was mostly around wage board demands and deliberations and was not realised below. The NCC also did not have state level bodies and bodies at other levels.

Thus, in the concrete struggles at the factory level against rationalisation, retrenchment and automation in industries, there was not much solidarity from newspaper workers; particularly in strikes like the Bombay textile strike and the jute strike, the rank and file newspaper workers did not join. The result was that due to the absence of solidarity with other plant level struggles against modernisation, the general effects of modernisation did not go down deep in the consciousness of the common newspaper workers. The only exception perhaps was the Statesman Employees' Union, which persisted in imbuing a resistant attitude towards automation in its members over the years. This was acknowledged in a particular reference to the union in the silver jubilee publication of the AINEF (AINEF, 1986b: 27).

Let us now see how the leadership developed its attitude towards automation and the confusion it continuously created in forging a tactical line vis-à-vis modernisation. We shall see later that this confusion left the individual unions defenceless against the relentless onslaught of technological modernisation. Even as late as 1986 when the AINEF had already issued several declarations against automation, its silver jubilee declaration omits the most important issue faced by the newspaper employees (AINEF,1986a). It contains platitudes against casteism, communalism, secessionism, a defence of peace and socialism but does not contain a single paragraph on the issues and course of struggle to be adopted by newspaper employees.

While modernisation was recognised as a problem before the trade union movement in the newspaper industry in the Silver Jubilee publication, as it pointed out the consequences of the Palekar Award, the corollary of the IMF loan, the OGL (open general licence), import of new technologies and the likely reduction of the labour force as a result of modernisation, the Federation could not formulate a tactical line to fight for positive demands vis-à-vis modernisation. It gave more stress to reports of talks with the Union Labour Minister and ILO recommendations. While the reference to recommendations of the ILO certainly provided a clue to the demands that the AINEF would have liked its members to pursue, no clear-cut suggestion was offered (AINEF, 1986b: 27–28). Basically, the recommendations as well as the AINEF's stand revolved round social security demands. As umemployment was the main concern, since 54,000 jobs had been lost in one year in 1978 in the printing trade according to the government, the suggestions included thirty working hours per week, increased leave facilities, guarantee of jobs, improved health and labour protection, sharing of the benefits of new technology among consumers and workers, and employees' retraining for new skills. But how were the demands to be framed in a charter? How were they to be projected nationally as well as at the unit level? What were the key issues among all these? What if the management refused to concede anything at all? How should protection and the enlargement of the rights of printers and their trade unions be pressed? On all these vital questions of tactic, the leadership remained silent. Thus, the unions could not find a skilful bargaining line, nor could they attempt to achieve a measure of control over the process of modernisation. Either most unions waited passively, or thought only negatively, or they deceived themselves that by extracting some financial benefits from their employers, they could manage the situation effectively.

The most clearcut articulation of views was from an article by the AINEF General Secretary K.L. Kapur (1986). Here Kapur refers succinctly to the background of automation, the survey work done by the AINEF and the Statesman Employees' Union, and the social security issues as well as the relevant contemporary demands. Though here too we miss the appropriate directives to be sent to member units, the line of approach is clear. In fact, the AINEF makes an efficient job of surveying the extent of modernisation in the Indian newspaper industry. (NCNNAEO, 1983).

Kapur's circular on modernisation to the affiliated units of the AINEF adds further clarity.[4] The circular mentions the inadequacy of tackling automation at the union level and refers to the need for parliamentary legislation. It asks the unions to keep abreast of technological developments and concentrate on a strong union defence against the consequent hazards (like radiation, chemical pollution, unemployment, lack of occupational safety and health). It directs the unions to demand full consultation at every stage and ask for comprehensive training and retraining schemes. But it cautions the unions also that they should care for the competitiveness of a paper.

The organ of the AINEF, *Newspaper Worker*, also bore the mark of confusion in its presentation of views on automation in its successive issues.[5] The organ speaks of a resolution passed in the Nagpur Conference on 3 and 4 August 1985 of the National Confederation of Newspaper and News Agency Employees' Organisations pertaining to automation. It refers to the demand for adequate interim relief, mentions the need for organisational coordination between journalists and non-journalists and reports in a big way the deliberations on the consequences of new technology in the third consultative conference of the Trade Unions of the Graphics (Printing) Industry in Asian and Oceanic Countries at Fiunze, 21–23 May 1986, as also deliberations of the Sixth International Consultative Conference of Trade Unions of the Graphics (Printing) Industry held in Sofia from 27 to 29 July 1986. But here, also, in none of the issues of the organ do we find a single clear directive as to how the Indian unions are to proceed against the technological onslaught.

However, even amidst the confusion, some clarity was gradually emerging both due to pressures from below and the increasing maturity of the leadership. Initiatives to tackle the phenomenon began. For example, the Bombay Union of Journalists organised a discussion on automation, where the President of the Confederation, S.Y. Kolhatkar, urged a line of introduction on appropriate technology and not indiscriminate high technology.[6] Earlier, trouble erupted in the *Daily Maharashtra Herald* (Pune) and the

[4] Circular no. 29/86, New Delhi, 23 July 1986.
[5] Monthly organ of the AINEF published from Calcutta, *Newspaper Worker*, March, May, June, July 1986.
[6] *The Statesman*, New Delhi, 30 November 1986, 'Press Employees Decry Automation'.

Nav Bharat, Hitavada, Lokmat, Tarun Bharat and *Yugadharma* (Nagpur). There was discontent in the *Hindu* (Madras), *Amrita Bazar Patrika, Jugantar, Ananda Bazar Patrika,* the *Economic Times* (Calcutta), and the *Indian Express* (New Delhi). Automation spread to *Bombay Samachar, Blitz, Hind Samachar, Jagbani, Kerala Kaumudi, Prabhat,* and so on, in Bombay, Jullundur, Trivandrum and Lucknow. Newspapers completely based on new technology, like *Ajkal* and *Bartaman* (Calcutta), were published. These became the likely fresh battlegrounds over new technology (NCNNAEO, 1982: 29–42). These battles would not resist automation per se, so much as increasingly demand social security services for common workers. For example, one Jugantar union handout complained of non-regularity of even a token pension service.[7] The same union had placed a sixteen point charter of demands which included several demands related to social security like pension, gratuity and health.[8] In a rebuttal of the management's charge that the union was deliberately helping overtime earnings of employees, it countered with the fact that the management was denying social security measures to the staff while it found enough money for new buildings, new machines and new coloured supplements.[9] The Bengali handout of the reception committee of the Silver Jubilee Conference of the AINEF at Calcutta on 4–6 April 1986 also harped on the dangers emanating from new technology.[10] Even a call of the West Bengal Newspaper Employees' Federation (WBNEF) for a demonstration on 30 June 1986 in Calcutta in support of the demands for interim relief and job security again spoke of social security measures needed to protect the workers from automation.[11] A small daily like *Satyajug* (Calcutta) witnessed conflicts and clashes regarding the introduction of automation.

Thus, the unions as well as the rank and file workers became increasingly articulate, which is a long way forward from the 1979 Ananda Bazar Patrika agreement on modernisation between the

[7] Factsheet No. One, issued by the Amrita Bazar Patrika, Jugantar and Amrita Employees Union on the dispute with the management, Calcutta, 25 June 1986.

[8] Bulletin No. 2 of the Amrita Bazar Patrika, Jugantar and Amrita Employees Union, Calcutta, June 1986

[9] Leaflet on the dispute issued by the Union, Calcutta, 20 June 1986.

[10] Reception Committee Circular, Silver Jubilee Conference of AINEF; Calcutta, 10 February 1986.

[11] WBNEF Circular, Calcutta, 27 July 1986.

owners and the employees. From submission to confrontation—that is the story of the development of the attitude of the Federation—the largest body of newspaper workers in India.

S.Y. Kolhatkar, President of the Federation, was to admit, late in life, that to understand the problems of the printing workers in the graphics industry, we would have to transgress the official history of the Federation referred to and briefly described earlier. As he saw when summing up his experiences, the movement for appointing the wage board in the mid-sixties was a step that helped the Federation grow vigorously, unionise the workers across the country in various plants, and coordinate the various unions along one central charter of demands—indeed one central demand. It is a commonly known fact among unionists today that, under the Working Journalists Act, the government had intended the wage board for the journalists only, who formed just 10 to 15 per cent of the staff in the newspaper industry. The Fifteenth Labour Conference had recommended similar wage boards for other industries. The Shinde Wage Board recommendations were mandatory regarding journalists, but non-statutory regarding non-journalists. The Shinde Wage Board's recommendations for interim relief for employees were the first such in the newspaper industry. A tribunal was set up to implement the recommendations for interim relief. The commercial printing section (popularly known in the trade as the job section) was included for interim relief. The wage board struggle for two months in 1967 for the implementation of recommendations developed the Federation as an all-India organisation. The next wage board, the Palekar Board, was statutory for both journalists and non-journalists, as the scope of the Working Journalists Act had been extended through an amendment. The award for interim relief was accepted by the government. The employers' representatives resigned from the board over it. An impasse was created. The board was changed into a tribunal. And even to implement the tribunal's award, the Supreme Court had to intervene. Kolhatkar was to say later that the wage board struggles had two lessons to offer to newspaper workers: first, the organisational capacity of unions still mattered and the lack of organisational capacity to get the recommendations uniformly implemented proved crucial; secondly, modernisation came as a reaction to the Palekar Award and disrupted the Federation's organisational progress by attacking its capacity to get the recommendations uniformly implemented, by introducing and pushing modernisation programmes at the plant level. Kolhatkar further admitted that the Federation had judged the question of new technology as one more 'technology' and had not considered the introduction of new technology as a deliberate anti-worker managerial strategy that reduced both the wage bill as well as the number of workers. According to him, the technology was brought piece by piece, hence the struggle could not be universalised. Sitting on the ruins of unionism in the *Times of India*, Bombay plant, with a large number of workers rendered jobless and defenceless, Kolhatkar talked of a useless expert committee appointed by the government to look into the working conditions in newspaper plants, the hurdles placed by a slow-moving Labour Ministry, the unprecedented wave of unilateral decision making by the management everywhere on technological issues and the immobility of the Federation to meet the new situation.[12]

The feeling of helplessness and pain expressed by the old lifelong unionist at the immobility of his own organisation is understandable. As I shall show in the course of this work, the leadership as a whole often missed the often mysterious connection between the wage board, wage hike, modernisation and demobilisation of workers in the industry. The official biography, written in 1986, did not mention it. Nor did Kolhatkar comment upon it in his preface to the biography. Even the arrangement of chapters in the book shows beyond doubt that the Federation leadership had not considered that the relation between wage hike, wage board oriented organisational strategy of the union, the side-stepping of the wage issue by the management through the introduction of modernisation and, finally, the defeat of the union movement were integral (AINEF, 1986b: Chapters 11–12).

Indeed, Madan Phadnis, a CPI(M) and CITU member and Secretary to the Federation, expressed surprise at any suggestion to explore the links between technology and the determination of wages. To him, there could be any number of determinants of wages, as the Fair Wages Committee showed, and modernisation could at best be a residual factor. To him, the appeal to social welfare and social justice contained in the Federation's submissions

[12] Talk with S.Y. Kolhatkar, President of the AINEF at Bombay, 13 March 1991.

on wage increase before the Bachawat Wage Board had been made on principle, and modernisation could not be invoked as an argument for increase of wages. 'Wage as compensation' was again a 'wrong view,' 'pension as a defence against compulsory retirement' was similarly an 'extreme view,' pension being just a retiral benefit. Phadnis, being a lawyer, had been instrumental in forging the arguments of the Federation before the wage boards. Yet, according to him, any alternative suggestion to explore the possibilities of challenging the 'terms of reference' of a wage board constituted in the wake of modernisation seemed 'unrealistic', and to him modernisation and revision of wage were issues at two separate levels, most likely unconnected and 'breaking new grounds in law' as far as fair wages were concerned in the form of invoking 'compensation' due to modernisation was 'not so easy matter'.[13]

Like Kolhatkar, K.L. Kapur, the General Secretary, in his circulars in the post-1986 phase showed an awareness regarding such a possibility of links between wage boards and modernisation, though only slightly. It is clear that the Federation, as a national union, thrived on wage board oriented struggles. It remained content with relying on the crutches offered by the State in the form of the institution of wage boards. It remained oblivious to the fact that the employers had devised a strategy to undermine the crutches, weaken the union movement, and modernisation, in course of just half a decade, would demobilise the movement built around wage board oriented struggles. Thus, the absence of such a discussion in the Federation's papers is stunning, though it is not surprising considering the state of the union movement in India. The silence in the official history of the Federation here is eloquent and, like the proverbial question of why the dog did not bark at the needed hour, I shall probe subsequently into what the Federation argued about before the Wage Board and what it remained silent about at the critical phase of technical change.

Consider the organisational structure of the Federation, a national union built entirely around the demand for revision of wages through the mechanism of a wage board, appointed by the government. The Federation is a union of newspaper unions, mostly plant-based unions. State federations are not its mainstay.

---

[13] Author's interview with Madan Phadnis, Secretary to the AINEF, Bombay, 12 March 1991.

A newspaper company having several offices with several editions at different centres may often not have company-based unionism. Thus, the *Indian Express* may have different unions at different centres of publication, with the management finding the task of dealing with the workers relatively easier as there is no single strong union representing the workers. A strike at the *Indian Express*, Delhi, may not thus be supported by a similar strike in Hyderabad or Madras, as happened in 1989–90. The Federation has its office in New Delhi with its General Secretary, K.L. Kapur, acting as the post office. The President stays in Bombay, with the leadership and Central Working Committee (CWC) meeting infrequently. The central office serves the purpose of only informing the member units of various developments in the industry. While informing remains an important task of organisation, leadership at the Federation level calls for other similar obligations which, as a one-man office, it fails to perform. The Federation has, we have to keep in mind, member unions whose members are in most cases only non-journalist employees. These are very rarely composite unions. As a result, the management is often able to drive a wedge between journalist and non-journalist employees, as happened during the *Ananda Bazar Patrika* strike in Calcutta (1984). This drawback is significant, particularly during the phase of modernisation and the consequent deunionising strategy of the bosses. As has been indicated, the Federation leadership becomes a collective and active only during wage board work and thus, in spite of repeated token strikes, indefinite strikes, participation in general working class struggles, and so on, the leadership is still not a collective. The most damning indication of this comes when a strike is conducted by a single union at a plant, when the Federation's aid and advice for providing leadership and solidarity are found wanting. Struggles in response to modernisation have thus collapsed and too often the unions have been left to themselves to manage their own barricades.

It is not that there is no link with journalists. Apart from few composite unions, there is a working relationship with the Indian Federation of Working Journalists (IFWJ). There is the confederation of various federations of employees—journalists, non-journalists, news agency employees, and so on. But again, as we shall see later, the meetings of the confederation are 'grand occasions,' hence a rarity, and even for the imperatives of long-term strategic leadership, are inadequate. Finally, in terms of forging unity among newspaper employees regardless of category and affiliation, its record has become increasingly bad. Its own strength as a union is not due to the number of affiliated units or workers who are members of these plant unions, but has been built up and is recognised due to two factors: the location of the affiliate unions in strategic newspapers, like the *Hindu*, *Indian Express* and the *Statesman* and its ability to conduct wage board oriented struggles. These two factors (namely, strategic strength in place of numerical strength and successful emphasis on wage revision), though sufficient at one time to make the story of the Federation a success, are not enough to take a resolute stand with respect to modernisation. For, as shall be explained subsequently, the introduction of micro electronics based technology raised issues of power, social security and organisation which could not be tackled with the old structure of the movement. The strategic strength due to the location of unions soon dissipated as the 'modernising' onslaught of bosses crippled strong unions at the *Times of India*, Bombay, *Ananda Bazar Patrika* and *Jugantar* at Calcutta and at several other places; rival federations cropped up, the journalists' organisation split and the Federation got involved in factional quarrels. We shall see further that the tactical emphasis on wage boards also backfired, as modernisation was legitimised through wage board operations, and issues thrown up in the wake of modernisation at the plant level remained unattended. The decline of the Federation is a story left out of the official biography, possibly because the Federation till the end remained blind to its own problems in the milieu of technological change in the industry.

A study of the circulars sent out from the head office of the AINEF at Delhi to the affiliates from 1981 to 1988 anticipate some of the problems discussed in the following chapters. About 138 circulars and letters were sent by the General Secretary from 1981 to 1988.[14] Of these, 42 circulars relate to the problems of modernisation (which include strikes, health problems, pension and information about computers); 12 circulars relate to international developments (like resolutions of the International Consultative

[14] This is a rough estimate as I could not get all the circulars from the office, in spite of assistance from K.L. Kapur. The period 1981–88 was the decade of changeover; in a way important circulars went out in 1989–91 also. The cut-off year, 1988, is purely arbitrary, as the circulars were collected mostly in 1989.

Conferences of Trade Unions of the graphics industry, ILO news, and so on to the members); 9 circulars appeal for solidarity with movements of other sections of the working class, with the general trade union movement and campaign; and the remaining 75 deal with miscellaneous issues like pay structure. I did not find a single circular that discussed organisational problems or advised members on how to conduct struggles against modernisation or, more importantly, how to update the organisation in order to face the issue of automation in the industry. Of the 42 circulars concerning wage boards, appeals for funds for wage board preparation were the most insistent. Almost no circular talked of mobilising and utilising the plant level unions for furnishing data on how the management planned to utilise wage board recommendations for modernisation. The 36 circulars concerning modernisation are, again, informative, not strategic. They do not discuss trade union strategy and tactics but mostly relay information from books and resolutions on micro electronics. In other words, a content analysis shows that throughout the decade, the Federation, in guiding its members, remained theoretical and abstruse, not strategic. It could rarely lay its hands on the heart of the problem—the problem of power at the plant and shop floor level in the wake of modernisation.

Throughout the decade, strikes erupted in many centres like Calcutta, Bombay, Nagpur, Bangalore and Delhi. In each place (except Delhi), the absence of state level federations was significant. Between the organisation in newspaper offices and plants, and Delhi, there was no middle tier. The Federation became a hopping exercise from conference to conference, one CWC meeting to another CWC meeting, wage board to wage board. In an industry where wage was the only crucial issue to be negotiated, this would have been enough. But the eighties were a different decade altogether though, in the consciousness of the leadership, the sixties and seventies continued to be crucial.

It is in this sense that the Federation's story has to be foretold before the narrative even begins. I shall take into account the structural constraints within which the union movement proceeded and met its worst fate. The union movement may concern itself with one issue—for example, wages. But the power matrix does not allow it to remain unconcerned, unaffected by the question of powers raised in the wake of a technological change. It robs it of power and strength, and demobilises it. When the President of the

Statesman Employees' Union was dismissed by the management of the *Statesman* in 1991, the workers thought that the defeat of the five day strike in the plant in 1990 had led to it. Some grumbled that the Federation leadership had not aided much. Many tentatively said, yes wages had increased, but power had gone! But few suspected that the process had its beginnings in the late seventies and early eighties, when modernisation had initially emerged, the union structure had started getting outmoded, wage board awards acted as a legitimating agency for modernisation and an onslaught of bosses started taking shape with which the workers had not previously been familiar at all!

I shall thus start not with strikes but with technology. I shall show, in due course, that it was a technology based not merely on microelectronics but on newer techniques of power as well.

2

Automated Technology in the Newspaper Industry

To begin, then, with technology. The ongoing scientific and technological revolution has taken one important form—that of information revolution. With the new technological means to collect, store, process and disseminate news, no news is really external today, and no news is really remote or late. With the development of novel means of mass communication, it is really the age of mass media.[1] No wonder then that the spectacular progress in the technology of automation has become really evident in the newspaper industry where the entire work process has been revolutionised within a decade or more.

What is the precise character of modernisation being introduced in the newspaper industry, which has in fact already been adopted in almost all the big newspaper establishments? In India, it was not accidental that immediately after the publication of the *Palekar Tribunal Report*,[2] the owners of big newspapers started a concerted drive to adopt computerised technology in their industry. Of course they remained silent about the possible effect of new technology on the labour force; in some cases, the management tried to lure the workers into accepting the new process in lieu of financial benefits, particularly when the workers were still unaware of the total nature of the new technology being introduced; at some

[1] Schreiber (1974), pt. 3, ch. 1.
[2] The Palekar Wage Board was instituted in 1979 to go into the demands for a hike in the wages of the employees of newspapers and news agencies. Subsequently, it was converted into a tribunal.

places, they linked up the question of introducing modernisation with their duty of implementing even the very few benefits for the workers due to the Palekar Award.[3] However, let us examine in the first place, what the modern electronic process is—the photo-typesetting system and the new technique of printing—that has automised the entire newspaper industry. The sudden leap from conventional linotypesetting to computerised phototypesetting is at the core of the introduction of electronics in the newspaper industry, and a thorough examination of this leap will make clear how the socio-economic aspects and the technical aspects of auto-mation are inextricably interlinked.

The Old Method

The hitherto existing method of production in printing, particularly in newspapers, required an extensive and elaborate process of work. The technical aspects of production could be divided into four parts: typesetting and composing, block making, paper print-ing and distribution. In newspapers, predetermined and fixed measured metal type lines are cast out mechanically by a linotype machine. By tapping keys, individual type matrices are set and sent off mechanically into the machine to cast out the typeline, called a slug, which is made of molten lead. The molten material is composed of tin, antimony and lead. Thus, a series of hot metal slugs are gathered in galleys, while the matrices of head-line types are arranged manually into a strip and cast out by APLs (All Purpose Linotype or Ludlow machines). This line casting output is then arranged as desired and proofs are pulled out of this solid made-up matter and read out with the manuscripts or copy matter. Corrections and instructions are marked on the proofsheets and carried out by operatives and working hands. Where necessary, blocks of picture illustration, and so on, are inserted together with the set type lines. This arranged matter and hand-set titles and headlines are then made into page forms called chases. Page proofs are then taken for correction and editing. Blocks of adver-tisements and news text matter are made in the process department through an elaborate method of manual and mechanical work, photographic and chemical processes and treatment.

[3] For instance the wage agreement in the Ananda Bazar Patrika group of papers in 1978.

From composing, the process now reaches the stage of printing. The finished made-up newspaper page, called forme, is put into a matrix punching press. A heat-resistant sheet, called a flong, is laid on the forme and compressed, thus creating raised types out of the imprints from great pressure and extreme heat. Two plates, cast out of these flongs and screwed opposite each other, make up a rotary forme. Then starts printing after the formes are arranged, ink rolled and reel papers set in order. The continuous roll of paper is printed out by a rotary machine, folded and cut into size. These are then automatically collated in correct order and leave the folding machine for despatch. For short run jobs and commercial work, flat bed letterpress machines are used. The method to print on an offset machine is to take a machine pull of the matter that is to be printed. A film negative is then taken to expose light on the offset plate to be made. This plate is then set on to an offset machine for printing. The method of printing in offset is the reverse printing method while for letterpress it is the direct printing method.

This has been the basic metal printing method, the principles of which were discovered by Johannes Gutenberg around 1445. Since the time of Ottmar Mergenthaler in 1884, a move from hand-setting metal types to mechanical setting was made. The teletype-setter (or the TTS) is the latest development in speeding up the hot metal system of typesetting, where to do away with manual attention regarding justifications or splitting of words, TTS is made to operate on a tape perforated by a computer already fed with the complete programme for splitting syllables.[4]

Cold Printing

Electronics has revolutionised the entire method of printing with the introduction of the phototypesetting system. This came about with the help of computers—the automatic typesetting system. The principle of phototypesetting is to generate characters or types by the photoset method. Phototypesetting produces no solid types. It produces photoset types on photosensitive papers—no relief or raised metal types, but printed images of characters on a flat surface.

[4] Smith (1980), ch. 1.

Now no metal or metal matrices, moulds, casting and blocks are required to make up images. Under the new system, newspaper pages are made by pasting galley formats of photoset characters onto a transparent dummy sheet according to the layout. Film negatives of pasted-up pages are then taken to produce plates for printing. Thus, it is at this initial stage of composing, preparatory to printing, that the most vital departure from the conventional method takes place and this departure produces the inevitable impact on the subsequent and interrelated stages of newspaper production. This departure is, of course, technological (an aspect which I shall briefly discuss), but the technological aspect is enmeshed in a web of socio-economic relations, such as the relation of labour to capital, the relation of capital ownership to the total structure of the newspaper industry, the effect of and on news gathering and news distribution, the import of foreign capital; and, more interestingly, the technological form is created or thrown up due to the complex web of economic and political relations.

Let us first examine the technological aspect. The integrated circuit, along with the microprocessor, has changed or done away with all the previous skills of the hot metal process. Computerised phototypesetting, the first major breakthrough in the revolutionisation of the entire industry, involves composing, correcting and editing text matter displayed on a videoterminal and stored on a magnetic disk. These machines are typically 5 to 150 times faster than previous hot metal systems and can compose 150 to 4,500 words a minute. Further improvements have been towards digitised systems that dispense with photographic paper to engrave the text and illustrations directly on the printing plate. The laser scanner helps colour separations of colour photographs or illustrations. Typically, various models of scanners, operated by one or two trained technicians, take anywhere between 15 minutes to two hours to produce colour separated positives, a process that earlier involved many more skilled process technicians and took 2 or 3 days to produce a set of acceptable colour separations. The transition from metal based printing to phototypesetting need not be very sudden. It can often pass through some intermediary stages, depending upon the investment capability of the employer, adaptability to new technology, degree of union resistance, availability of foreign inputs, and so on. Thus, computerisation may first be introduced only through teletypesetting. Or, without resorting to offset printing press, photopolymer plastic plates may be used to adapt photocomposed text to letterpress rotaries. In the case of a newspaper with more than one city edition, facsimile transmission can also be gradually modernised. Direct transport via airways, STD use and faster facsimile transmitters can lead to the use of satellites. In India, while transmission methods still remain backward,[5] in the developed West today, the use of satellites has become a common reality.

The crucial point in this whole computerised system of newspaper publication and distribution is obviously computerised composing, which is at the nerve centre of news collection, analysis, editing, disseminating and finally news preserving in most modern methods of archiving. There are two ways of generating characters by the photoset method: the successive assembly of individual letters by photographic printing from film matrices instead of metal matrices; and cathode-ray tube generation of individual characters, individual lines of types or areas of text.

Though, for activating photosetting devices, manually operated film lettering 'enlargers' or machines based on the hot metal principle may be used, where photographic printing heads are substituted for metal pot and pump, the modern method is the computation of images through CRT (cathod ray tube) displays or the high speed assembly of individual characters by electronic computerised devices. So the basics of photographic typesetting to obtain the image of a character on sensitive photographic paper, or a paper printing plate, require the existence of the character in a negative form on a master usually made out of film or treated glass through which light can be exposed to imprint the image on the paper. Thus, by repeating the process, sets of images of characters may be obtained in required measure and the full text can be done in the same way.

However, to obtain characters by keyboard operation, either rotating negative discs or movable lenses are used. One or several fonts (a set of characters in one style) on a master and one or several masters may be loaded on the machine at one time. A slit opposite each character and each timing mark is counted by a

[5] 'Printing Technology Takes off,' *Business India*, 18–31 July 1983. A few years ago, *Ajkal* used to transport the fascimilies by van for its Asansol edition, which had to be discontinued later on.

special optical sensor. When the mark for the character selected comes under the sensor, the flash lamp is activated. The light from the flash lamp passes through the master image and enters a path that often takes the light through a lensing system. Lenses of various sizes in a rotating turret may be used to get the required type size. By a mechanical device, the light sensitive photomaterial moves with the speed of exposure and takes the image of the character. Increasingly, the movable mechanical parts have been reduced to enhance speed. Now, instead of imprinting images of characters directly, the method is to store the data of characters in a magnetic type of sheet by the tapping of keys. Photoset characters can now be assembled at the rate of 200 to 600 characters per second by an electronic computerised device.

The first generation machines were barely faster than metal typesetting. Their aim was not to improve the speed of setting, but rather to produce a printing base for the then new photoprinting offset process. The second generation of phototypesetters of the fifties and sixties were guided by a perforated tape and used glass discs by scanning or rotating negative discs with the letter produced by a flash. The real breakthrough came with the third generation machines, the cathod ray machines, where glass or film grids are not used, but the letter and symbol are data-stored. These machines can therefore work without materials and at the speed of the flashing light with which the cathod ray photosets line by line. The sole technical procedure that remains is to insert a magnetic film or a magnetic sheet the size of a gramaphone record.

Today, all typesetting functions, from original keyboarding, playing and editing to camera-ready reproduction, are controlled by a computer brain attached to the heart of the machine. The required margins, alignments, size and points, justification and hyphenation can be programme set for automatic functioning of the photocomposing system with a revolving magnetic disc or cassette. Any type size or showing of types can be obtained by automatic lensing devices. The usual practice is to type blindly and continuously to record the information (data and symbol) on to some form of storage media—cassette, magnetic disc or perforated tape. When required, the recorded jobs can be rerun, and corrections, insertions, resetting and updating can be done. The justification and hyphenation would be automatic by computer programming.

Sometimes input devices use a video screen (cathode ray tube) to display the copy being typeset and edited. Letters are scanned by an electronic beam (according to the symbol and data being programmed) which is generated at the back of the tube. It is then deflected by the deflection coil to various locations on the face of the tube (screen). The CRT characters are made up of groups of dots creating a visual pattern of the characters on the face of the tube. The number of dots within which characters are constructed is called dot-matrix. In a way this system is like displaying pictures on television. From the data and symbol displaced on the screen, light sensitive photographic paper can receive the print. CRT computation can extend up to the astronomical figure of more than 5 lakh characters per minute printed out in column formats. This output may be produced on film (bromide) or photosensitive paper in long strips like galley proofs, developed through an automatic developing process, which are then cut and pasted on sheets of paper (or astrolon sheets) to make up the pages. A photograph is taken of the assembled sheet by placing it on to a flatbed machine and, within a few seconds, the whole negative comes out. From the negative either an offset plate is made for offset printing, or a plate polymer is made for letterpress printing.

The photographic keyboards are designed in such a way that two or more languages can be worked out by the same machine by shifting devices. Only the master disc needs to be changed. In a cathode ray machine, this is done by computer programming. With record and playback capability, most direct entry phototypesetters can accept inputs from off-line input devices, thus forming the nucleus of higher output systems with multiple input sources. Depending on the ability of the PTS, six or even more input sources can often be accommodated. Besides, a magnetic sheet can be erased and used several times.

The Work Flow

For newspaper work, then, the whole process—from keyboarding to photosetting—is divided into four stages. The first is the key to the magnetic disc or film. Then the disc is taken out and fitted on to a machine called a dot-matrix printer or solid matrix line printer. This works as a proofing machine. From the magnetic code of the disc this machine gives a hard proof copy for correction purposes within 2 minutes, which requires a PTS operator half an hour to complete. In the third stage, the disc is fitted on to an editing machine similar to the keyboard operating machine, except that this machine has an attachment like that of a television screen. On this machine corrections are done by reading the matter through the screen and operating the keyboard as necessary. After this, for the final output, these discs are inserted into the photosetting machine having automatic devices for development also. A newspaper set-up generally requires 10 to 12 key-to-disc machines, one dot-printing machine, one editing machine and a typesetting machine.[6]

In the field of administration, too, electronics has had a profound impact. Accounting, making ledgers and bills, preparing paysheets, stocktaking of inventories—all such work will be shrinking drastically. The need for non-productive hands (like peons, orderlies, bearers, sweepers, watchmen and drivers) also diminishes as production switches from one basic type to another. This reduction starts taking place as the vast area of possibilities opened up by photocomposing begins affecting the number of editions—indeed the entire pattern of circulation.

With the advent of so much new technology in this field, one cannot be sure of knowing what the latest developments are. However, what is certain is that typesetting methods have already entered into the fifth generation stage with the laser typesetter. Innovations in science and technology have eliminated the need for expensive silver halide films, processing units, dark rooms and petrochemicals. In future, papers will be printed and assembled in remote plants, with instructions coming via satellite communications systems, computers providing electronic control and information processing, plateless imaging and variable data input producing packages of information in individual types, word processing and telephone hook-up, laser facsimile, with fibre optics and electronics page make-up providing speed and flexibility. Display advertisements and the classified columns will be thus drastically affected. And, finally, computers will monitor and control the printing presses and distribution.

In short, as the intention of the whole process is to optimise,

---

[6] Help for this section has been taken from James Craig (1978).

integrate, maximise and automate all the operations connected with the newspaper industry, the work flow will be hugely altered. Though all innovations do not appear simultaneously, or may not be used simultaneously due to social, political or economic constraints, the fact remains that these have to be used as a system for maximum utilisation; and a distinct possibility remains of furthering the system. There is no question of stopping midway once some part of a system has been introduced. For each system has its own logic, and admitting all adaptations and modifications, all the components of the system both individually and as a whole drive the newspaper industry towards accepting the whole system. Newspaper plants, in particular, have to adopt the technical system as a whole.

Two examples of the system may be given. In the United States, the *Sun Times* has 10 computers—5 for handling the materials from reporters and 5 for wire services, editing and processing. All the 10 computers are controlled and coordinated by a multi-processor bus—a giant computer. Separate sets of electronic computers are used for classified and display advertisements which are also hooked up at one end to make-up terminals and on the other to a typesetter. In India, at the *Hindu*, the typesetter works on 24 video display terminals, which are handled by editorial staff as well. Any story to be printed, once fed into the terminal, is immediately transferred through electronic impulses to a central processing system capable of storing several million works. All such technical functions (like altering the sequence of paragraphs, inserting or deleting a line somewhere, changing a word or correcting a spelling mistake) can easily be performed with the push of a button, thus completely eliminating the manpower needed in various stages of production. The typed text is thus stored in a computer. On command by pressing a button, a lasercomp phototypesetter produces bromides or matter which are made into complete pages. Thus, each fully made-up page (consisting of text, pictures and advertisements) is then photographed by an automatic computerised camera to get the negative. The negative is printed by contact on to a thin plastic plate under high-intensity lights. Within minutes after etching, the plate is ready for printing the city based edition. And it now takes only 7 or 8 minutes to send each page by facsimile through telephone cable. So far-flung editions (such as the *Hindu* at Bangalore, Hyderabad, Coimbatore and Madurai) start printing simultaneously.

Discussion on work flow leads us to the question of job potential. A PTS keyboard operator has to type from copy—either blind or by a visual display terminal like a television set. This keyboard is just like a typewriter, with some additional keys. Once set for inputting, one need not look at or attend to the machine or handle any attachment. This is unlike a lino operator or typist. The speed for a lino operator is as fast as the machine can go (that is, 6 or 7 lines per minute), where the PTS is essentially as fast as the operator. The intake capacity of this machine is between 20 to 30 character lines and 50 to 70 or more character lines per minute. Therefore, the input rate of a PTS keyboard operating can be anything a human being can attain.

Assuming that a PTS keyboard operator can, on an average, produce at least 2 columns of 7 point matter in an hour, he can produce a minimum of 8 columns (*Statesman* measure) of 7 point output per shift. However, a PTS operator obtains much higher production.

In short, two results follow: One, higher productivity and intensification of labour where, in the initial stages, labour is puzzled, has to find his new moorings, has to cope suddenly with the intensity and pressure of work, has to learn new methods of adjusting himself to the rhythm of work, has to find new ways of rest and relaxation during work, has to feel, estimate and conclude the intensity of his work, consequently also the intensity of his exploitation. Second, the redundancy of an entire set of jobs, with the elimination of the previous necessity of arranging metal types and of previous speed. Thus, the elaborate chain of work from block making, type making and page making to printing (that is, up to the stage of casting cylindrical rotary forms) is abolished, at the same time abolishing all the grades of workmen involved in that elaborate system of solid set composing. The role of the journalist also changes in the production process. Here also the change is reflected in two ways.

First, the journalist becomes an operator in a sense. Though he or she may resist the function of keying-in or may be saved by operators from performing the said function (as journalists in the *Times*, London tried a few years ago), yet imperceptibly his or her role changes and the white collar job becomes a little 'blue'. Second, with the development of the composing method, computerised assemblage and classification of data and sophisticated news gathering apparatus, journalism undergoes a change in role. It becomes more investigative, the final copy being often the result of team-work. The journalist starts resisting conventions of news writing that seem to oblige the reporter to conduct himself compliantly to the point of complicity. New journalism in the post-Gutenberg set-up avidly grabs any opportunity for self-expression, vividness of style and political purpose, the absence of which had previously cut the reporter from the mainstream of national information.

The work-flow can be further influenced by the introduction of robots. In manufacturing printing equipment, robots are increasingly employed. One such unit, controlled by dual microprocessors, has a 'sense of touch' to detect missing components or substandard parts. One such can lift varying size bundles, or shift pallets and place them automatically where they are required. The computerised control of robots thus increases productivity, eliminating the producer with his various complaints, breaks from work or absence. In the PRINT 80 exhibition in Chicago, the Womac Machinery Co. of Sweden demonstrated the BA 100 Palrob Robot Palletising system. This is presently available and being operated in conjunction with adhesive binders for book lines and the product from magazine and newspaper presses. At the newspaper industry's production management exhibition in Atlantic City, Womac again demonstrated the prowess of its system for use in palletising newspaper bundles in brick piles, taking products from a conveyor belt and transferring them directly on to skids or plastic wrappers. The ultimate system also bundles and wraps the completed newspaper and delivers them, addressed, to the trucks allocated to delivery in each zone. The cut-throat competition for profit sets a general trend and becomes the basis of this rapid development. The adverse effects on employment, the resultant social discontent and working class protests become universal and can never be harmoniously settled under the anarchic nature of competition and technological upgrading.

The unevenness in adopting and developing the new technology makes for the fact that there is no 'given,' 'once for all' new system. Just like the hot metal system development spanning centuries, here too it proceeds over a period of time, only now the theatre of development is wider, from Japan across the entire globe to the US. In Japan, larger newspaper units like *Ashai Shinbhum* are using the 'Automated Newspaper Editing and Composing System' (a full page photocomposing system) for laying out pages. They have developed devices to automatically join rolls of paper without having to stop printing, together with transistorised monitoring equipment to control the operation. Speeds of 140,000 papers an hour have become common. Techniques for preventing paper breaks, more important in Japan than in other societies, have been developed. The Japanese have successfully concentrated on the problem of long print reams. Here, under such innovations, technicians increasingly take the place of foremen and mechanics, and the 'blue' job becomes a little 'white'. In Germany, new offset presses can be run by three men. In the US, the latest PTS can produce 3,000 or more newspaper lines per minute. In the *Los Angeles Times* an editor can request a listing from the computer of all the stories in a particular category (for example, on the Lebanese hostage crisis) and this list will appear on his visual display terminal (VDT). It can even furnish a synopsis of stories. A computer storage bank can receive wire services that are coming at a speed of 1,500 words per minute.

Even in advanced countries all the processes have not been introduced in a single institution. But one must remember that at the back of the mind of all designers is the idea of an ultimate system, an integrated whole. All the basic elements of this system already exist and are used in newspapers in one part of the world or another. But the trend among newspaper magnates is to adopt such an all-comprehensive system. As India is technologically and economically dependent on advanced countries, newspaper magnates here may not be able to put together all the elements of the new technology at one go. But here, too, the same trend is asserting itself gradually. Electronics technology is constantly developing and, once adopted, one must keep pace. Thus, the use of laser and optical fibre, microcomputers, sensors, and so on, in PTS, has led to a chain of interrelated developments of far-reaching significance. Just like phototypesetting, there is word processing, and a modular system has also been developed. A colour scanner, electronic page make-up, facsimile transmission system and automatic printing, binding and packing are other related developments.

Word Processing: Similar to phototypesetting, word-processing also involves the conversion of paper written texts to a coded format on magnetic disc or tape. In the former, manuscripts are converted into camera-ready copies. In word processing the copy is made suitable for editing, communication and other electronic manipulations. Like the development of PTS, its scanning ability too has advanced by using advanced emitter coupled logic (ECL) technology. The most up-to-date word processor can scan and enter, in 60 seconds or less, what a typesetter can perform in 7 to 12 minutes. The merger of word processing and PTS has driven the fundamental work process of a newspaper towards further automation.

Modular System: The modular composition (MC) system combines a keyboard and screen, disc storage, a digital CRT typesetter and a controlling system. MCs can accept input from other commercial and newspaper front-end systems. A front-end system is a computerised one that files and stores all information fed into it. It sends this to the typesetting machine with all the typesetting commands after the information has been edited.

Wire Services: The direct linking of transmission of news from agencies and other sources, on teleprinters to computer banks installed in newspaper offices, eliminates work in the composing room. Transmitted news may be passed on to the PTS directly or through a front-end system.

Colour Scanner: Scanner technology has literally cut days out of the manufacturing process through the computerised breakdown of a piece of colour work and photographic transparencies for colour printing.

Electronic Page Make-Up: This is achieved by assembling set-news, editorials, advertisement matter and pictures in an actual size VDT system. Reference has been made earlier to this.

Facsimile Transmission System: Using a special light source, the facsimile transmission device scans made-up pages and converts the resultant light reflection into electronic signals. These signals are conveyed via co-axial cables, micro-wave or satellite channels to a recorder at the receiving centre. The recorder signals back light reflections which are exposed on a film. This is then processed to get a negative used for printing. Thus, the simultaneous publication of several editions has become possible today and the circulation of big newspapers commanding the latest technology has gained by leaps and bounds. The small ones face inevitable decline.

The Composite Set-Up under the New Technologies: Let us now draw a composite picture of the various innovations and see where the old system can be demarcated from the new. To quote one report:

> Typesetting and presswork were the heart and lungs of the newspaper. Today, the newsroom is finally coming to the fore, because it will more directly than in the past command the production operation, in conjunction with the advertising department (another input department). Executive roles will also presumably change to take account of this fundamental power-shift (NCNNAEO, 1983).

But how does the newsroom come to the fore? The central point is the CPU or the central processing unit. The PTS was initially meant for, as has been earlier mentioned, the off-set photoprinting process. But with increasing computerisation, photocomposing has reached a very high technical level. Now, with computerisation, it is possible for a newspaper plant to have at the centre of its operations a central processing unit, which stores the copy digitally in its memory, where formerly trays of completed metal type covered a large floor area of a composing room. The computer performs text corrections according to editorial instructions and dots the 'i's and 'j's, which used to be done line by line manually by the typesetters.

Journalists and editors type their copy on the visual display terminal and correct the copy as needed, the VDT being attached to a CRT. Then the copy is sent to the CPU, from where it can be recalled when needed by anyone whose logging in code permits him or her to receive it. The text can be displayed on one half of the screen, while another version of the same story is recalled from the CPU for comparison, review or incorporation. Each VDT user has his or her own small electronic scratch pass for holding material not ready for the main file. Thus, the more 'intelligent' a terminal, the more elegant the report can be. The journalist then becomes almost like a 'typist' of the hot metal composing days. In the case of an advertisement, the VDT permits the operator, while taking down a telephone-dictated classified advertisement, to check the credit worthiness of the customer, plan for future insertions of the advertisement in subsequent editions, inform the customer of the exact cost and bill him automatically. For display advertisements, large VDTs are used for complex designs and alignment operations with all possible manipulations: a function that would have otherwise needed many hours of elaborate physical design and layout work as well as complex procedures of filing and checking.

For entry into the CPU, an optical character reader or OCR may be used in place of a VDT or in addition to it. Here, what is typed on a fast electric typewriter is passed into the CPU though electronic signals of the OCR. But here the copy must be near perfect, only the 'dots' will be done by the CPU. In handling wire service copy, (syndicated materials), the OCR is used, as syndication agencies are able to supply scannable copy directly to their newspapers.

Laser technology goes further: With the help of laser, it is possible for the central processing unit not to take each character when required out of the file, but to have the whole thing in a design, thus making the operation a matter of seconds.

Once matter is in the CPU, it starts to perform its second task (after that of memorising the copy). It sends out a stream of text, offering back all the material it has been given, laid out in neat columns on strips of paper obeying all editing instructions. Whereas, formerly, there would be the laborious task of laying out trays of type and correcting them, today the matter comes out from the CPU composed and laid out, with space left for photographic materials. Only a few pieces of material (like pictures or special headlines) remain to the added. Through a highly intelligent terminal, the pasting process for making a page is eliminated and the whole page can be laid out.

In a sophisticated system, a large pair of CPU units are combined with small pairs of computer units giving wider scope for information processing, graphic printing, circulation, advertising, accounts and administration—practically all the jobs connected with newspaper work.

Fundamental Trends

All these changes give rise to two fundamental trends: one, a reduction in human labour and the intensification of its exploitation, and, second, monopolisation of the information media.

The scientific reason for such a reduction is clear from the foregoing description of various innovations. With regard to the intensification of labour, the crucial factor is the speed of computer-aided typesetting. A hand-compositor would take 22 hours to produce a single page of text in the black and white section of a large size newspaper; a machine compositor 5.5 hours; a teletypesetter 1.3 hours. Once the text is available in machine readable form, it takes the electronically controlled film setting machine exactly 15 seconds.

As regards monopolisation associated with computerisation, the issue is no less clear. The system, logic and equipment now come from giant companies like IBM and RCA, in addition to the old giants of printing and composing machinery. Computerisation spreads further as news agency reports are fed directly into the computer as finished type matter, ready to go to print. To overcome the obstacle of a large number of characters in a certain language, a new system can store them in digital form in computer memory, as has been recently developed in Japan. Thus, had it been merely a question of introducing one new machine into an old set-up, the question of command over the entire gamut of production would not have arisen. But, inexorably, it is a new system introducing new arrangements. It is not that it cannot be adopted half-way, singly or piecemeal, but to gain optimum utilisation, and bring into full play the whole potential of phototype-setting, big capital in newspaper ownership in the present market based economy is a must. Technically, it may mean a proliferation of production centres, guided by a system or an allied arrangement of systems. But financially and command wise, the whole thing is poised for oligopolistic control under a competitive set-up. Thus, all the technological innovations and developments in the four main sectors of industry—typesetting and data input, graphic reproduction and platemaking, printing, and binding-finishing—have to be combined and, when done, they effect a revolutionary leap from the Gutenberg days of technology. The information medium comes increasingly under monopolistic command with the formation of a system that combines the innovations in all the four sectors.

It must be noted that this technological transformation is part of the worldwide leap in electronics technology, and the particular case of newspapers helps us understand the basic features of this universal phenomenon. The experience of the industrial revolution is always a ready reference here. There is now a similar shift in all aspects, a rapidity of change, a remorseless dynamism, and that terrible shrinkage in employment, a shock which the *existent order in industrial relations cannot withstand*, a momentous portent of the coming of which only 'the gallantly misguided Luddites had any glimmering of insight' (Evans, 1979).

In a sense, the electronics revolution, particularly in the information industry, is bringing about the death of the printed word. Newspapers, as one of the most vital parts of the information industry, are no more an arrangement only of printed words, but rather an arrangement of instant news and views, a gamut connected with the whole electronics media. Thus, it is true that 'it has a tendency to stress the short-term, if not the immediate'.[7] With the above technology, newspapers become more photographic, instant, and display oriented. With the adoption of new technology in newspapers, occasionally there is an accompanying collapse of general magazines.[8] The newspaper turns into a half-magazine, full of special supplements and sectional displays, of special interest to different sections of readers—a development of zonal advertisements. Reality and public opinion get intertwined. Instability constantly exists with instant news. Politicians are in search of cameras. Bosses are the communicators, the consumers of information at the mercy of the media giants. This is one particular feature of the transmission explosion.

The other feature is that even the news, which the consumer buys (retail or wholesale) is so much the subject of monopoly control today that one should ponder on how much the freedom of the press is a reality, whether only the rich are really informed, and what reforms remain on the agenda of information. Though, technically, as one author suggests,[9] the transmission explosion turns into news wherever it happens, whenever it happens, whatever may happen, wherever it is wanted and whenever it is wanted, it is this universality of the potentiality of new technology that makes

---

[7] Schreiber (1974), p. 201.
[8] Ibid., pt. I, ch. 1
[9] Ibid., pt. 3, ch. 1, pp. 165–77.

it the victim of the bosses of media. Accurately, only the big bosses can command such technology and resources as make available this universality. The more the command over all the possible sources of information which are merged in newspapers, the more opinionated the latter become. Paradoxically, more news leads to more commitment to opinion creation. Thus comes the trend towards newspapers acquiring the features of a magazine. With sophisticated consumer and reader research, there is more and more market segmentation. The miscellaneous newspaper is broken into sections. The tendency towards zoning and supplementing helps the profitability of the paper.[10] Thus, the new techniques of printing and distribution make feasible a new role for the newspaper as a 'hold-all' for information products, whether these are offshoots of the main paper or foreign products altogether. The Calcutta *Telegraph* is on example.

One of the most rapidly developing techniques of newspaper advertising has been the preprint—sheets of carefully zoned advertising slotted into the daily or Sunday edition just prior to delivery and printed by the newspaper's own plant or by some other local printing house. Thus a newspaper is sliced into component parts, repackaged, redesigned and 'zoned'.

A computerised newspaper is not simply a labour or cost saving one (which it undoubtedly is where, for example, in the US, typesetting means a saving of 40 per cent of setting labour or where new technology signifies more columns per page and lighter weights of paper, thus reducing the amount of newsprint to be used), but it is a new medium with a new purpose. This arose from a series of technologies that originated with the space and missile programme. It later infiltrated, or was made use of, in a range of industries that had become crisis-ridden and technically obsolete. The whole new organisation in a newspaper reveals certain features about the nature of the reading public itself also: about its assumed attention span, about its preferences for kinds of materials, about its homogeneously shared interests as well as its various other preferences. More accurately, the newspaper moulds the public more into its own preferred design. Since today's newspaper has to be a completely new one, the real problem in applying computer science to the newspaper industry is that of breaking down habitual attitudes,

---

[10] Smith (1980), sec. 4.

methods and relationships within the newspaper organisation itself. Another crucial issue is the market structure. The new phenomenon is the monopoly over news as well as readership. For example, computers help a paper to embark on its own programme of consumer trend analysis. The editorial department uses the same service to learn more about its readers and conduct opinion surveys for the feature page. The same logic leads to computerisation of the circulation department, even for small newspapers, thus raising the survival level in the market. More and more departments are thus being supplied with video display terminals to operate the computer on-line. All the new inventions in the main function of a newspaper and its ancillary wings help to confirm the newspaper as a medium of zonal control and zonal monopolies. As the market goes through a general boom, the advertisement revenue increases; during a depression, too, its shock absorber is stronger because of its capacity of fall back upon advertisement revenue and its role of presiding over the spending power of the community. Establishing total command over its universe of households, a newspaper can then bring into full play its total range of extra functions and services. For instance, it can become a localised general research institute with its collection of back copies and clippings. And it can bring increased expertise in the field of librarianship with 'deep classification' techniques.

Finally, behind all this lies the idea of an ultimate system.[11] Introducing computers to newspapers is no longer experimental to the supplying company or the receiving one. But as computerisation proceeds, not one at a time but according to need, improvisation, ongoing technological improvements and competition, we can say that the newspaper does not buy 'the system off the peg' and get the whole staff in the right frame of operation. But the ultimate system of cold type printing is emerging—on-line computerisation from the newsroom to the loading dock. The VDTs of the newsroom and advertisement staff lead to the main computer where pages are automatically made.Then the laser beams are activated by the plate maker to create the necessary printing plate, which goes to the offset printer. Bundling, wrapping and delivery to the designated trucks are all computer directed. Auxiliary functions relating to administration and finance are similarly computerised.

[11] Ibid., sec. 3, pp. 85–86.

Finally, the newspaper becomes a giant database. But very few employees remain to make the whole system work and tick.

This is not a far-fetched scenario. Small publications have already ·started this process, and have thus rendered themselves more vulnerable to information producing giants and giant newspaper companies. According to a story by William E. Brooks Jr., editor of the *Sun Commercial*, filed in *Presstime*, two US small daily newspapers have reached the plate making stage almost entirely through the use of PCs. Editorial matter, display ads, and full page ads all are handled by network systems. The services of Associated Press, Datastream, Datafeatures, Laserphoto, Access for Graphics, and so on, are linked to computers. The *Sun Commercial's* daily circulation is 14,518 for weekdays and 15,939 for Sunday. Nearly two dozen Apple Macintosh plus personal computers in networks connected to Monotype Blaser typesetters comprise a front end system that produces the Vincennes *Sun Commercial*. The key to making the complete editorial conversion to Macs was to find a software package to process wire copy. The answer has come from Lorenz Management Systems Inc., of Ann Arbor, Michigan which sells a Mac package embracing both wire and local editorial copy. The people who developed desktop publishing had not seriously considered the daily newspaper as a potential user of the technology. Weekly newspapers picked it up because of the fact that the cost of a sophisticated, computer driven system was suddenly within their reach. Producing a newspaper with networked personal computers, off the shelf software and laser typesetters is, for the small newspaper, as exciting as converting to offset press and cold type was almost a generation ago.[12] Who knows, desktop technology may soon capture the big press too.[13]

The newspaper has become multidimensional. It stores and disseminates information in totally new ways and has the capacity to give a person only what he wants, and relieves him of the necessity of paying for what he does not. Thus, editing, distribution and economies of scale all are involved in reorganisation. Conversely, one can see in this process the evolution of the journalist into an information technician, the transformation of the metal

[12] *RIND Survey*, Monthly Bulletin of the Resarch Institute for Newspaper Development, Madras, Vol. IX, No. 12, December 1988.
[13] Desktop technology invaded the big press in India within a year of writing this section.

compositor into a computer operator, the emergence and increase in power of media giants and oligopolies in the newspaper industry, the conclusive hold of information monopolies over the newspaper industry and a shift in the response of the workers to the change in the industry.

Motives behind this major change certainly existed, which I shall now discuss. But here the point is that the emerging 'ultimate system' changes the whole medium. As Anthony Smith states:

> This was also in the earlier days of printing, when the Gutenbergian principle was introduced to reduce the labour of copying text, but stayed to change the nature of the text itself and its role in society (Smith, 1980: 85–86).

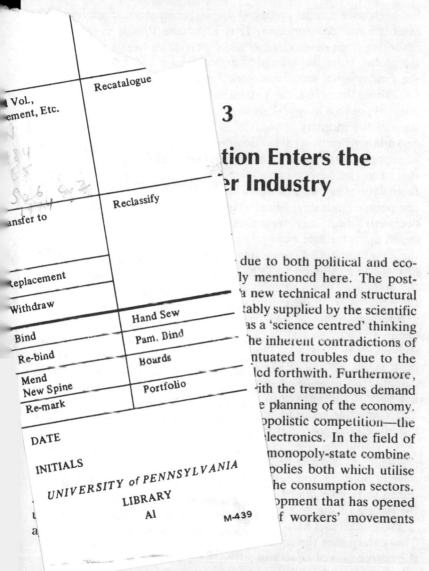

3

tion Enters the
er Industry

due to both political and eco-
ly mentioned here. The post-
a new technical and structural
tably supplied by the scientific
as a 'science centred' thinking
he inherent contradictions of
ntuated troubles due to the
led forthwith. Furthermore,
ith the tremendous demand
e planning of the economy.
opolistic competition—the
lectronics. In the field of
monopoly-state combine.
polies both which utilise
he consumption sectors.
opment that has opened
f workers' movements

Monopolies and Newspapers in the Market Place

Let us now see how far these factors operate in the newspaper industry and in what way. I shall first present a general picture. As has been shown in the preceding chapter, computerised printing is an international development. It is a process that is continuously emerging from developments and experiments over a huge part of the globe, from the United States to Japan. I shall first examine the fundamental factors at work here. In citing instances, I shall sometimes draw on the experience of the US communications industry, as that may give us an idea of the advanced technological state of the industry.

Anthony Smith writes, 'Computers came to the rescue of the newspaper at the end of the 1960s when demographic changes with regard to the newspaper audience had started to undermine the financial nexus through which the medium worked'.[1] A naturally competitive industry, founded in the market of a nineteenth and twentieth century city, turned into a naturally monopolistic medium based upon the late twentieth century megalopolis. Further, with the development of communication facilities, newspapers started growing in a chain ownership. Tastes developed and varied among the audience, needs developed, printing technology boomed and the newspaper, in the course of this changeover that itself entailed a complete financial and dynastic restructuring of the industry, began to acquire too high a quantity of text for the existing technology to cope with. 'Industrial relation problems, rising newsprint costs, escalating distribution costs all took their toll and computerisation—like a *deus ex machina*—represented an important part of the answer to the newspapers' mounting problems'.[2] The computer reduced the setting costs, but, at the same time, introduced the possibility of a further series of changes. Continuing these would, in the long run, change the whole nature of the medium. As already mentioned, it was the same with the earlier days of printing, too, when the Gutenbergian principle was introduced to reduce the labour of copying text, but stayed to change the nature of the text itself and its role in society.

The crucial fact here is that the *newspaper is in the market place*. This determines the intrinsic logic of monopolistic development, the correlation of news and advertisement, the structural relationship between the newspaper industry and other industries and, finally, the zonal character of its hold over its constituency, which

[1] Smith (1980), p. xii.
[2] Ibid.

includes the lay public as well as the business of that area and the existence of different social movements that also clamour for attention.

There are basically two factors that continuously fuel the newspaper economy towards acquiring a monopolistic character or, more appropriately, two reasons why monopolies acquire a ;ewspaper. First, post-tax profits here are more, in fact almost double the average rate for Fortune 500. Secondly, it is the advertising base and not total circulation that determines the profitability of a newspaper. In a society where most big newspapers have local monopoly distribution zones, a newspaper is able to preside over the total spending power of a community without any comparable medium threatening to undercut the rate at which space is sold (though television poses a challenge to the newspaper by holding similar sway over time sale). But here, too, the main competition is over editorial content and time of the audience, for the newspaper can get its advertisements into the vast majority of homes within a given geographical area and can thus hold great power over every enterprise attempting to sell goods within that region. The relevance of new technology is most clear here, for this is the tool by which its hold over the region can be accomplished in depth and fast. During general boom conditions, a newspaper grows as the advertisement expenditures of every enterprise active in the market go up. More significantly, a monopoly newspaper can reduce its size and losses and make use of its greater cushion capacity to perhaps even make a profit during times of general slump. Its greater manoeuverability comes to the rescue then.

The continuous stability of a newspaper thus encourages a monopoly medium to go ahead with drastic or revolutionary technical change and adopting a new technological base. Its relative immunity to the cyclical performance (of course, relative) of the surrounding industry helps it look forward to a long period of continuous technical improvement for reducing the cost and increasing the sources of revenue. Moreover, while an increasing information load forces the owner of a newspaper to search for new technology so as to survive in the market, it becomes the vested interest of the owner to acquire and distribute more and more information through this medium so that it can become a 'hold-all' for all the information products of its constituency. Its monopoly position is thus asserted and strengthened through hegemony over the products not only at a material level but at an ideational level as well, where the newspaper industry, coupled with its literary supplements, extends its domination over ideational products. This cultural domination is an urge that can hardly be overestimated in assessing the trend towards monopoly.

The way in which newspaper barons perceive their tasks and imperatives for modernisation is thus a very crucial factor, though the facts may not always correspond to their supposed imperatives and perceptions. For example, they always perceive the introduction of automation as effectively labour cost saving. But exactly how much nobody can say, for even in the previous system much was superfluous. Here, it is their perception of the problem that matters and sets the pace of change. Most publishers, again, are keenly aware of the amount that the new system costs them. However they are more vague about how much it saves them. There are plenty of out of context figures available for the number of typesetters removed from the composition room and the number of pressmen 'saved' in the press room. Several overall calculations end up with a figure of around 15 per cent as the amount of reduction in total costs effected by the introduction of a modern front-end system with full photocomposition, in an existing hot metal newspaper. Most analysts claim that the necessary investment can be paid for within two years from the savings in the wage bill, although this figure, too, is questionable, as an examination of the dozens of variables that must be entered into the ledger will show. Due to inefficiency in previous operations, much superfluous expenditure already existed, and a saving on this could hardly be claimed as the cost saving capacity of the new system. Since it is the perception of the bosses that counts along with haggling with the union, no evaluation can be made per se. All the changes in the organisation can be phased in and out, and a firm calculation is thus almost impossible.

Nonetheless, monopolies consider the introduction of new technology cost effective. Also, it offers them the scope to use the 'broomstick' to revitalise the organisation. Above all, there is the economics of new information technology, against the background of which the modernisation of newspapers like the *New York Times*, the *Los Angeles Times* and the London *Times* assumes significance. As I have already indicated, a modern newspaper is very much connected with a modern information network, and for that it has to possess or have access to suitable modern information technologies and techniques. Thus the technical base of a modern newspaper, whether in the United States or India, is influenced and controlled by information monopolies like IBM and AT & T.

In fifteenth century Europe, Johann Gutenberg started the print revolution by printing Bibles and other religious works. Today, a new print revolution connects the newspaper with electronic data banks, dispensing with paper, printing and binding, with terminals bringing in news on cathode ray screens. Such electronic publication means information monopolies spreading information through home computers, word processors, telephone and satellite transmissions, and so on, at an unbelievably low cost per unit. This means the large scale use of holography—an electronically squeezed-in information storage process that can fit the equivalent of large libraries of data into the space of a table-top. Holography uses lasers to record and retrieve information. Its ability to compress prodigious amounts of data into small spaces makes it useful for archival tasks. There is also the photocopier and mimeograph—the intelligent copiers. Whoever might be the actual user of these instruments in an information establishment, the top information monopolies will gain.[3] Thus, no doubt monopoly capitalism correctly grasps the significance of the basic relevance and domination of information technology and system. As a 1979 OECD report describes it, the information industry is the 'pole around the productive structure'.[4]

The market of the information industry dictates the job pattern in the newspaper industry also. For example, professionals and managers will now increasingly hold more jobs. This is equally

---

[3] Dizard (1982), ch. 3, p. 81. Indeed, even developed western Europe is dominated by American firms like IBM and UNIVAC, without whose information machines western Europe would become a lame duck within a day, and who continue to hold over 70 per cent of the market (over 90 per cent if one includes computers licensed from US firms). In western Europe, only four firms can be mentioned: British International Computers, French Campagnie Internationale, Siemens and AEG-Telefunken in Germany, and Philips, a Dutch firm. See Kinter and Sicherman (1975), pp. 86–87. Regarding holography see, for example, Ostrovsky (1977).

It is interesting to note that just like all electronic technology, holography has also had an impact on social science, particularly on methods of social analysis. See, for example, Ganguly and Ganguly (1983–84).

[4] Cited in *The Economist*, 3 January 1981.

true for the entire communications sector. In a 1979 report (cited in Dizard 1982) two sectors in the United States showed gains in a productivity survey of eleven industries from 1973–78, that is, banking and communications. In 1979, for instance, AT & T System handled 185 billion telephone calls with one million employees—185 thousand calls per employee. The economic hold of the information giants was revealed in studies on the information sector by Fritz Machlup and Uri Porat (1962; 1977, cited in Dizard 1982). There is intense competition now. To cite examples again from the United States, new names in innovations are making breakthroughs in information systems like ITEL, Racal and MCI. Monopolies are rooted very deep. In the information sector commenting on AT & T, one observer has remarked, 'Economics dictate a monopoly since a universal system cannot be built without cross subsidisation between high density profitable and low-density unprofitable services'.[5] Newspapers are customers to most information gadgets; thus it is a hybrid information system. Should it be called communiputers? Computercations? Compunication? Many giants are involved in this hybrid besides IBM and AT & T—Xerox, Comsat, RCA, ITT and Hewlett & Packard. The hybrid is the most integrated, thus excluding from the outset any haphazard economic orientation. The Satellite Business System of IBM transmits information to small earth terminals through its own satellites, all the Fortune 500 corporations being its clients. GTE, another giant, conducts electronic mail systems, whose worth in 1987 was $122 billion. Xerox Corporation makes computerised photocopying products. General Electric provides centralised storage and data-bank services. There are also newcomers like Exxon, an oil monopoly. They dominate the means of production in the newspaper industry where the tools today are word processing machines, terminals, long-distance facsimile equipment, phototypesetting machines, high speed printers and related communications gear.[6]

There are novel branch-outs of new technology. In the United States, the *New York Times* runs an 'information bank' that serves on terminals to customers throughout the country. There may be such specialised banks like the Middle East data section of the *New York Times*. Other firms are also in this business, like *Reader's*

[5] Dizard (1982), ch. 4, pp. 98–99.
[6] Ibid. ch. 4.

Digest or *Dow Jones*. Another newspaper, *Columbia Despatch*, transmits its entire editorial content to home terminals. This offers a new challenge to regular television viewing—a real electronic newspaper. Formerly there were several media operating at different levels within an urban conglomerate. Now, wholescale urban systems are sought to be built up by communication conglomerates dominating all the levels, cities being the important prizes. Several media have to be coordinated in a single system that becomes the medium. This is the result of monopolisation in information business.

The Political Factor in the Modernisation of the Newspaper Industry

Automation in the newspaper industry has not created information giants; rather, the latter has preceded the former. Against such a perspective, it is pertinent to note here that the very political-economic nature of a newspaper is such that it has always been, so to say, almost a sitting duck for monopolies ever in search of effective instruments of political-economic control.

The clash between the editorial staff and the owners of a newspaper has been a frequent occurrence in the post-War era, when the economic potential of a newspaper was revealed in an unprecedented way. The ideas of Bryce (who said, 'It is the newspaper press that has made democracy possible'), Laski ('A people without reliable news is, sooner or later, a people without a basis of freedom'), Victor Hugo ('The greatest invention of all times'), or Locke ('Freedom is inconceivable without free speech,' which was quoted with relish by the Press Secretary of President Johnson, George E. Reedy, speaking on the attitude of American politics towards the freedom of the press—a politics that, within a few years, would create the Watergate scandal and Pentagon Papers scandal) are today being realised in a dialectically opposite manner where, in a big paper like the *New York Times*, over 400 journalists have been on the roll of the CIA for over the past twenty-five years! The famous journalist Salburger also kept up a regular liaison with the CIA. Syndicated columns now increasingly rule the roost. For example, the column of Jack Anderson is publihsed in 700 daily papers. A conservative news baron of Germany,

P. Goete, admitted that news freedom is only for 200 moneybags who can command the media to express their opinions. One of the dinosaurs of the press, which became a victim of modern electronics propaganda, the American journal *Life*, found its ex-editor Thomas Griffith admitting that the newspaper is purely a business, dishing out paper notes instead of paper news. He bemoaned the decline in the role of the editor, a point supported by the Director of the International Press Institute, Peter Galliner, who also commented on the decline in democracy in the press.[7] The publishers, of course, maiñtain that only a new type of editor is required, and other press freedoms remain unimpaired. In fact this is a round-about way of saying that the newspaper is a full-fledged part of a business economy, and the editor has to adapt himself to it. The domination of the business economy over journalism is a point over which the Press Commission in India also lamented during Nehru's days. Thus, old doyens like Ramananda Chattopadhyaya, Satyendra Narain Mazumder or the old editors of the *New Statesman* would be misfits today in newspapers under monopoly business commanding huge chains through modern electronics technology.

Hence, it would be wrong to assume that the essence of mono-polistic control over the modern press, particularly a computerised press, has only been economic. Besides economic reasons, there is a political aspect too. A little has already been said about structural changes in a city and the problems of a modern urban society that necessitated the transition of a 'Gutenberg newspaper' to an elec-tronic one.

The twin factors active from opposite directions in the drive towards computerisation are the drive of monopolies for greater technological-political control over society (stricter command based on detailed information of all social aspects), and the drive from the opposite direction, that is, from the democratic aspect. This is embodied in the demand for more information, a decentralisation of decision making sources, and the demand for an end to discre-pancy over access to information. Both these trends—from the angle of the monopoly bourgeoisie as well as from the broad mass of people—have made computerisation a reality at all social levels. And both make up the dialectical unity of the information order of a capitalist society, of which the newspaper is an integral part.

---

[7] All these facts and citations are from Mukhopadhyay (1984), pp. 118–19.

Take, for example, some random cases of these overlapping trends. Modern society is so complicated with new social issues (like ecology, health, education and women's liberation) that public decisions at the grassroots level have become imperative. At least decisions at the top must reach the grassroots public level. As one commentator remarked:

In the thirties, the great dams of the Tennessee Valley Authority were the prototype for future technocratic success. In the sixties, the model was the Apollo space programme and its systems-analysis path to the moon. The new computer-based age would bring similar analytic efficiency to such earthbound problems as education, poverty, foreign policy, transportation, and the cities.

Writing in March 1967, a team of researchers studying inner city problems in Detroit declared, 'We feel that, in a very real sense, the age of the computer has ushered in a new age of urban planning (Dizard, 1982: 118–19).

Four months later, Detroit went up in flames, urban renewal projects included. The smoky pall that hung over the city for days was a pungent reminder that stubborn social problems were not amenable to computer print-out solutions. Civil disorder was followed by the escalation of war in Vietnam, economic setbacks, and public setback that culminated in the Watergate scandal. The experience with new information technologies during the first computer decade, however overblown, was useful in defining the limits of computerised shortcuts. The result has been a more realistic view of the role of communications and information—an important but not a cure-all resource in reducing economic and social problems. It is clear that the monopoly bourgeoisie tried for a 'science' centred solution to the social problems of a capitalist order; which was reflected, among other things, in a technological system of more news, quicker news, greater storage of news, further dissemination of news and wider variety in the collection and distribution of news, in short, the essence of an automised newspaper. But it is not clear if the bourgeoisie has forsaken such a solution, for the basic issue before it is still the more effective management of society with the help of the control over distribution of power, enhancement of the ability to manage through the new technologies that permit massive centralisation and manipulation of a wider range of information resources than ever before. It is thus not a purely spontaneous development of electronic technology spilling into different communications media; it has been a policy consideration. As John Debuts, a former board chairman of AT & T (one of the transnational information giants) frankly admitted, 'It is not technology that will shape the future of telecommunications in this country. Nor is it the market. It is policy'.[8] In this policy consideration, the State is heavily involved. For example, in the US, the country with the most developed electronics communications, there are many State agencies immersed in developing telecommunications, for instance, the Department of Transportation handling air and maritime communications, the State Department negotiating agreements, the International Communications Agency operating the Voice of America, NASA handling satellite communications, CIA analysing telecommunication developments abroad or the National Security Agency engaged in highly secret monitoring of foreign communications, and the Social Security Administration controlling and handling millions of separate files of information relating to jobs and social security. Thus, there are all kinds of data banks, formerly autonomous, now gradually being interrelated, that find a reflection of their technology in the post-Gutenberg newspaper. Since this system of interrelated information networks involves massive start-up costs, it is only a certain structure of business that can undertake such investments to reap the economic and social gains inherent in the productivity increase and seek a coherent flow of information. There is thus a political-social motive that urges the conglomerates to go for high-capacity communications circuitry and data banks.

But, ironically and conversely, the avenues for rapid dissemination of information create information-seekers below. Though exaggerated, Alvin Toffler's image of a democracy in communications is a possibility, increasingly contradictory to the centralised ownership and control above. Newspapers can effectively come from small and medium towns and have instant access to all information sources; data banks can be situated in a decentralised form too; there may be local community interest channels; finally, decision making too can become possible at the local level.

[8] *Communications News*, September 1980.

Finally, there is another intermingling trend—that of exporting information or the urge of the conglomerates to export capital in the form of information—that engenders the telecom revolution abroad. Once again this creates an offshoot in the shape of a revolution in information media in other countries, including some countries and regions of the third world. A newspaper must send matter/facsimile through satellite to its chain publications, and must receive the same for quick publication. Automation, as was explained earlier, is a system. It may start from any vantage point depending upon local specificities, but will finish as a front-end system, which will become an integral part of the telecom revolution based on electronics. Thus, though satellites do not by themselves destroy Gutenberg, they pave the way for its destruction. There is also a motive to amplify the Westernised ideas and values abroad—certainly an ideological motive, helped by the 105 nation Intelsat satellite network providing high-grade communications wherever there is an earth terminal. Again, there are vital interests at stake here: AT & T, the US link in the massive spurt in world telephone traffic; Xerox, the exporter of PTS machines; RCA, Global Communications, ITT controlling telex business and other text and data traffic, even from high speed terminal to computer. A report indicated a 16 per cent annual growth in such services in the early eighties, with total revenues reaching $14 billion by 1985.[9] The economic stakes, plus the political motives, are, thus, really high. Telenet's specialised data network, thus, has access to the New York Times Information Bank. There is stiff competition in this high-stake international field where Japanese firms compete with American ones, and with European firms steadily registering their presence as well. As the *Economist* noted, patenting has almost collapsed and a technological lead in electronics survives usually for only 18 months.[10] Hence governments back up their communication firms in the scramble for bigger shares. IBM remains the leader in this field with its research, innovation and mainline servicing. Others use IBM systems, at least for economy. However, yet others are fast coming up. The worldwide development of photocomposed printing is a direct result of this international development where the technology pushers remain system builders

[9] Ibid.
[10] *The Economist*, 23 July 1977.

like IBM, or information storage managers like Control Data, Xerox, Systems Development Corporation and Honeywell. Take, for example, the sale of information by TNCs like Associated Press. Since literally millions of people are its captive audience, one can now understand how communication networks are crucial to these media agencies. There is a plea on behalf of the victims of this monopoly for 'information sovereignty'. But without imposing political curbs, it is hard to see how the victims, particularly the third world nations, can go ahead without a Reuters, UPI or even a *Reader's Digest*, *Time* or *Newsweek*. Elite readers of the third world cannot do without *National Geographic* type exoticas. Thus, a separate information system for the third world may remain merely a rhetoric, lacking the capital and expertise for achieving it. Even if a *new world information order* is a slogan worth rallying for, it can come about not by dispensing with technological progress but on the basis of that—an 'open information system' free of monopoly control.

This mix of political, ideological and economic factors in the introduction of new technology in the newspaper industry has been clearly observed by trade unions in the newspaper industry. For example, the Confederation of different organisations of newspaper and newsagency employees in India commented in a report on modernisation:

Monopoly over an industry enables industrialists to dictate prices. Moreover, monopoly in the newspaper industry is capable of refashioning readers, ideas and tastes and diverting their attention from people's agony and sufferings under the existing exploitative system—the very basis of their existence. It is not accidental that the number of glossy Indian magazines—catering to base instincts like sex-perversions and crime—has increased in the recent past. The latest technology in printing has come handy to Indian employers as well. Such being their philosophy and practice, all this talk of progress is rubbish. In view of the increasing trend towards monopoly and concentration of newspaper production in fewer and fewer hands, the situation will go from bad to worse. The economy in production resulting from computerisation will in no way benefit employees in general or the readers. Real wages will not go up. Newspapers will not become cheaper. Even the few receiving comparatively high wages will, in reality, be duped. Under the present set up increased productivity of labour means more intensive exploitation from which there is no escape even for workers drawing relatively high wages. The workers' alienation from the instruments and processes of production as well as the products will increase. There will be greater monopoly of work (NCNNAEO, 1983: 2–3)

This report further admitted the possibilities opened up by the new technology, but clearly stated: 'We demand modernisation for social progress as a whole, social ownership, social control, social planning and social benefits of and from all technological progress. The new technology in the printing industry cannot be excluded' (NCNNAEO, 1983: 52).

This adequately sums up the counterdemands and countervailing tendencies operating in the process of automisation in the newspaper industry. Thus, there are different views as to why automation enters the newspaper industry, and we can see the differences that arise because of the differing social nature of those comprehending the objective phenomenon—in short, class differences and ideological differences generating differences in perception.

Illusions certainly exist in perceptions regarding change. We can consider the dreams of Alvin Toffler (which undeniably contained the seeds of a correct perception of new technology), who spoke of the *third wave*—the decentralisation of production, the arrival of the home-office, customised production, a switch over from 'series production' to 'tailor-made' production, a transition from the 'Cartesian' system (products broken into pieces to be painstakingly reassembled) to a 'holistic' one, and a 'presto effect' in manufacturing by intervening at the molecular level, by using computer-aided designs, by integrating more and more functions into fewer and fewer parts, and substituting 'wholes' for many discrete components.[11] It is true that at the concrete level of a newspaper one can note the appearance of the following: a VDT combining the tasks of a newswriter, sub-editor and proof reader, and a multi-processor bus combining the many functions of composing, archiving, proofreading, news gathering, and so on. Then again, there is the

[11] Toffler (1980), p. 185.

increasing integration of photography in journalism, due to modern forms of printing. Again, there is a wide variety in the classification of advertising and zoning. Thus, a more 'customised production' exists due to electronics technology.

But, still, this vision of the future may remain an illusion. For, despite such compelling reasons and the effects of automation, newspapers continue to operate under market laws; and without any concomitant socio-political change, the above changes both at a general and particular level only reinforce the capitalist working of the general economy, the newspaper economy inclusive of it. The workers may resist such change if these threaten their life and security; the wage level may influence decisions to introduce technological change; market competition and monopoly control may induce or halt change; finally, change may or may not occur in a structure of centre-periphery relations in the capitalist world. Thus, there is no scope for technological determinism here.

So the question remains: how are we to view the various levels of interaction between the objective reality (that is, automation in the newspaper industry) and the act of perceiving the reality (that is, the forces pushing forward, forcing back, amending and stalling)? As will be shown through concrete examples of the Indian situation, these levels are indeed very complicated, with the latter definitely influencing the former.

When discussing political factors in the introduction of microelectronics based technology in the newspaper industry, we have to locate the crucial role of the State in the general 'electronic development' of the economy as well as in any branch of industry. In India, at the concrete level of the newspaper industry, the government liberally permitted the import of PTS machines under OGL (open general licence); the periodic revision of wages led the owners to pursue methods of rationalisation; the use of satellite for the dissemination of news and the lending out of post and telegraph facilities for facsimile transmission, and so on. The general science and technology policy of the government acts as the overall backdrop against which this transformation proceeds. The semiconductor industry and computers could not have developed at all in the capitalist world without State aid, and the consequent information revolution would not have become a reality. I need not repeat the well-known story of semiconductor and computer giants like IBM getting their fillip as a continuous process from the State. Suffice it to note here that public policy plays an extremely important part. There is public procurement of semiconductor devices through military spending. When military specifications fail, these are sold to private sector customers at discount prices.

Talking of public policy, we have to consider the entire policy of the State in promoting microelectronics technology. The silicon transister and integrated circuit are consistently in demand by the military and, hence, are continually under research. For example, in the US the National Science Foundation and the National Bureau of Standards have helped Bell Labs. Miniaturisation is encouraged by military specification. There is then public support for higher education, by means of which a technological climate of a certain orientation can be built up in a country, and it may out-compete another in the development of electronics and other areas of frontier technology. In a survey of the semi-conductor industry of the US, it was found that of the related patent holders, government institutions were prominent like the navy held 11, patents, the army 15, NASA 21 and the Department of Energy 56. Thus, State orders and requisitions placed with vertically integrated electronics firms producing both soft and hardware (like IBM and RCA) have contributed greatly to technological diffusion. In producing and shipping semiconductors, manufacturing integrated circuits, developing microelectronic technologies and equipment and in the application of electronics to industry, the hold of vertically integrated firms like IBM and RCA is important. They act as the gatekeepers of State activity in the technological field, and particularly in the communications industry.

Assured defence orders made assembly line products possible for commercial use, and early losses were amply compensated. MIT recommended IBM to the government to work with Lincoln Labs in the design of SAGE systems for the air force. The IBM 701 computer arose out of the Defence Calculator Project, whereby it required the coordination of several computers in real-time calculations: 'if alien aircraft were detected, the system was to select the appropriate interceptor aircraft and determine anti-aircraft missile trajectories'.[12] This ultimately resulted in the IBM 704 and 705. The story of Remington Rand and LARC is also the

---

[12] The original cost stipulated was $2.85 million; the actual cost $19 million. This alone points to the huge risk factor, so ably minimised by a captive market in the form of State policy. See Katz and Phillips (1982), pp. 162–221.

same. These have been crucial for the development of solid state technology, again a factor which made the application of electronics to a wide area of industry possible. The State provided the captive market. Government R & D contracts, purchase and sponsored conferences enabled the application of transistors in computers, pioneered by Bell Labs.

What made the 'electronic transformation' of an intellectual industry like newspapers possible was the fact that from 1964–65 on, processing of time-sharing and real-time applications of computers became important aspects of the continuing development process in the industry. With this, there were vast improvements in memory, control and input-output peripherals. Partly as a result of various governmental interests in miniaturisation, increased speed and improved process-control techniques, a number of 'mini-computers' and 'intelligent terminals' appeared. The 'old transistor' developed into monolithic 'chips'. Random-access memory gave rise to 'virtual memory' computers that ostensibly operated as though there were no bounds to memory capacity. Microprocessors with advanced chip technology appeared. Computer technology changed so rapidly that, in a very short period of time, a VLSI (very large scale integrated) circuit hardly larger than a fingernail became possible. This was the starting point of the development of microelectronics and its subsequent introduction in the field of communications.

Three Questions

If one recalls the technological innovations in the newspaper industry described in the preceding chapter, the theoretical importance of these developments in the context will become abundantly clear. But, in the process, some interesting questions also arise. They are: What is the precise role of an exogenously driven technology in shaping an endogenously determined structure? Is the growth of electronics in the newspaper industry a case of Schumpeterian enterprise, or is it the old story of predominance of monopolies? Can we standardize the computerisation process in the newspaper industry as one of having two stages: government-university-research (first stage) and commercial use (second stage)? In other words, how does a 'near technology' get transformed into a 'becoming technology'?

These are indeed the questions that this whole enquiry is about and, while winding up the various threads of discussion, these are the issues to be concluded upon. The newspaper industry, till the mid-sixties, was in a hothouse which was an endogenously determined structure, so to speak. It had monopolistic control over itself as well as over the news-hungry public. It contained archetypal articles and a narrow advertising base. Then electronics technology—exogenously driven—came like a hurricane to change or initiate total change. Competition grew with the boom in television and magazines. The response of the trade unions was haphazard and indecisive. The workers felt that a technological change was coming which could not be resisted, yet the change was coming at their cost. In such a situation, how could they respond properly to the crisis? Would they obstruct it? If obstruction was the only way out, could they do it at the trade level, or at the still larger national level, or wherever possible (at the unit-plant level)? It was this lack of decisiveness that helped the press barons push through automation everywhere, from the United States to India.[13] I shall show in the next chapter dealing with the response of the working class, the scenario around the automation of the newspaper industry seemed extremely complicated to the workers and their unions. It was this complexity that speeded up technological change and engulfed the workers in massive change in the technological set-up, workflow and management. They were virtually left with a fait accompli.

Again, competition was certainly an augmenting factor. In the US, old dinosaurs like *Life* died. The basic technology was being enriched with innovations from medium sized firms, which were later eaten up by big firms like IBM. Small magazines, newspapers and information bulletins began emerging in towns, leaving the megalopolis to big newspapers. Then again it showed that like the field of basic technology, here too the vertically integrated firms in publishing had an intrinsic advantage (that is, the ones who could combine newspapers, magazines, information services and job work could reap the advantages of new technology best).[14] It is they who pushed modernisation the quickest, be it the *New York Times*, *Los Angeles Times* or *Dow Jones* in the US or the *Times of*

[13] For an account of such a dilemma, see Smith (1980), Section 6, where the position taken by the ITU (International Typographers Union) is discussed in detail. On the strike in the *New York Herald Tribune*, see Kluger (1986).

[14] A fascinating account of the scenario can be had from Williams (1978), chs. 6, 7, 12 and 13.

India or *Indian Express* in India. It was again a new management strategy that made automation a reality in the industry. Compared to earlier rationalisations, this was far more fundamental and total, far more revolutionary, and far more at the cost of the life and livelihood of the workers. Yet it was achieved with far less friction. Why? As I shall show later, one reason was the new management strategy, which tamed the union into accepting automation, or rather involved the latter as an official partner in the whole process.[15] The earlier excessive 'sectional politics' in unionism had given birth, possibly as a reaction to it also, to what has been termed as 'new syndicalism' among the organised workers. It facilitated the adoption by the management of a new style of management, which encouraged the unions into co-sponsoring modernisation. Moreover, while researches and further advances in computerised printing technology continued in the West, in India they were adapted to local limits—a classic case of centre-periphery relations. In short, the afore mentioned questions show how technology in a given situation is not mere technology, but politics and economics as well, a technical issue becoming in its entirety a social issue.

In Great Britain, journalists who were opposing attempts by newspaper managements to get them to 'key-in' their own copy directly into a phototypesetter (thus dispensing with a separate composing department) asserted in a booklet published by the National Union of Journalists called *Journalists and the New Technology* (1981): 'The reasons why managements seek to introduce new technology may be broken down into five main areas; (*a*) rationalisation and re-equipment; (*b*) manpower saving; (*c*) deskilling; (*d*) undermining the power of the trade unions, and (*e*) assertion of management control.'

Press in India and New Technology

Coming to the concrete example of our country, let us see how this mix of various dimensions has been active in the modernisation process in the newspaper industry.

---

[15] Such a management strategy has been used in, for example, Scandinavian countries. See Timashkova (1981), ch. 4.

Availability of Machinery

In India, deskilling is not such an important factor, given the generally low level of wages. But the outdating of technology, given the external source of the basic printing technology, is very much a motivating factor here for modernisation in the newspaper industry. As the Executive Director of the Printers (Mysore) Ltd, publishers of the *Deccan Herald* and the Kannada newspaper, *Prajavani*, K.N. Harikumar told the correspondent of *Business India*, their linotypes and letterpress rotaries were 30 to 40 years old and needed replacement. Foreign suppliers, mostly American or German, now no longer manufactured these, so they had to shift to phototypesetting and offset printing. Even if any new letterpress rotaries are imported, for example from the CIS where high speed letterpress rotaries are still manufactured, the management cannot be sure if spare parts will be available ten years hence, although these machines can last for at least 30 years.[16]

Tax Planning

Differing tax rebates are also an important factor. Depreciation allowance, import liberalisation speeded up by the IMF conditionalities in 1982 and 1991 and (corporate) income tax rebates have turned the trickle of imports of microprocessors and computer controlled printing machinery by large Indian printing firms into a flood.

Some companies have opted for an intermediate process and use photocomposed text on existing letterpress rotaries by using photopolymer plates. This is no doubt expensive, each plate costing around Rs 70 after import and other duties. Thus it works out to around Rs 15 lakh a year for 64 plates needed every day for a 16 page newspaper. Still, this is lower than the interest payable for a high speed web offset printing press. This is how the *Bombay Samachar* has effected the transition; the *Statesman*, too, has done it in this way. As the *Business India* report cited earlier shows, the gradual introduction of facsimile transmission machines in the *Hindu* and scanners in the *Times of India* had been planned

---

[16] *Business India*, 'Printing Technology Takes Off,' 18–31 July 1983.

with different tax rebates in mind. The union-management correspondence which I shall discuss in detail later also testifies to this. Modernisation and tax planning go side-by-side. Tax planning induced both by government policy and the company's own budget and accounting have acted as a catalyst.[17] Referring to tax rebates, an executive of the *Hindu* admitted, 'Between 1978 and 1982 we have spent Rs 3.5 crore. In the next three years we intend to spend another Rs 7 crore towards modernisation.'[18]

Labour Saving

Job shedding is also an important factor. As unions are understandably perturbed and strongly opposed to any direct labour cuts, there may not be any direct retrenchment. But gradually, through retirement and premature voluntary retirement, the management will push towards eventual cuts in the labour force As has been pointed out already, while the Palekar Award hiked up wages, the management sought a way out via the backdoor. A Statesman Employees' Union study (1982) estimated that the changeover to photocomposition and offset printing would ultimately result in a reduction in the press workforce from 706 at the hot metal stage to only 192 people after modernisation.

All ILO report observed a cut of 50 to 70 per cent of manpower requirements as a result of new printing technologies. Though new technology may help large establishments bring out new editions from other, particularly smaller, centres, or newer papers may come out, yet it is universally acknowledged that additional manpower requirements would then be restricted to additional editorial staff for local news, coupled with a small complement of composing room and print shop workers. The addition, in other words, cannot compensate the reduction. The newspaper and magazine revolution, however, will be a revolution at the tip of the iceberg only, for as the *Report on a Survey of Printing in India* (1982), carried out by the ORG (Operational Research Group) (cited in *Business India*, 18–31 July 1983) pointed out, the 188 newspaper presses and elite presses like Thomson (bringing out *India Today*)

[17] Tax rebate was the reason cited by the Statesman management when asked by the Employees' Union about the need for speeding up modernisation, talk on 8 January 1986.

[18] *Business India*, 'Printing Technology Takes off'.

or Tata Press form only a miniscule proportion of the 43,000 printing presses in the country, though the former handle large quantities of print. As the survey has pointed out, nearly 88 per cent of the printing presses are letterpress with handcompsoing facilities, nearly 70 per cent employ less than 10 people and around 80 per cent have an annual turnover of less than Rs 42 lakh. The printing industry employs 5.33 lakh persons. Of this, some 69 per cent are accounted for by presses having less than 10 workmen. Printing in India is mainly a small scale industry, depending mostly on letter press technology. And the computer revolution will modernise only the top. It is difficult to see any percolating effect, though with the top cornering as much job work as possible, it is conceivable that many below in the business may go red. It is clear that the basic new printing technology is not cheap by Indian standards, nor are the products therefrom coming on the basis of a low scale of operation. Thus, both the possibilities remain. While one section below may be ruined as in West Bengal, another section may yet survive by their incredibly low cost of production, with almost no depreciation cost and extremely low wages. Computers, thus, have arrived, but not very much or to an overwhelming extent.

Low wages also act as a damper. The average pressman/compositor, according to the ORG report, earns Rs 500 a month, a mere pittance. According to the same report, of the 1.1 lakh printing machines, 90 per cent are letterpress treadles, platens or cylinder machines. Of the rest, some 7,000 are sheet-fed offset printing machines and 116 web-fed offset machines. The ORG survey put the total investment in machinery in the industry in 1977 at Rs 450 crore (or 12 employees per every one lakh rupees of investment). At this level, it appears that another few hundred crore rupees would be required to modernise the entire industry. Some 600 phototypesetters and 20 direct screening scanners have been imported, according to one estimate, within the last four years. Offset printing units are fast expanding in the small scale sector, thus setting a standard for vernacular press coming out of small/medium towns. However, vernacular press based on PTS is costlier, sometimes 50 per cent higher than English.

There are snags too in the race for computerisation among the top groups. Opting for photocomposing means opting for quality improvement, which often amounts to becoming an unwilling victim of high pressure salesmanship. Then there is dumping of equipment, for technological obsolescence is faster in a PTS machine. Unlike hot metal machines which have a lifetime of 30 to 40 years and have a comparatively high resale value even after their supposed life span, the normal life of a PTS machine, in the sense of keeping abreast with technological development, is much shorter. Sometimes, the reorganisation within a newspaper set-up is not done in such a way as to take full advantage of phototypesetting. Computers which can take on many keyboards are not fully utilised, perhaps either due to trade union resistance or due to insufficient infrastructural facilities, or maybe even due to a lack of sufficient funds to fully computerise the entire set-up: It may even be that the management wishes to rush in computerisation to score a victory in the constant tug-or-war against the union without overall planning and arrangement. This is the story of the *Statesman, Jugantar* and even the *Amrita Bazar Patrika*.

As the home market is small for even non-newspaper big printers, some of them have begun exporting phototypesetting prints. For example, Macmillan India Ltd, armed with a unit of 4 monotype film setters, 20 keyboards and 5 editing terminals worth Rs 1 crore, does publishing jobs from abroad. Others like Tata Press and Printwell also aim at such a market.[19]

One thing that can be said is that as long as costs remain higher than traditional presses and there is no large spread of literacy and no adequate supply of cheap paper (in other words, as long as there is no lowering of printing costs that bring the printed word within the reach of a majority of the country's population), we cannot expect a real boom in photocomposed printing. Apart from some notable national and vernacular newspapers, and more particularly glossy magazines like *India Today* and *Debonair*, there will not be much percolation below, however much Arun Mehta, the president of the All India Federation of Master Printers (AIFMP) might expect and suggest.[20]

Competition from Magazines and the Growth of the Middle Class

Kicking newspapers upwards (that is, forcing them to adopt new technology) was the magazine boom of 1977–87. Magazines

---

[19] Ibid.
[20] *All India Federation of Master Printers (AIFMP) Annual Report*, 1983, New Delhi.

fight tooth and nail for the quality-conscious limited market, and the result is worth studying. The market that English national dailies and magazines aim for is a select market. The middle and upper middle class market is quality conscious. The magazine boom, and the consequent or accompanying modernisation of newspapers, is a direct result of that marketing effort. Colour printing has become cheap and there is advertising gloss and packaging punch. All this serves a function that is similar to slick chromeglass shops, fast food restaurants, videos and packaged foreign tours.

There are several factors behind the magazine boom: growth in the number of literates, fast urbanisation or growth of the urban population, development in communications and investigative reporting are some of these. As a leading magazine *India Today* remarked in an almost autobiographical tone, the Emergency and the post-Emergency liberal atmosphere gave rise to investigative writing, and the floodgate of saucy story writing mixed with Anderson's *All the President's Men* style of reporting opened with magazines quickly cashing in on it.[21] They started competing with dailies in circulation. Delhi Press prints 17 lakh magazines a month and this accounts for an overwhelming proportion of their Rs 4.5 crore turnover. In-house magazine printing of *Sarita* (fortnightly, 300,000 copies), *Grihashobha* (2.25 lakh copies) and a few others accounts for 92 per cent of its capacity. Another press, Thomson Press, has shown how printing as a precision technology can help magazines like *India Today* and *Readers' Digest*. The poster campaign for Hot Shot camera in the pages of these magazines exhibited the potential of the new combine. By modernising the entire printing equipment and cashing in on the magazine boom throughout the seventies, Thomson Press increased its assets by 11.46 per cent in 1980, 21.07 per cent in 1981 and 38.61 per cent in 1982. At the end of 1982 its net assets stood at Rs 8.68 crore. Along with printing has come packaging modernisation. Corporate consciousness of status and the corresponding emphasis given to image building activities have emphasised the production of increasingly volumnious corporate literature like brochures, balance sheets, diaries and calenders. Label designing and the packaging of home appliances (like mixers, toasters, irons and cooking ranges) is now an

[21] *India Today*, Tenth Anniversary Issue, 31 January 1985; see in particular, Aroon Purie, 'The Inside Story,' p. 6.

expert field. 'As a rule of thumb,' explains one businessman, 'the cost of packaging should work out to between 5 and 10 per cent of the retail price for necessities such as tea, oil, foods and detergents.'[22]

However, even if retail prices have increased, the demand for quality printing and packing has not lessened. The price of offset machines has soared. A two colour offset machine cost Rs 6 lakh in 1976 and Rs 40 lakh in 1987–88. In 1982–83, when printing equipment could be imported under OGL, more than 500 printing machines were ordered by printers in the Delhi region alone. There is a mushrooming growth of small printing units almost remniscent of the Schumpeterian pattern, but perhaps in a closed circle, for the hierarchy in the printing business (machine-wise and location-wise) in the modernised set-up is obvious! Apart from packaging, there is processing which also helps the magazine grow. Scanners have been introduced. Artwork from the printer, or advertising agency, consisting of design and transparencies, are scanned quickly. An earlier requirement of two hours on an enlarger is now reduced to 10 to 15 minutes on a Magnascan two module scanner. The recent generation of scanners provides for electronic retouching facilities with automatic colour correction. Once the transparency has been analysed according to the intensity of its colours, it is loaded on cylinders, sized and exposed by laser light. The exposed film is developed, fixed, washed and dried. Then the type is photoset, screen tints are provided and the automatic camera exposes various components in the format indicated by the layout. The printer receives either the plate or chromolia depending on capacity. Thus, at a process speed of 35 transparencies a shift, say, of IPP (International Print-O-Pac), small printers can have the photographic work done cheap. Again, here the opposite face of Schumpeterian growth is the growth of the hold of monopoly over processing. Big business in processing will ironically help small printing.

To go back to the story of *India Today* narrated in its tenth anniversary issue (1985). The magazine *India Today* started with a circulation of 500 in December 1975. This jumped to 370,000 at the end of 1985. It has openly claimed that this jump in a decade

---

[22] All the above figures are from *Business India*, 'Printing Technology Takes off'.

was mainly due to 'new freshness, a new breed of journalists breaking new ground, new technologies such as the word-processor and the computer terminal, a broad basing of mass media owner- ship following a new entrepreneurship in journalism, increasing advertising support and much more.' (p. 7) The magazine, within a decade, expanded its staff, invested in a national teleprinter net- work and 'acquired the most advanced computer system that any publication has in the country, so that all staff in New Delhi now write, rewrite and make-up pages on computer terminals, all of which make for shorter lead-times and more up-to-date coverage.'

This is the magazine which, along with *Sunday* of Calcutta, initiated a new kind of journalism which ultimately had a decisive impact on dailies. These magazines were unlike the old lady of weekly journalism, the *Illustrated Weekly*. Human stories, incidents of violations of human rights, corruption, caste and communal riots, scientific breakthroughs and public interest litigation became lead stories in these publications. *India Today* even instituted an award, in association with the PUCL-PUDR, on the best human rights story of the year. During election time, the fortnightly gave prominence to psephologists, a word virtually unknown before. It ran an election forecast that started a whole new trend in journal- ism. This, again, needed a sophisticated computerised system, just as without computerised processing we would not have enjoyed the work of Raghu Rai, India's best known photographer, the picture editor of the magazine. This was the signal for a now established running battle between photographers and writers over the visual space of a paper. Cartoons flourished, the business section became one of the major features and today, it is not individual writing that is the hallmark of the magazine, but superb team-work in writing and consequent editing. This is, of course, the line popularised long before by the American weekly, *Time*, which would have been impossible without editing terminals. Thus, story writing is more a production line and the outcome is the symbol of a collective style of operation. This, too, has caught on with newspapers, with the *Telegraph* and the *Hindu* taking the lead. Today, visual format, photo features, collective reporting and business reporting have all become inseparable parts of a modern day newspaper.

However, if we ascribe all the reasons behind this technically modernised new vintage of journalism, pioneered by the weeklies and fortnighties, only to a technological source, the whole perspective may not be comprehended. For, apart from the technical reason, the social reason that encouraged technical changes was the rise of the middle class in the seventies and early eighties. Education spread among the rural people; electronic consumer goods like televisions and cameras became increasingly popular with the middle class; the service industry absorbed many in banking and insurance; technical education gained prominence in sharp contrast to a weak primary base; cooperative housing boomed in the cities; prosperous farmers sent their offsprings to towns like Meerut, Pune, Varanasi, Cochin and Patna; synthetic cloth pushed cotton and handloom out of the middle class market; this was also the time when urbanisation resulted in the colonisation of vast tracts of land in different areas like the Delhi-Meerut corridor, the Bombay-Pune corridor and the Trivandrum-Cochin corridor; the middle class started buying shares, the stock market received a boost, and the Annual General Meeting of the shareholders of a company like Reliance Industries looked like a public meeting, and was actually held in Brabourne Stadium in Bombay; the number of two wheeled vehicles and cars rapidly increased; fashion garments came into their own and perfumeries started business in an unprecedented way; along with this, personal income tax was continuously slashed; import rules were liberalised; in short, the world of the middle class was invaded by the 'quick buck' culture. It was this milieu which encouraged new glossy publications based on photocomposed offset printing. This milieu resulted in a new type of political culture of the middle class. It acted less, but desired to know a great deal. It remained immersed in publications which were more often than not mystifying representations. We must keep in mind this middle class market and culture, albeit narrow, which gave birth to a new media boom. This was, in the final analysis, a constricted expansion of capitalism in India and the cultural reflection of this phenomenon. A few figures may be cited from the tenth anniversary report of *India Today*: The number of investors in 1975 was 1.5 million; in 1985 it grew to 7 million. Every fourth Indian now lives in a town. In the beauty business, there are 50 different kinds of shampoos, 500 shades of lipstick and the total business is worth Rs 150 crore. In the decade 1975–85, the production and sale of refrigerators increased four times to six lakh annually; the production and sale of cars increased in the eighties to around 90,000; the per capita consumption of synthetic clothing increased to 150 per cent; the production and sale of two wheeled vehicles increased 5.8 times to 10 lakh annually; in 1985, the number of television sets in the country grew to 5.5 million.[23]

It was this economic scenario which also gave rise to business literature on an unprecedented scale. Arun Shourie, a freelance journalist, remarked: 'The Emergency affected the politicisation of the Indian middle class, with the result that they wanted to know more and more about the people ruling them.' M.J. Akbar, former editor of *Sunday* and the *Telegraph*, said that the new situation demanded that editors and reporters 'take the cobwebs out of reporting'. Some magazines like *Society*, *Stardust*, *Sunday Observer*, *Sunday* and *Debonair* 'made a religion out of irreverence'. The personality factor entered the newsrooms of the largest selling business periodical too, *Business India*. With this, several senior journalists have quit secure cradle-to-grave positions to strike out on their own as syndicated columnists. The result of all this has been a dramatic rise in circulation. In 1975 there were about 225 publications, including newspapers and magazines, with a combined circulation of just over 14 million. In 1985 the total number of publications shot up to 300, with a combined circulation of more than 26 million. This means that one significant periodical with a circulation of 12,000 has appeared on the newstands every month during the last ten years. This is a phenomenal growth by any standard, considering that the price of newsprint as well as that of newspapers and magazines rose during this period. In fact, in the case of newsprint, the price rose threefold. This consumer demand for the media product is definitely connected with the rise of India's 80 million strong middle class. The Express group commands a combined net circulation of 2 million, and is engaged in a Rs 4 crore revamping and expansion programme. In Andhra Pradesh Ramoji Rao's Telugu *Eenadu* is selling some 400,000 copies. Thus, the vernacular press is not lagging far behind; in fact, with the growth of a regional bourgeoisie in India and the fast expansion of the petty bourgeoisie, the 'revolution in the language press will continue for some time'. Due to the forementioned two factors, there will be both capital for vernacular press as well as a readership for it.

---

[23] *India Today*, Tenth Anniversary Issue, 31 January 1985.

Big Capital and Modernisation in the Indian Press

We should also examine the monopolistic structure in the newspaper industry. While associations of individual newspapers are not unknown in press circles, very little effort has so far been made to determine the ownership and control structure of the Indian press as a whole: this has been the opinion of S.K. Goyal and Chalapathi Rao, authors of the *IIPA* (Indian Institute of Public Administration) *Report*, 1981, on the Indian press.[24] While the Annual Reports of the Registrar of Newspapers of India (RNI) provide a large volume of data and information on the Indian press, the analysis undertaken is a limited one. For example, the RNI treats each newspaper edition as an entity by itself, even when the editor, printer and publisher happen to be the same. Then again, while the names of the trustees, directors and shareholders of the newspaper establishments are published regularly, no attempt is made to determine the identity of the individuals or the corporate bodies involved in the ownership and control of the newspaper establishments. Similarly, RNI reports make a distinction between 'news interest' and 'non-news interest' publications, when there is a need to have an overall perspective to determine the significance of a unit in the press as a whole. To understand the relative strength of a newspaper or any one unit in the industry, one has to take note of the overall assets and other resources within the reach of the press units. To put it simply, commercial printing (that is 'job work') has to be seen as an effective limb of the overall printing business of a newspaper house. Then, again, the phenomenon of press reporters and senior staff of a newspaper being employed to promote the non-newspaper interests of their managements has not yet been quantified. While the use of press for the promotion of house interest is known, it is not very often realised that newspaper managements exercise their choice to ignore or build up the public image of chosen political personalities, official and private decisions, and commodities. In other words, this is once again a manifestation of big capital in the newspaper industry.

[24] S.K. Goyal and Chalapathi Rao, *IIPA Report*, New Delhi, IIPA, 1981, Vol. 2 of the Second Press Commission Report, p. 233. This was the opinion of the Fact Finding Committee on Newspaper Economics also: See *Report of the Fact Finding Committee on Newspaper Economics*, Ministry of Information and Broadcasting, Government of India, 1975.

There is one more aspect to this. As has been mentioned earlier, newspaper monopoly houses are, more often than not, a part of larger newspaper establishments. This is a position which secures for them constant revenue as well as an investment source. There is an uninterrupted supply of advertisements and 'job' work. And its economics are better managed in the overall framework of ownership and control structure, and other linkages of the total establishment.

It is not my intention to analyse the monopoly structure as such in the newspaper industry, but to find the link between monopoly and modernisation, if any, in the Indian scenario. One thing is immediately noticeable here. It is the monopolies (that is, the common ownership units or COUs[25]) which first opted for modernisation. Examples are the *Hindu, Times of India* and *Ananda Bazar Patrika*. Meanwhile, single ownership units have also opted for the same technology, like the *Patriot, Bartaman* and *Aajkal*. In fact, the last two were born with new technology. The importance of COUs can be seen from Table 3.1.

It is clear from Table 3.1 that the higher the circulation range,

Table 3.1
Share of COUs in the Circulation of Significant Newspapers (1979)

Circulation Range	Total Circulation (in thousands)	COU Circulation (in thousands)	% Share of COUs in the Total Circulation Range
1 lakh and above	5,415 (50.53)	5,190 (58.06)	95.84
50,001 to 99,999	2,074 (19.35)	1,471 (16.45)	70.93
15,001 to 50,000	3,227 (30.12)	2,279 (25.49)	70.62
Total	10,716 (100.00)	8,940 (100.00)	83.43

Source: Registrar of Newspapers for India, *Annual Report*, Delhi, 1979.
Note: A significant newspaper is one with a circulation of more than 15,000.
Figures for Total Circulation and COU Circulation are in thousands.
Figures in brackets are percentages.

[25] A COU is a newspaper establishment owning two or more 'news interest' newspapers, at least one of which is a daily. *IIPA Report*, 1981, p. 237.

the greater the dominance of COUs, now virtually run with PTS technology. The Express chain has a 10.68 per cent share in the national circulation of all languages. Bennett and Coleman 8.79 per cent and Hindustan Times and allied publications 4.37 per cent. The combined share of the top nine newspaper establishments in 1980 was 41.61 per cent of the national circulation. The Registrar of Newspapers has identified a total of 82 common ownership publishing units which publish 218 newspapers out of a total of 645. Of these 82 COUs the top 9 form the big league, the remaining 73 share 30.93 per cent of national circulation.[26] Here, the monopolistic trend is evident even among the top (that is, the COUs). This is evident from another angle as well.

Table 3.2
Big COUs and their Relation to Average Circulation

Express group	59 times average circulation
Bennett and Coleman	48 times average circulation
Hindustan Times	24 times average circulation
Amrita Bazar Patrika	21 times average circulation
Malayala Manoram	20 times average circulation

Source: *IIPA·Report*, New Delhi, IIPA, 1981, p. 238.
Note: The total number of newspaper establishments being 561 with an overall circulation of 132.29 lakh, the average circulation per unit comes to 23,581

In the regional languages too, monopolisation is evident. *Malayala Manorama* commands 37 per cent of the Malayalam circulation; *Thantri Trust* 42 per cent of the Tamil press and *Amrita Bazar Patrika* more than 50 per cent of the Bengal press. In New Delhi, India's capital, a single newspaper, *Hindustan Times*, run by the Birlas, commands 40 per cent of the English circulation: Its sister paper *Hindustan* commands 33 per cent of the Hindi circulation. Again, out of 81 COUs, the Express group publishes newspapers in six different languages. Bennett and Coleman, Hindustan Times, Tribune, Indian National press and associated journals and Amrita Bazar Patrika publish in three languages each.[27] The geographical coverage of the Express is the largest, followed by Bennett and Coleman. The dominance of the still greater monopolies among the monopolistic 81 COUs can be ascertained from another angle (see Table 3.3).

[26] Ibid., p. 238
[27] Ibid., p. 238.

Table 3.3
Distribution of 81 COUs According to their Share in the National Circulation

Percentage Range	No. of Units	Share in National Circulation
More than 5	2	19.47
4–5	1	4.37
3–4	3	10.68
2–3	3	7.09
1–2	13	18.22
Less than 1	59	12.71
Total	81	72.54

Source: *IIPA Report,* New Delhi, IIPA, 1981, p. 239.

The phenomenon of the domination of big capital is easily discernible from some other facts also cited in the following tables. The late seventies was the period when the big newspapers seemed poised for a technological jump possibly because, even in the hot-metal period, enough capital had been accumulated, funding sources secured, the market expanded and competition, even among the big fish, had reached such a stage that the introduction of new technology was the only answer out as a greater market-capturing and cost-cutting device. Hence, let us look at a comparative picture (Table 3.4)

Various facts can be noted from Table 3.4. The high degree of

Table 3.4
Number of Newspapers According to Circulation

Group Size	1979		1969	
	Number	Circulation ('000)	Number	Circulation ('000)
Above 100,000	30 (4.3)	5,415 (40.9)	16 (3.3)	2,239 (28.7)
50,001 to 100,000	31 (4.5)	2,074 (15.7)	24 (5.0)	1,708 (21.9)
15,001 to 50,000	115 (16.7)	3,227 (24.5)	80 (16.7)	2,240 (28.8)
5,001 to 15,000	212 (30.7)	1,899 (14.3)	134 (27.9)	1,181 (15.2)
Up to 5,000	302 (43.8)	614 (4.6)	226 (47.1)	422 (5.4)
Total	690 (100.0)	13,229 (100.0)	480 (100.0)	7,790 (100.0)

Source: *IIPA Report*, New Delhi, IIPA, 1981.
Note: Figures in brackets are percentages.

concentration has increased. In 1969, 3 per cent of the newspapers commanded 28.7 per cent of the circulation. In 1979, 4 per cent commanded 40.9 per cent of the circulation. But, simultaneously, there was a certain entrepreneurial growth among the top league, and their number has increased from 16 to 30. Among the smaller papers, too, the jump was from 134 to 212. In fact, the total number in every category has increased along with circulation increase. But within this Schumpeterian growth, in which technology plays a vital role, is hidden the phenomenon of monopolies. In Table 3.4, only the growth at the top is evident. But the fact remains that out of 30 newspapers at the top, 28 belong to the COU category, controlling 96 per cent of their circulation. The share of COUs in the 15,001 to 1,00,000 circulation is 70 per cent. In 1979, it was found that nearly 16 per cent of the newspaper establishments in India controlled more than 72 per cent of the national circulation whereas, in 1969, small newspapers consisted of 47.1 per cent of the total newspapers. In 1979, it went down to 43.8 per cent. In circulation, too, the reduction was from 5.4 per cent to 4.6 per cent.

An upgraded technology implies upgraded circulation. For that, what is primarily needed is more newsprint. We have to remember that the newspaper industry is an area where most of the inputs are imported. Except for labour, all the items from newsprint to machinery are mainly brought from abroad. Here, too, monopolies are at the gaining end.

Again, we have seen the widening of the advertising base of newspaper economics—yet one more instance of the connection between big industry and big press. Tables 3.5 to 3.10 illustrate the present financial position of the big presses in all major aspects like circulation revenue, and advertisement revenue.

Since the Palekar Award, there have been hikes in the selling price of newspapers as well as an increase in the advertisement tariff on four or five occasions. Yet newspaper circulation, as well as circulation and advertisement revenue, have grown (Tables 3.7 and 3.8).

Tables 3.9 and 3.10 show that between 1986 and 1988, the price of newspapers and advertisement tariffs rose more in relation to the rise in newsprint price from 1986 to 1988.

More than three-fourths of the newsprint is obtained from abroad, just as the new technology is almost wholly foreign obtained. This

Table 3.5
Consolidated Position of 60 Newspaper Establishments (in Lakh Rs)

	1979	1985	Percentage Rise
Gross block	5,725	14,909	190.91
Net worth	2,354	5,068	115.29
Borrowings	3,494	11,391	226.01
Total finance	5,850	16,457	181.31
Gross revenue	16,884	47,580	181.80
Newsprint cost	7,949	25,368	219.13
Net revenue of newsprint cost	8,933	22,209	148.61
Interest	472	1,708	261.86
Depreciation	244	1,433	487.29
Gross profit	1,401	3,319	136.90

Source: *AINEF's Submission to Wage Board*, 27 February 1989, p. 26.
Note: Before the Bachawat Wage Boards, employers' organisations had filed financial data for the past few years relating to 60 newspaper establishments, accounting for 95 per cent of the circulation of newspapers.

Table 3.6
Classwise Gross Profit of 60 Newspaper Establishments (in Lakh Rs)

Class	1979	1985	Percentage Rise
IB	514	670	30.35
IA	224	632	182.14
1	415	1,179	184.09
II	89	304	241.57
III	112	412	267.85
IV	20	74	270.00
V	15	16	6.66
VI	12	27	125.00
VIII	0	5	500.00

Source: *AINEF's Submission to Wage Board*, 27 Feburary 1989, pp. 52–59.

obviously implies expenditure in foreign exchange. And, again, it is from foreign exchange that the technological revolution in the newspaper industry is being financed today. As data shows, in 1973, 83 per cent of the total newsprint consumed in India was imported (for instance, out of 180,000 tonnes, 140,00 tonnes came from abroad).[28] Even in this scarce resource, the big papers have

[28] *Report of the Fact Finding Committee on Newspaper Economics*, 1975, Section on Newsprint.

Table 3.7

Circulation Revenue of 60 Newspaper Establishments

Year	(in Lakh Rs)
1979	9,076
1980	10,889
1981	13,055
1982	13,702
1983	17,678
1984	19,842
1985	23,640

Source: *AINEF's Submission to Wage Board*, 23 January 1989, p. 41.

Table 3.8

Advertisement Revenue of 60 Newspaper Estblishments

Year	(in Lakhs Rs)
1979	8,274
1980	9,890
1981	12,790
1982	16,610
1983	20,235
1984	21,009
1985	24,657

Source: *AINEF's Submission to Wage Board*, 23 January 1989.

Table 3.9

Price Rise in Newsprint (Rs Per Tonne)

	1986	1988	Percentage Rise
Imported	6,135	9,555	49.41
NEPA	7,860	8,934	14.00
Mysore (1983)	9,319	10,360	11.00
Kerala (1983)	8,660	10,360	20.00

Source: *AINEF's Submission to Wage Board*, 23 January 1989.
Note: Data are for the period July to September.

the lion's share, for they are the main beneficiaries of newsprint allocation. In Appendix X-2, the authors of the *IIPA Report* have observed:

Table 3.10
Price Rise of Nine Newspapers and their Advertisement Tariff Rise

Newspaper	Price Rise			Ad. Tariff Rise		
	1986	*1988*	*Per-centage*	*1986*	*1988*	*Per-centage*
Times of India (Bombay)	1.00	1.20	20	125	290	132
Times of India (Delhi)	1.00	1.40	40	95	165	74
Hindustan Times	1.00	1.40	40	125	180	44
Amrita Bazar Patrika	0.90	1.00	11	70	75	7
Ananda Bazar Patrika	1.00	1.40	40	125	160	28
Deccan Herald	1.00	1.50	30	55	75	36
Free Press Journal	0.90	1.00	11	32	40	25
Statesman (Calcutta)	0.90	1.25	38	102	115	13
Sandesh (Ahmedabad)	0.75	1.20	33	65	80	23

Source: *AINEF's Submission to Wage Board*, 23 January 1989, pp. 67–68.
Note: The figures for Ad. Tariff Rise are in Rs per column cm.

The share of small newspapers (an overwhelming number of which consisted of individual or family based regional language newspapers catering to local readers) in circulation was 23.1 per cent but these papers received only 5.9 per cent of the newsprint in 1976. On the other hand, the big newspapers accounting for about 50 per cent of the circulation received 67.6 per cent of the overall newsprint. Thus, the big business controlled press was not only the main beneficiary, it also received more favourable treatment from the government in the matter of newsprint allocation.[29]

When considering monopolies in the newspaper industry, it is worthwhile to recall the Report of the Vivian Leigh Commission, which laid bare the takeover of the Times of India group, formerly run by Bennett and Coleman, by the Dalmia-Jain group. To briefly

[29] *IIPA Report*, p. 305, ch. IV conclusion.

narrate the story, Bennett and Coleman was a private limited company, whose paid-up capital by the end of 1945 was Rs 39 lakh, and whose reserves were about Rs 30 lakh more. They owned government securities worth Rs 30 lakh and a bank balance of more than Rs 14 lakh. This was the time when there was a great rush for the purchase of shares of British enterprises by Indian capitalists. In 1946, an enterprise of the Dalmia-Jain group, the Dalmia Cement and Paper Marketing Company, suddenly started buying Bennett and Coleman shares. They took an overdraft of Rs 80 lakh from the Bank of India and bought shares worth Rs 1 crore. The Bank of India itself bought shares worth Rs 84 lakh and sold them to another Dalmia-Jain concern, the Gwalior Bank, at Rs 3 lakh less. The Gwalior Bank subsequently wound up and its assets and liabilities were taken over by another Dalmia-Jain concern, Delhi Glass Works Ltd. Some time later, the Dalmia Cement and Paper Marketing Company sold its own stock to Indian Insurance and Indian Fire and General Insurance, among others, and then repurchased it. Many of these companies subsequently closed down, and thousands of small and medium shareholders were ruined. The Vivian Leigh Commission indicated that the robbery was to the tune of Rs 3 crore. Thus the Dalmia-Jain company bought over Bennett and Coleman totally with other people's money.[30]

Similarly, Birla took over *Hindustan Times, Searchlight and Leader*—the three papers it had financially supported for, essentially, anti-British political reasons. The Free Press of India, a nationalist news agency of Bombay, started by an eminent journalist, S. Sadanand, was taken over by Ramnath Goenka. He thus came to own two of its concerns, *Indian Express* and *Dinamani* (in Tamil). After the death of Sadanand, the owner of the chief patronising advertising agency of the Free Press, the Publicity Society of India—the Karnani Group of Bombay, took over the Bombay paper *Free Press Journal*, as well as a Gujarati and Marathi newspaper also run by the Free Press.

These are small examples to show how monopolisation took firm control over Indian industry, and it is now the monopolies which have the requisite scale of production, capital, technical

[30] *Gana Andolan o Sangbadpatra*, pp. 216–29.

knowhow as well as an advertising base to opt for a new technological base.[31]

However, this growth of monopolies in the newspaper industry is not surprising, nor is their undertaking of new technology, if we keep in mind the overall monopolistic trend in our economy as well as the 'modernisation wave' among the big businesses in India.

We know that from 1972 to 1979, the total assets of MRTP listed companies doubled from Rs 5,597.74 crore to Rs 12,456.79 crore. The top twenty were worth Rs 3,058.87 crore in 1972; in 1979 the figure shot up to Rs 6,618.69 crore. According to the Reserve Bank Report, in 1964 (cited in Chakraborty, 1984: 55) monopolies controlled 46 per cent of the total industrial assets; in 1972 they controlled 70 per cent, and in 1978 83 per cent.

It is again these monopolies whose scope has now been allowed to be expanded in regard to their assets, imports, technical collaborations and field of production by the government. Consequently, they are going in for modernisation of production technology, especially in engineering, textiles, metallurgy and electronics. We have to view the monopolisation and modernisation of the newspaper industry against this overall perspective.

However, as stated earlier in the discussion, this is not a phenomenon specific to India. The country from where modernisation of printing technology originated (namely the United States) has witnessed the same phenomenon. It is well known that the famous American newspaper tycoon, William Randolph Hearst, had tried to instigate the US government to declare war upon Mexico through a three-month incessant campaign in his paper. This was done not to create or augment news but simply to save his mining business in Mexico, which the Mexican government had ordered to be confiscated. In 1979, Senator Morgan had stated in the Congress: 'We are losing independent newspapers to chains at the rate of one a week.' An avid observer of trends in journalism, Ben Bagdikian, made a famous comment, which has subsequently been often quoted:

---

[31] While government stipulation is that in a newspaper, advertising may occupy at most 40 per cent of total newspaper space, the rest being news, at least six newspapers are grossly violating the rule to the extent of more than 60 per cent space being occupied by advertisements. Of these six, three are monopolies. See Rathin Chakraborty (1984), 'Ekchitia Punji O Sangbadpatrer Bhabishyat,' in *Gana Andolan O Sangbadpatra*, p. 219.

'Half to three quarters of all media are owned by corporations run by 100 executives, and these 100 executives constitute a private Ministry of Information and Culture . . . . Today there is a greater potential for the use of journalism as a by-product by large conglomerates which have an explicit desire to influence public opinion and government policy in their favour.'[32]

Limits to Modernisation

However, there is no doubt that this modernisation of the newspaper industry, aided and abetted by the State, the magazine revolution, market segmentation, domination of big capital and the imperatives of controlling unions, has its own limits too. First, the type of journalism that is growing is obviously more story-oriented, investigative, clamouring for headlines, and hence competitive. But with the rising public demand for more facts and analysis thereof, even journalistic coups may fast become a banality. Human stories are already becoming dreary, which can be illustrated by the falling circulation of *Sunday* to reportedly below a lakh; the *Herald Review* of Bangalore's Deccan Herald group which has been a disastrous flop; and the Hindu group's *Frontline*—a glossy newsmagazine with splendidly reproduced colour pictures—which has slowed down after an initial spurt.

Second, as has been repeatedly stressed earlier, this modernisation and expansion was eventually a response to the rise in the middle class market. And given its overall limited nature, this modernisation too was bound to be limited. As long as the costs remain higher than in the traditional letter presses, the new print technology is going to merely serve, entertain and seduce the rich and the affluent sections of the middle class. The real boom in printing still awaits the further spread of literacy, an adequate supply of cheap paper and newsprint, and a lowering of printing costs that would bring the printed word within the reach of a majority of the country's population.

Finally, with the number of growing organisations and the unionisation of newspaper employees, the retrenchment of employees is getting more and more difficult. Unless workhands are reduced in number, the main purpose of automation is lost. Thus, a continuous

---

[32] Cited in ibid., p. 218.

union awareness to modernisation is bound to act as a brake upon the speed of modernisation, and there are indications that labour is not going to take it easy. With a concurrent rise in wages and the demand for social security benefits, like pension and shorter working hours, the game is back to square one, where the initial economisation as a result of rationalisation of the production process is lost or neutralised again.

To speak of this is to speak of the absolute limits of the growth of Indian capitalism. And it is this point which must be grasped while concluding this issue.

Earlier, the question was raised in the context of the introduction of automation in the newspaper industry: what is the precise role of an exogenously driven technology in shaping an endogenously determined structure? This led to other enquiries, like has this technology obstructed the monopoly character of the ownership or otherwise? And can we say that this technology is going to be the dominant technology, or will it remain on the border for the time being?

We have seen that hot metal technology is still being used in most small presses, though computerised technology is fast expanding. We have also seen that it is the big groups who have introduced PTS technology and the COUs are the base of this technology. This is because the more the matter to be printed, the greater utilisation of new technology. We have also seen that there is a range of political, social and economic factors which together determine how far the new technology will advance to a dominant position from its initial borderline existence. We have also seen how the international background was prepared for the advent of photocomputerisation, how the basic technological breakthroughs were utilised by the communication giants, the initial entrepreneurship was gobbled up and how a 'near' technology became an 'existing' technology. But, here, concretely in our country, it can be safely predicted that the small will survive by the side of the big in two senses: ownership and technology. For, fundamentally, capitalism is proceeding here on a weak basis. Moreover, it is witnessing daily the tenacious survival of small and medium capital, which together set the limits of microelectronics based technologies in India.

We find that the new technology arrived on the scene when the industry as a whole was monopolistically built. This new technology could help the small units and gave a boost to the growth of enterprises. Yet, above all, it was inherently suited to a monopolistic structure. It is the monopolies (or rather the oligopolies) which have gained the most from the computerisation of newspaper technology.

Very naturally, what is called the national press was the first to adopt the new technology, though we have seen that the vernacular and small presses too have proliferated, and the latter might have also gained somewhat. Yet we must remember the overwhelming presence of COUs and understand that the vernacular press need not always be a small press.[33]

The presence of big business is a further boosting factor; for, in our country, the newspaper industry may stand on its own, yet in the top league, it is often an arm of overall big capital.

Again, we have seen the role of the State in helping the newspaper revolution pioneered and led by monopolies, in two clear ways: allowing the import of computers and PTS machines under OGL and, second, allowing foreign exchange consumption for raw materials like newsprint. This technological revolution has altered the content of newspapers, and has given new shape to the reader's taste.

Finally, we have seen that the magazine and newspaper revolution was a product of the growth of Indian capitalism, particularly the growth of consumption goods. As such, it signified the rise of the middle class. And, again, the limits to the burgeoning phenomenon of middle class growth determined the overall limits of the growth of photocomposing technology; in other words, the extent of the electronics revolution in the newspaper industry—one form of mass media.

In the context of staggering overall illiteracy, circulation cannot increase much. Still, since the cost of switching over technologically is staggering, small publications will remain with letter and lino press. Finally, the cost of newsprint is still prohibitive and there can hardly be sufficient output to satisfy the news-hungry literates and illiterates in remote areas of the country.

So, if this is a revolution, it is still a limited one—a revolution aborted from within. Originating from abroad, catapulted to the top, thriving on sensational news presentation, and depending on state largesse—how far can such a revolution go? It is a revolution to which the doors of small presses in India are still closed. As in

[33] *Report of the Fact Finding Committee on Newspaper Economics*, ch. XIV, para. 14.5.

the case of all revolutions, this too is extracting a price—the price of reducing employment and endangering job security. Hence it is a revolution opposed by the workers in its present form. A technological revolution cannot but be partisan in the dominant struggle between capital and labour that is going on today.

Hence, we have to now shift our attention to the resistance against such a partisan revolution. We have to see how workers have responded to this partisan character; how the question of power at both the plant and industry level has engulfed the whole introduction of new technology; indeed, how by breaking the power of the workers, modernising technology could come about!

4
The Lengthening Shadow of New Technology over the Institutionalised Process of Wage Settlement

We have seen how new technology changed the work flow in a newspaper, deeply affecting the very organisational set-up of a plant in the industry. More fundamentally, we saw its impact on the labour process. This impact can be seen not merely from the technical changes that it has brought in the work process, but also from the way in which labour has conceptualised and comprehended the change and linked the issue of technology to the crucial question of wage—wage revision and wage struggle. After all, the introduction of new technology had been hastened due to the Palekar Award for wage revision. And, by 1985, the question of another wage board—the Bachawat Wage Board—had come up in the industry. How was the issue of technology going to affect the struggle of workers for wages? For this, we have to now look elsewhere in order to understand labour's response to technology.

One of the relatively less discussed aspects concerning the relationship between the labour process and the institutionalised process of wage settlement is the formal separation of the two. The process of wage settlement takes place outside the production process, the contract is bargained outside and the terms settled. The worker, again formally, after agreeing to the terms thus concluded, enters the production arrangement and becomes an integral part of the labour process. But a close study of the labour process will show that this process cannot be separated in a substantive manner from the process of wage settlement. The process of wage settlement also cannot be meaningfully understood without constant reference to the labour process. The introduction of new technology has deepened the organic relation between the two, and has made the labour process a compulsorily substantive issue in the institutionalised process of wage settlement. Clearly, the imperatives are today that the entire range of work conditions be debated, argued, challenged and changed in the process of wage settlement. In this section, I shall try to show how it is the employers who stand to gain from the forementioned formal separation. For them, this formalism is a 'fetish' that has to be continued. For the workers and the trade union movement, however, the need lies in ending that formal separation. New technology has made it all the more imperative. In order to understand the crucial issue of technology and the labour process, let us examine the Bachawat Wage Board and the trade union submissions to it.

The setting up of the Bachawat Wage Board settlement requires political analysis for a number of reasons. The Board was appointed by the Union Government at a time when new technology had become a reality in almost all big newspaper establishments— national, regional, English and vernacular. Software had developed to a certain extent. The government's electronics policy was clear, in the sense that it indicated an encouraging attitude to the technological switchover in the industry. Most of the unions had accepted the switchover either passively, or had remained content with the employers' as well as government's assurance to Parliament that there would be no retrenchment consequent upon the introduction of new technology.[1] However, fear loomed large everywhere, with the growing realisation among workers that manpower would be reduced anyway—now or later. The AINEF had shown earlier no clear-cut lead in responding to new technology, and its policy had been, to say the least, haphazard. It had, of course, brought out a working paper on modernisation (NCNNAEO, 1983), had spoken in glowing terms of the Statesman Employees' Union's pioneering attempt to grasp the reality of automation in the newspaper industry (Statesman Employees' Union, 1982), had talked of the hazards of

---

[1] Labour Minister's Statement in Parliament, referred to in the AINEF Circular 5/85 (30 April 1985).

new technology and, as the various circulars of the time show, it had tried to keep the affiliated unions abreast of advances in technology in the graphics industry culling news items from international literature.[2] But, on the whole, it had left its affiliates and the broad mass of newspaper workers to fend for themselves in the face of the massive switchover in the entire industry. The Bachawat Wage Board was appointed in 1985 at such a time.

Wage revision was overdue. The period of the Palekar Award was over. The attention of the workers now shifted from modernisation to the wage board. The questions became paramount: how would the bosses, after successfully introducing new technology, face labour's demand for an increase in wages that could now offset the gains achieved by them consequent upon modernisation? Again, how would the AINEF, after dithering for almost over a decade, now squarely face the issue and try to bring in the reality of modernisation in its wage board negotiations? As the wage board was essentially a process of tripartite settlement, how would the State look at the issues of pension and occupational health and safety, for on that depended how the terms of reference would be constructed for Justice Bachawat? Would the reality of modernisation be inbuilt into the legal arguments before the Board, or would it appear as only one intervening section in an otherwise general construct where the focus remains only on wage increase? These were all complex issues, for they enveloped the interpenetrating realities of technology, union consciousness, unionisation, wage settlement, managerial strategy and the state. Finally, would the reality of technology react upon industrial relations in the process of tripartite settlement in the same way in which it would in a bipartite process? Moreover, the relationship of capital-labour in the form of wage settlement can be different, say, in a case where it is being determined at the national level from the way it is

---

[2] For example, circular no. 5/81 (17 May 1981) spoke of the declaration of the Fifth International Consultative Conference of Trade Unions in Graphics Industry; see also circulars 1/83 (16 February 1983), 2/83 (2 March 1983) and 3/83 (14 March 1983). Circular no. 22/85 (3 October 1985) even gave lengthy extracts from a book *Electronic Illusions*; circular no. 21/86 (6 June 1986) reprinted the Communique of the Sophia Conference of trade unions in the graphics industry; other circulars, notably 26/86, 28/86, 29/86, also continued the Report; another circular, 31/86 (31 July 1986), reprinted the Global Charter for Work Environment; circular 25/87 (9 November 1987) circulated the Declaration of the Moscow Symposium on New Technology. Apart from these, excerpts from some journals were also circulated from time to time.

fixed at the company level. To put it simply, thus, would the Federation's response be something different, and at a higher level, than a union's response at the plant level? And, consequently, how would it affect the union's performance in response to modernisation? For, one notable phenomenon surprisingly neglected in the literature on industrial relations in our country is that wage settlement would be standardised as a result of wage board-centred struggle between the employers and the workers, and the union's performance at the micro level might become irrelevant in the face of the determining reality of a tripartite settlement with the State acting as the guarantor. This may or may not affect unionised strength in the face of new technology at the plant level. But, conversely, with the institution of the wage board (the wage board would hereafter mean the Bachawat Wage Board), the management's introduction of new technology free from the shackling constraints of wage revision, reduction of the working day, occupational health and safety, and so on, also cannot be pursued unilaterally at the plant level. In other words, the Bachawat Wage Board holds the prism where the complicated interactions between technology and class relations can be seen in a clear light. Marx wrote:

> Whenever machinery is employed—let us first consider the case in its immediate form, i.e., that a capitalist, instead of expending a part of his capital on immediate labour, puts it into machinery— a part of capital is taken away from the variable and self-multiplying portion of capital, i.e., from the portion which exchanges with living labour in order to be added to the constant part whose value is merely reproduced or is maintained in the product. Yet this is done *to make the remaining portion more productive* (Marx, 1987: 198, emphasis in original).

In other words, it is more productive of surplus value as well as profit. As we shall see, the whole struggle of labour in the form of its submission to Bachawat was against this imperative to make it productive. The employers also understood the real point of the contention well. But the employment of machinery, with its consequent effect upon the 'variable and self multiplying portion of capital,' was not going to take place in a vacuum. The objectification of labour and alienation of labour—the twin results of the introduction of machinery—were being challenged by living labour itself. Either it demanded a voice in introducing, planning and managing new technology, with a broader demand for a national modernisation policy to be jointly formulated by the trade unions among others, or it tried to control the work conditions in which the worker would be working. This resistance to objectification and the alienation of labour echoed through the Bachawat proceedings. As Marx significantly observed:

> Obviously, the worker cannot produce without the objective conditions of labour. These are now separated from him in the form of capital and independently confront him. He can relate himself to them as conditions of labour only, insofar as his labour itself has preciously been appropriated by capital. From the standpoint of capital, the objective conditions of labour do not appear as necessary for the worker. What is essential to it is that they should *exist independently over and against him, that he should be separated from them, that they should be owned by the capitalist,* and that this separation could only be abolished by his giving up his productive power to capital, in return for which capital should maintain him as an abstract labour capacity, i.e., precisely as a mere capacity to reproduce wealth as a force dominating that capacity and confronting it in the form of capital (Marx, 1987: 201–2; emphasis in original).

To put it simply, with each act of introducing technology, the employer would try to increase the conditions of domination over labour; in fact, technology would be the form through which this domination would be articulated and, conversely, with each new act of introducing technology, the worker would be presented, fait accompli, with a new set of dominating factors—a new type of domination—through the technology and its introduction, and a struggle for power would ensue. The Bachawat submissions of the AINEF need to be examined from this perspective.

Knowledge, Technology and Power

Challenging the domination which stems from the introduction of new technology requires knowledge of that technology. The institution of the Bachawat Wage Board was the occasion when the union had to acquire knowledge of the technology and contest the terms of the wage board arguments placed by the bosses: the INS (Indian Newspaper Society) and others. For, if the terms were accepted per se, then the main battle would be lost in the first round itself, and peripheral wage increases would mean nothing in the face of the severe domination epitomised through new technology. As we shall see, the Federation certainly acquired knowledge and tried to place hurdles in the path of a unilateral increase of power and domination of the bosses in the plants, industry and work-organisation by contesting many individual features of the new technology set-up, through wage board arguments. Thus arguments pertaining to work organisation, machine deployment, plant safety, occupational health and safety, work hours, allowance for a modern and humane living and pension became crucial during deliberations. These were the grounds where the domination of workers by bosses through the introduction of new technology was being contested. Knowledge and power, here, were obviously interlinked. It is amazing how the leadership of the AINEF painstakingly gathered knowledge of the new technology and its terms, conditions and effects, which would put many professional researchers to shame. Yet the paramount question remains, as pointed out at the outset: Was this knowledge built into the entire argument of the wage board or was it just 'another section' alongside many others in the wage board submissions? In other words, how were power and authority being contested: sectionally, 'other things remaining the same' or pervasively, in an overall way, along the entire range of domination existing in class relations inside the factory, even at a shop-floor level? Was knowledge sufficient for mounting such a wide ranged challenge over new technology? The Bachawat submissions probably gave a negative answer and showed that something beyond knowledge was required. It demanded a new form of argument, a new form of contest and a new form of organisation. But we must not anticipate the story.

It is clear that at both the plant level and the industry level, workers (particularly union militants) in big newspapers were gaining professional knowledge and, in the placement of workers under the Bachawat pay scales, would be getting supervisory status.[3] Professionalisation going hand-in-hand with reskilling meant that

---

[3] In *The Statesman*, Calcutta, this was most apparent where, from the implementation of Bachawat onwards, transition to new technology and new placements were almost simultaneous.

knowledge would no longer be a monopoly of the management. For example, in the *Statesman*, the Statesman Employees' Union had the 'termerity' to suggest a clause to the management and force its inclusion in the proposed agreement on modernisation in a letter of 12 May 1986: 'The whole technical plan with detailed specification of equipments for modernisation and their installation must be put before the Union so that the Union may give its views upon the matter.'

The subsequent history of industrial relations in the *Statesman* suggests that this clause was not enough. The management could revoke the agreement by killing it and the terms of automation could be pushed unilaterally, the power of the union could be curbed and order reimposed.[4] Thus the question arises, more after going through the eight volumes of the AINEF submissions to the Bachawat Board: Is knowledge inherently a basis of power? What is the relation of knowledge as a power resource to other bases of power, especially those of an economic and political nature? From the start of the decade of the eighties, there was an increasing professionalisation and, along with professionalisation, came increasing knowledge of technology and of industry, both at the Federation and union level. The Bachawat proceedings reflected the challenge to power of the bosses on the basis of knowledge gathered by the Federation. Yet the paramount point remained, to which one must seek an answer: Was this knowledge enough to mount an effective resistance?

The functionalist interpretation of knowledge, which follows naturally from a political position of industrial unionism as well as new syndicalism, in fact, overemphasises the role of knowledge in curbing management, mounting new forms of struggle and contesting managerial prerogatives in running the plant and the industry on a new basis. The knowledge base of the professionals is given huge importance in the analysis of union struggles. As Serge Mallet argued, the 'new' workers took the lead in 1968 in France and, in C G T France, the professionals were the vanguard in effectively confronting management.[5] But conflicting reports have come from

[4] This happened particularly after a new General Manager was appointed in a shuffling of managerial personnel, or rather, cards. The new incumbent succeeded in suspending the union president, chargesheeting him for violation of work discipline and, finally, terminating his services. The union had to accept this order.

[5] Mallet (1975); see also Touraine (1965).

another set of case studies, which challenges the theory of the natural growth of new syndicalism on the basis of new technology and professionalisation and shows it to be untrue (Nichols and Beynon, 1977). Thus, through an analysis of the Bachawat Wage Board, we can see how far the functionalist interpretation holds true, and how far professionalised knowledge can be effective in mounting a challenge to the power of the bosses.[6]

First of all, let us see what type of knowledge was accumulated by the Federation to strengthen its arguments before the board. The list of books and documents is amazing—ILO documents, wage agreements in some non-newspaper industries and companies, excerpts from journals on computers regarding health and safety, and the pay Commission Report on pension. Documents of the International Graphic Federation and the balance sheets of some non-newspaper companies were also used and provided for the consideration of Justice Bachawat. The list is being reproduced here.

1. Pakistan and Bangladesh Wage Board Awards.
2. Settlement dated 22 August 1986 in Bharat Petroleum.
3. Settlement dated 18 September 1986 in Hindustan Petroleum.
4. Reserve Bank of India settlement dated 12 October 1984 in regard to Class III staff.
5. Reserve Bank of India settlement dated 23 November 1984 in regard to Class IV staff.
6. Latest wage agreements for 1982–83—an AITUC publication—containing wages structures in:
   (a) Steel Authority of India
   (b) Coal industry.
   (c) IDPL, Hyderabad
   (d) Bharat Electricals.
7. Report of the Committee on Revision of Pay Scales of Teachers in Universities and Colleges (n.d.).
8. 4th Bipartite settlement in the banking industry dated 17 April 1984.
9. Indian Standards Guide for requirements of low income group employees by the Indian Standards institutions.
10. Self-financing scheme of the Delhi Development Authority.

[6] See, in this connection, Rueschemeyer (1983), pp. 38–58.

11. Registration Scheme of New Pattern (1979) of Intending Purchase of Flats to be constructed by the Delhi Development Authority.
12. Human Stress, Work and Job Satisfaction—an ILO publication.
13. The Impact of Micro-Electronics—an ILO publication.
14. Automation, Work Organisation and Occupational Stress—an ILO publication.
15. Visual Display Units: Job Content and Stress in Office Work—an ILO publication.
16. Occupational Hazards and Diseases in Commerce and Office—an ILO publication.
17. The Socio-Economic Impact of New Technologies—an ILO publication.
18. Trade Union Demands and Activities aimed at Ensuring Health Protection and Labour Safety and at Humanising the Working Environment in the Graphics Industry—Standing Committee of International Trade Unions of Graphics Industry document.
19. International Trade Union Guidelines on Visual Display Units—an International Graphics Federation document.
20. New Technology and Media Concentration: International Capital Links in the Media Sector and Demarcation Lines between Editorial and Technical Departments—a joint International Geographical Federation/International Federation of Journalists Conference documents, Geneva, 1986.
21. Reserve Bank of India Award dated 16 January 1981 on the introduction of computers.
22. 'The Hindu Cares for you'—brochure brought out by the *Hindu* eight years ago on modern technology.
23. Three ILO Reports:
   General Report—Geneva, 1981.
   Report on: Training and Retraining Needs in the Printing and Allied Trades—Geneva, 1981.
   Report on: Technological Developments and their Implications for Employment in the Printing and Allied Trades, with particular reference to Developing Countries—Geneva, 1981.
24. *Computers Today* (February 1987), article entitled 'VDUs, Health Risks and Hidden Dangers'.

25. ILO publication: Profession Journalist—A Study of the Working Conditions of Journalists.
26. Minimum Wage Fixing—an ILO publication.
27. Revision of Pension Benefits (Fourth Pay Commission) by P. Muthuswamy.
28. K.T. Desai Award in the banking industry.
29. Shinde and Banerjee Wage Committee Awards.
30. Distribution of Income and Level of Living Report, 1964.
31. Monopolies Commission Report.
32. S.K. Das Report on Dearness Allowance.

Balance Sheets of the Following
Non-Newspaper Companies

33. Rallis India Ltd., year ending 31 May 1987.
34. Lakme Limited, 1984–85.
35. May and Baker, 1984.
36. Crompton Greaves, year ending 30 June 1985.
37. Hindustan Lever, 1986.
38. Hindustan Lever, annexure to Report for 1986.
39. Mahindra and Mahindra Ltd, 1983–84.
40. Mahindra and Mahindra, annexure to Report for 1983–84.
41. Tata Oil Mills, 1984–85.
42. Tata Oil Mills, 1986–87.
43. Copy of the Petition, including the National Industrial Tribunal Award in Grindlays Bank on Automation, dated 13 November 1985.[7]

The arguments were built on the forementioned material, which was also submitted to Justice Bachawat. The main body of submissions also carried the imprint of professionalisation. The text itself showed that this massive body of submissions could hardly have been the product of the work of just a labour lawyer accomplished in arguing before labour tribunals, pay commissions and wage boards, unless the union/federation itself was gaining in professional knowledge and could thus help its lawyer. The Federation filed three volumes of *Memoranda in Reply to the Wage Board Questionnaire* and the statement of case, two volumes of

---

[7] Circular no. 13/88 of AINEF, 31 May 1988.

Supplementary Memoranda, two volumes of *Surrejoinder* in reply
to employers' memoranda, one volume of *Reply to the Supplementary Information* memorandum submitted by the INS to the
board pertaining to the latest selling price and advertisement rates
of newspapers, plus one volume of 'additional material', one
volume of 'fresh material' and one of 'new material'. But this was
not all. A separate memorandum, *Advantages and Disadvantages
of New Technology*, was filed on 28 December 1987. *Chart on New
and Old Systems of Work in the Newspaper Industry and the
Required Work Force* was filed on 7 April 1988 and, finally, on 15
April 1988. A note was filed on *Clubbing of Establishments for the
Purpose of Wage Fixation*. In all, this was a massive 2,216 pages:
an eloquent testimony to the interacting relationships between
knowledge, power and division of labour.

Yet, as already mentioned, the Bachawat submissions raised the
question: how were power and authority being contested? Sectionally, as one more side of wage bargaining, or a crucial chapter
on which modernisation was being based, and relentlessly introduced, and which itself assumed a new character basing itself upon
new technology? It seems that the more the submissions were
being loaded with knowledge, the more yawning and clear became
the gap between Federation leadership, at the top, and the unions
below. Modernisation demanded nothing less than a restructuring
of the organisation of the Federation which, as we have seen, had
grown and remained essentially a wage board oriented body. It
thrived on wage board preparation and arguments. But modernisation demanded that technical knowledge, and the challenge to
power based on that knowledge, percolate well below, that the
'new' concepts of occupational health and safety be grasped by
grassroots unions, that the traditional divide between white collar
and blue collar (in this case, journalist and non-journalist employees)
gradually be bridged and mutual animosity done away with the
setting up of composite bodies at the plant, regional and Federation
level,[8] that regional bodies be formed as the main pillars of the

[8] In fact the Nagpur resolution of the Confederation, for the first time, proposed
that resistance to new technology cannot be effective without the joint preparation
of journalists and non-journalists and, hence, organisational preparations should
proceed along those lines. But this remained only a resolution on paper. Wherever
joint struggles were launched, for example in the *Indian Express* in 1990, it was in
spite of the Federation and not because of the Federation. See, in this connection,
the Nagpur Resolution of the National Confederation of Newspaper and News

Federation and the concept of social security be made the cutting edge in wage negotiations as well as productivity deals at the plant level. As we shall see, the Federation responded to the demands of the wage board splendidly, but failed at the grassroots level. Thus, if the power and authority of the management, buttressed by new technology, were challenged successfully to some extent by the Federation at the wage board level, the loss for the bosses was amply compensated at the plant level. For example, one agreement over wage board implementation at the plant level included a clause like this:

The parties hereto confirm the provisions contained in the Memorandum of settlement executed on different dates with different unions as well as the letters written by the Management to the unions on the subject of introduction of new systems of work/production new technologies.

It is agreed by and between the parties that, as and when necessary, new technologies will be introduced in this company in its production and journalist lines.

The union and the management agree that there will be no termination of service nor any reduction in wages and benefits on account of the introduction of new technologies.

It is further agreed by and between the parties that the unions will extend cooperation in the matter of rehabilitation, redeployment, training and retraining of workmen whose functions have been taken over by new technologies, and encourage them to acquire new skills and adapt themselves to the resulting new environment.[9]

Agency Employees Organisations on *The Perspective and Tactical Line on Modernisation in the Newspaper Industry*, Nagpur; 3–4 August 1985.

[9] Clause V of the Memorandum of Settlement in the Ananda Bazar Patrika Ltd., signed between the management and ABP, Hindusthan Standard and Desh Employees and Workers' Union, Ananda Bazar Group Employees' Union, Ananda Bazar Group of Publications Journalists' Union and IJA (Indian Journalists' Association), Ananda Bazar Group Unit coordinated by Ananda Bazar Sangbadik Asangbadik Jukta Committee, signed on 26 October 1989.

In the section *Short Recital of the Case* (p. 4), there was a revealing para:

In the course of the discussion, the management pointed out that things have been rendered further difficult on account of the present low productivity of the workmen, heavy absenteeism and late attendance, non-implementation of devices and systems meant to reduce wastage and improve business efficiency.

In another company, the Agra unit of *Amar Ujala*, there was simply no agreement between the company and the workers for, as the management said, 'there is no grievance of the workers that is left unattended'. Further, there was no cause for unrest, as the management claimed that *Amar Ujala* was the first newspaper establishment in Uttar Pradesh to implement forthwith the Bachawat Award. Leaving aside the claim of the management, the example of *Amar Ujala* is revealing from the point of view of trade union struggles on the issue of wage increase and modernisation.

Amar Ujala is published under new technology from Agra, Bareilly, Meerut and Moradabad. It is one of the premier vernacular regional papers in northern India, particularly Uttar Pradesh, with a combined circulation of 2.35 lakh. The Agra edition is photocomposed and then printed on a web offset rotary machine. In Agra, it has very successfully challenged *Hindustan* and *Navbharat Times*, the Hindi edition of two major groups—the Express and Bennett and Coleman—which are published in Delhi and reach Agra early morning. It competes successfully with *Aaj* and *Jagaran* also—the two other notable vernacular papers in Uttar Pradesh. The Agra edition has a circulation of 90,000. In 1980, it was 35,000. The switch to new technology took place in 1984–85. The PTS machines are from Linotron, and are third generation machines. The rotary can print a 12 page edition, its hourly print capacity being 36,000, and its output 26,000 per hour. The computer has an image setting system. In the days of hot metal printing, they had 21 compositors for an eight page edition. Now, with 14 PTS operators, 8 processing men, 5 proof readers and 6 rotary men, the paper comes out daily at a very early hour. Clearly, with expansion through increase in editions and circulation, an immediate reduction in the level of manpower has been avoided. When asked about *Amar Ujala*'s success, the editor-in-chief Ajoy Agarwal made no secret of the causes that he perceived to be instrumental. 'New technology (*nayee taknik*, as he said in Hindi), Sir,' was the prompt reply. Pressed further he argued that sending facsimiles, prompt printing, a proper mixture of decentralisation through multiple editions and centralisation through editorial-managerial control, regional variation, the local look of the paper as well as cost optimisation were the crucial reasons. All these, in turn, owed their existence to new technology. Ajoy Agarwal sounded absolutely natural and convincing when arguing that implementing the Bachawat Award had in no way hindered the modernisation programme of the company. In fact, he implied that the management, like a benevolent patriarch, was looking after the workers, and, like a prudent manager, was quick to introduce new technology, though in stages, in a careful and discerning way.

Getting the opinion of the workers was an altogether different experience. The sub-editors said that their night shift duty was continuous, in one case it was 3 years at a stretch. One employee had not been promoted for 8 years and, under the new techno-logical dispensation, with several grades being removed and job scope getting limited, the scope for promotion was severely narrowed. Why was there no union? Who would risk initiating union activity? As there was no other newspaper in Agra, the chances of getting a job elsewhere in the case of being fired was remote. Most eloquent was the reply from the workmen in the PTS room—the operators. Was the Bachawat Award not satis-factory for them? Did they have any further complaint? What about their eyes and their lungs? The answer was *meethi jahar* ('sweet poison'). The temperature of the airconditioning was often below the stipulated requirement—18° Celsius. 'Machines are more valuable than machine men' and the management has to take care of the machines first. Yet, their eyes get red, they burn and double vision may occur. They sometimes get their eyes checked by the doctor. But what else can they do? They cannot get the required 15 minutes break after 2 hours. The number of operators is the minimum and the work load heavy. So the Bachawat Award is okay. But nothing can be done about these! Already, within a year of implementation of the Award, wage revision was becoming irrelevant even to a non-unionised worker in a non-metropolitan city.[10]

In another newspaper being published from a district town in West Bengal based on new technology, I found labour relations following almost the same pattern. The paper is the *Uttar Banga Sambad* of Siliguri. It had no recognised union for long; one had recently been formed but functioned ineffectively as most of the employees in printing and some in composing belonged to a legally

---

[10] This entire account is based on my visit to *Amar Ujala*, Agra, on 16 January 1990 and my conversation with Ajoy Agarwal, editor-in-chief of *Amar Ujala*.

separate printing unit, not connected with the *Uttar Banga Sambad*. It has a Nepali daily edition, *Himalchali*, one Bengali daily coming out from Calcutta, *Kolkata*, and publishes an employment news-paper as well. Obviously, Justice Bachawat's directive regarding 'bunching' has been ignored by the management. There is no question of providing various social security measures, though the workers feel strongly about occupational health and safety and other related issues. Modernisation has been introduced unilaterally, and Bachawat will be introduced unilaterally too. Though the workers are restive over the non-implementation of the Award, the basic discontent stems from something more fundamental—the non-relevance of the union at the grassroots level, whether regarding modernisation or wage revision.[11]

At this point, certain observations are in order in the context of the close relationship between new technology, unionisation and the wage board. As the example of *Amar Ujala* shows, wage increase may not defer modernisation but, on the contrary, may enhance the process of modernisation by taming an already beleaguered workforce as well as by depriving the union of the ground on which it had concentrated its fight against modern-isation—that of 'reciprocal' wage increase. Two possibilities may emerge out of this close relationship. The struggle against modern-isation in the form of wage board submissions and arguments may give rise to and strengthen unionism at the grassroots level, parti-cularly after the wage board verdict. But it may be the opposite also. With the apex body of the Federation fighting the battle in the form of wage board deliberations, workers and unions at the grassroots may have little to do, and the prompt settlement of Bachawat claims at the plant level may kill any possible unrest below, thus clearing further the path to modernisation. How exactly the outcome would be, of course, depends on the specific nature of the relationship between new technology, the union and the wage board at a particularly determined moment. But, given the absence of any overall perspective on modernisation and the inclination to treat it as just 'one' issue, as well as given the structural weak-nesses of the Federation and of the process of unionisation among newspaper workers, the second outcome is more probable. The hard work of five years of preparing the Bachawat submissions,

[11] This is based on my visit to the *Uttar Banga Sambad* plant on 28 April 1990.

the enormous amount of money, that the workers had to contribute,[12] and the brilliant and skilful arguments vis-à-vis new technology would probably all be lost. Surely wage increases have been
won and social security demands vis-à-vis new technology (like
pension or health and safety measures or reduction of the work
day) have been raised to some extent. But caught in the quagmire
of a tripartite system of industrial relations, particularly wage
board bargaining, the possibility of the Federation inspiring the
unions and workers at the plant level as a consequence of downward
filtration of wage board judgements seems remote. Knowledge,
after all, does not necessarily lead to power!

As mentioned, the Federation did not err in collecting information
from affiliated units for the purpose of building up its case on new
technology. A recent example[13] is being reproduced here.

To All Affiliated Units

Friends,
Modern technology has been and is being introduced with
utmost speed. The Expert Committee, set up by the Government of India, will soon call for submissions on many issues,
including modern technology, in order to decide about various
allowances, health hazards, etc.

You are therefore requested to send us the replies to the
following questionnaire within three weeks.

Questionnaire

1.A. Has your company adopted PTS technology in your
   plant?
  B. How is the paper printed—by letterpress machine or
   offset machine?
  C. If your unit is a part of a chain, how is the facsimile
   transmission done—by mail, microwave or in cassette
   form?
  D. Has your company modern processing equipment?

---

[12] Between 1985 and 1988, the circulars of the Federation would often desper-
ately ask for contributions towards the cause of the wage board from the unions,
and announce extra levies for that purpose. Indeed, one out of four circulars would
be asking for additional contributions.

[13] Circular no. 2/90 (19 January 1990).

2.A. When did the switchover take place?
   B. How many years were needed for switch over?
   C. How many stages did the process of switch over pass through?

3.A. Did you enter into any agreement with the management over the introduction of new technology?
   B. Did the management link or try to link the implementation of the Palekar/Bachawat Award with new technology/ productivity norms under new technology?
   C. Did your union confront the management in any way over the introduction of new technology?

4.A. Have you any say in the planning and scheduling of modernisation?
   B. Has there been any reduction in the level of the workforce by retrenchment, voluntary retirement, non-filling up of vacancies caused by retirement?

5.A. Is there any provision of pension?
   B. Is there any medicare, or any provision for medical checkup, or any other medical scheme apart from ESI?
   C. Have you noticed any impact on occupational health consequent upon the introduction of new technology?
   D. Have you raised any demand for (*a*) lesser working hours, (*b*) pension, (*c*) medical care, (*d*) sharing of power in deciding the plan and programme of modernisation?
   E. Does any union in your newspaper have links with journalists or journalist organisations?

(K. L. Kapur)
General Secretary

Earlier, at the start of the decade of the eighties, the Federation had issued a similar circular.[14] But nothing came of it. Probably this circular also ended similarly as just an information gathering exercise, for honestly it was meant for collecting information for the purpose of the wage board only, and not to hone out a well devised strategy on modernisation. Hence we are back to the original question: how does the wage board feature in the conflicting

---

[14] Circular no. 13/81 (12 December 1981).

relationships between technology and labour—in this case, new technology and the newspaper workers?

In India, historically labour relations have been built on the assumption that the State has the bounden duty to intervene in industrial relations before they deteriorate too much. The assumption of State neutrality is strongly rooted in various labour relations acts dating back to colonial days, strengthened further over the last forty years. Labour has not merely fallen prey to such an assumption umpteen times, but it has often been caught in a web of industrial relations agencies, tribunals, boards, and so on, that have made it difficult to stand on its own feet. Labour laws and legal practice in labour relations are today a fast expanding field. What has definitely been a casualty in this quagmire of the tripartite structure of labour relations in the strengthening of unionisation at the grassroots level. The State will often not allow employers to run berserk against labour; but then it will not allow labour to go all-out against the bosses. By perpetuating a state of tension, the State becomes the arbiter and, in the name of collective bargaining, it is often either bailing out labour or bailing out the bosses, though mostly the latter. We have to situate the policy of instituting wage boards in this perspective of State dominated industrial relations—the triad of the State, bosses and the worker. The Bachawat Wage Board was no exception. Instituted against the dark background of new technology, redundancy and long overdue wage revision claims, the Bachawat Wage Board stole the limelight. As noted earlier, victories were won by the workers certainly at the wage board level, but the larger question remained as disturbing as ever: would it help the workers in encountering new technology at the plant level?

The Structure of Industrial Relations, New Technology and Wage Bargaining

Early policy makers in the field of labour relations in post-independence India were worried about the prospect of labour and management knocking each other out or knocking too much at the doors of the courts and tribunals to sort out their problems. This would have resulted in excessive legalisation of industrial relations. Instituting wage boards is a form of conciliation—a formula that would put both labour and management on a tight leash and yet enable them to reconcile their differences over wages without going to court or resorting to prolonged and often violent strikes. Wage boards, thus, have been the form of State intervention—an extension of conciliation. In the usual forms of conciliation, parties are technically free not to come to an agreement. But the wage board has a judicial status and its award is guaranteed by the sanction of the State. But, at the plant level, the award has to be transformed into a concrete agreement, and there the mandatory implementation of the award is turned into another instrument in the hands of the employers to restructure, rationalise, regulate and control labour relations as well as the work flow within the factory. New technology and the control of labour thus always remain paramount in the whole institutionalised process of wage settlement.

It is important to comprehend the significance of this situation. The leadership of the AINEF naturally viewed the institution of the wage boards—Shinde, Palekar and Bachawat—as victories for the trade union movement, which had compelled the State to initiate a process whereby employers are bound to revise wages successively—a right undreamt of in many other industries. This may have really been so. But then, wage boards as a form of adjudication, as well as an extension of the conciliation principle, represent a soft option. In a bargaining situation, what a trade union at the plant or industry level can get out of the employer depends squarely on the size and commitment of its membership. The union draws its power from its industrial strength. In proper conciliation as well as adjudication, by contrast, industrial strength still counts, but only indirectly. For adjudication replaces the pressuring of bargaining with persuasion, State intervention and the legality of the award that can be enforced on an otherwise recalcitrant employer. Thus trade unions quite incapable of securing a demand industry-wise on the basis of strength can always hope for a favourable award. Bargaining is abandoned and the painstaking task of organising the workers for wage revision and coping with new technology is also neglected. The soft option turns into the sole option. Workers and unions in such a State fix their attention on the adjudication process taking place over a number of years, probably four or five, hope for a quick outcome and, meanwhile, the steamroller of modernisation starts moving, for all resistance has been concentrated at one place only. Thus, wage boards do not delay modernisation, they hasten it—not merely in terms of economic calculations, but in terms of power calculations too, representing a way by which modernisation can be introduced by overcoming labour resistance.[15] Thus, it must be repeated that it is important to comprehend the significance of the situation, for otherwise a very militant unionism may also run into a dead-end faced with the monolith of State intervention. Even perceptive observers have failed to note the significance of the interacting relationships. According to one lengthy comment:

> Two propositions can be derived from our discussion so far. One, gain in a system of state regulation is a function of the quality of one's claim on the political executive. Two, labour can be reasonably certain that the state will protect its right to employment whereas the management has the greater say with regard to economic compensation and production levels. Given this position, are we to regard the state as favouring labour or capital? The answer clearly is, neither. Both labour and capital gain in some ways, but both also pay a stiff price. . . . In a system of bilateral bargaining, trade unions have no choice but to engage themselves in the arduous task of building up their industrial strength. State regulation presents them with a choice of offering a crutch which can substitute for industrial strength.
>
> Indian trade unions have leaned heavily on this crutch. They have lulled themselves into the belief that a benevolent state will safeguard the legitimate interests of their members (Ramaswamy, 1984: 200–1)

The significance of the functional role of State intervention through forms of conciliation or adjudication in the structure of relationships between the State, labour and the bosses is completely' missed in the forementioned excerpt. The point is not that the employees should not have demanded State intervention but what

[15] On the role of the State in industrial relations in India, see Ramaswamy (1984), ch. 2. It is significant that the various reports of the Working Groups on Labour Administration sent by the National Commission on Labour failed to link the three crucial elements: labour unrest due to modernisation, the State and the employers. Ramaswamy is also silent on this. In fact, in trying to concentrate on the State's role, he has forgotten the milieu—the interpenetrating relationships between the three components of the triad.

grounds it should have chosen for the said intervention—the point is identifying the territory on which to articulate demands on the State in industrial relations. This would have made the referee role of the State more difficult and the assumption of neutrality and guardianship in industrial relations more hollow. Instead, unions have chosen the grounds offered by the State. One cannot expect that the fight against the State in labour relations can then continue fruitfully. Concretely, this means that the AINEF could not have ignored the wage board. Also, that it was right to concentrate its energy on it, but it was for the AINEF to challenge the very terms of reference by which the board was set up and prepare its legal discourse on wage revision and modernisation in such a way as to challenge the 'naturally' assumed absence of connection between wage revision and modernisation, or new issues of social security and modernisation. By allowing the various issues of modernisation to boil down to 'wage questions' in the course of the entire legal exercise, the ground was conceded from the start. A different outcome was hardly possible. Wage increase and increase in modernisation were to be, henceforth, twin companions. Demanding 'justice' from the wage board against the stark background of modernisation remained nebulous, just as the concept of 'fair wage' remained so, even after the massive volumes of submissions. Power, justice, State intervention, the decline of union strength and modernisation all remained mutually inextricable.

For the analyst of the labour scene, then, viewing the whole process of industrial relations vis-à-vis new technology would involve four crucial areas: the subjects of bargaining, the structure of bargaining, the legal framework of bargaining and the role of the State in the bargaining process.[16] But how these four crucial areas shape up depends on how workers are responding to the impact of technology on the work process and work environment. In other words, how the subjects of bargaining are being conceptualised and defined, and how they are accepting the structure of bargaining (as a fait accompli or as given, whether grudgingly or simply trying to change it from a sense of disbelief and distrust); then again, how much they have internalised the legality of the process (the legal discourse in industrial relations) and, finally, how they view the existence of the State in the whole domain of labour relations. We

[16] For a relevant and interesting discussion, see Rowan (1973).

must remember that the institution of the wage board was preceded and accompanied by strikes, *dharnas*, marches and *morchas*, resolutions and the observance of rallies on protest days. There had already been a token strike against modernisation. Yet, surprisingly, the issues of bargaining (that is, the contents of submission to the wage board) were not defined afresh, though as I have initially noted and we will subsequently see, these issues were formulated in the course of submissions, but feebly, sectionally. The centrality of the wage question could not be dislodged and the issues against modernisation remained peripheral to the master-argument. Thus, the Bachawat submissions represent both historic continuities and contrasts. The most striking contrast is the issues raised before Bachawat, and for that we shall have to go into a brief comparison with the Palekar submissions. The most striking continuity is the emphasis on wage revision—the continuing centrality of the wage question even under the shadow of modernisation over the entire industry. All in all, the period from Palekar to Bachawat (1978–89) shows that despite the modernisation debate, collective bargaining and adjudication were successfully accommodated by technological change. The process of bargaining and State mediation showed that negotiations, attrition, gain sharing, productivity deals and wage revisions could accept the general principle that yes, workers have an interest in modernisation and existing job conditions, but modernisation as a secular tendency was going to stay, primarily as conceived and introduced by the bosses. Indeed, bargaining and State intervention, as argued earlier, helped technological change.

Trade unionists often miss this point, for often popular understanding is that collective bargaining, adjudication and conciliation are forced upon the management by the workers, and it is often ignored that the management may also have a deep interest in the process (Mamkootam, 1982: 65). It is the institutional arrangement where the management also has a stake, as it legitimises the existing state of affairs at both the plant and industry level. Take the case of the Bachawat Wage Board. With the setting up of the wage board, attention shifted to the issue of wage revision, indirectly helping the furore over modernisation to subside. The conditions in the wake of modernisation were thus not challenged. In a way, as the working of the wage board showed, modernisation has been able to subsume the question of wage revision and other

allied matters under it. The specific factors of modernisation succeeded in going beyond the realm of challenge and were accepted
as 'given'. The management, further, can easily appreciate the fact
that State dominated industrial relations may breed worker apathy
in the trade unions at the grassroots level, which is why a tripartite
process of wage settlement will be welcome. The framework of
power, status and the award/reward system in the form of a State-
appointed wage board is such that, as we have already noted, the
unions at the grassroots level have very little to contribute to the
process. Modernisation being delinked from wage revision, this
became all the more true. The unions below can wait for the award
from the top, but the problems emanating from modernisation can
hardly be expected to be tackled in the award. Thus, worker
apathy increases. I have already noted the professional input into
the AINEF's wage board submissions in the form of knowledge,
but it seems this went hand-in-hand with growing worker deinvolve-
ment in the whole field of industrial relations where modernisation
and wage revision became the dominant twin factors. The defeat
and subsequent crumbling of the Ananda Bazar Patrika Employees'
Union after an abortive 54 day strike at the Ananda Bazar Patrika
group of papers, as well as the victory of the Bennett and Coleman
management by inducing worker apathy in the Times of India
group of papers at Bombay and elsewhere, are a pointer to that.
We shall have occasion to discuss in detail some such examples in a
subsequent chapter. Only the *Indian Express* strike in January
1990 in Delhi after the refusal of the management to comply with
the Bachawat order for 'clubbing' showed worker involvement.
But that was more an exception, where the Bachawat Award acted
as a stimulus to the workers and the trade union.

Except at the apex level (that is, at the wage board level), at the
plant and regional level the Federation did not take up issues of
modernisation with the management or the government. Thus,
given the nature of the wage board oriented organisation and a
combination of attention on wage revision through the wage board
and disregard of issues of modernisation at the plant and shop
floor level, an almost oligarchic leadership as well as worker
apathy in the trade unions were bound to emerge. This tendency
was simultaneously reflected at the top as well as at the grassroots
union level. The AINEF rightly claimed to be the sole bargaining
agent of the newspaper workers and refused to acknowledge the

existence of other rival organisations like the NUJ (National Union of Journalists) or its opposite faction, the IFWJ (Indian Federation of Working Journalists), led by Vikram Rao. But did it take up issues of modernisation, where workers would involve themselves, thus legitimising its status? The structural, organisational and environmental factors, we have seen, foreclosed the growth of the AINEF from a wage board oriented body to a dynamic federation of unions of newspaper workers—both journalist and non-journalist—at the regional and plant level. The existing pattern of union-management-State relations as well as the structure of the union contributed to foreclosing that development. It is against this background that we have to see the lengthening shadow of new technology over the institutionalised process of wage settlement. The history of the AINEF and the dynamics of the institutionalised process of wage settlement against the background of new technology show that an oligarchic leadership was not inevitable, but was the concrete result of the particularities of the process.

According to Michels' classic conception, power in organisations must inevitably become oligarchic. He laid down his 'iron law of oligarchy' thus: 'It is organisation which gives birth to the domain of the elected over the electors, of the mandatories over the mandators. Who say organisation, say oligarchy' (Michels, 1962: 365).

This is typical of the popular conceptualisation of bureaucratic politics, for political factors are largely ignored in such a setting down of the iron law of oligarchy. The organisation becomes oligarchic not because leaders are intrinsically callous to democratic values, but the more the union fails to respond to changing times and issues and to adopt changing forms of organisation, the more an oligarchic leadership starts developing. A wage board oriented organisation fails in this respect as it breeds inactivity and passivity below. There is thus irony in the situation, for while at the wage board level the Federation tries hard to link the issues of modernisation and wage revision, at the plant level the live issues are not fought owing to a lack of orientation and direction—the issues consequent upon the introduction of modernisation—and thus an oligarchic leadership starts controlling the union movement.

Let us go further into the dynamics originating from the triad of the State, union and bosses—the three active agencies in industrial relations—and see how the relations between union leadership and the rank and file are affected by the tripartite structure. A trade union is, after all, a communication system also, and communication plays a crucial role in the making of the organisation. The decision-making process in the union organisation and the communication system, on the other hand, are mutually related and dependent. The AINEF circulars and letters during the entire Bachawat period show a one-way communication—information flowing from top to bottom only. The formal structure of the Federation and the informal networks of the Federation provided the necessary channels that controlled the flow of information. But this very controlled flow of information showed that ground-level information and a two-way flow of communication were not needed as a major input in the decision-making process leading to submissions to the wage board. Rather, the nature of wage board organisation and the concentration of energy at the top dictated that the communication flow be simply one way. An oligarchic leadership and wage board oriented industrial relations are thus mutually linked. Bosses were helped in unilaterally introducing modernisation against this background.

Yet there is no inherent reason for such oligarchic tendencies in organisations, particularly unions. The Federation certainly consisted of fighting unions whose militants were ready to fight, participate in organisational activities and deliberations in conferences. But the very structure of industrial relations ordained that a one way flow of communication would characterise the organisation, and oligarchy may become a possibility. Lipset noted in the case of the American newspaper workers that the ITU (International Typographers' Union) had succeeded in nullifying the oligarchic tendencies due to the free flow of communication, non-monopoly of power, professional knowledge and skill of the union leaders, homogeneity of membership and a strong informal association of printers growing from extra union groups, as many of them did night work and, therefore, had little opportunity to interact with others outside the trade, on political and union matters. Lipset found that the high status of printers narrowed the status gap between leaders and the members. These were the causes that contributed to the development of what Lipset called 'occupational community' (Lipset, Trow and Coleman, 1956). In this community, various circumstances promoted democracy through cooperatives, annual conferences, clubs, cultural organisations and monthly bulletins. Yet this union democracy (whose variables Lipset outlined in the case of the ITU) seems to have been inadequate here in stopping oligarchic tendencies, for the determining factor was not the presence or otherwise of the said variables of union democracy but the very structure of industrial relations, whose characteristics were centralised wage bargaining, state guardianship over it and a centralised union leadership to concentrate on wage related issues.

During the Bachawat deliberations, all eyes remained fixed on the top. Thus the level of worker participation and involvement in union resistance against modernisation declined. Though unions were not divided according to party affiliation, yet factional tendencies and shifts emerged in such a milieu. Worker participation, union democracy and the openendedness of the organisation were not enough; they were defeated by the very structure of industrial relations. Everywhere, at the company level, agreements had to be negotiated with the master criterion laid down by the Award. Thus, positions were reworked, placements redesigned and the Award acquiring the character and status of inviolability, ambitions had to be curbed, social security demands summarily dropped, and workers placed according to placements dictated in the Award. Though the employers were never taken in by the 'inviolability' of the Award and implementation depended largely on how they sought to view it, the unions were bought by the 'sacrosanct' character, and once again the introduction of new technology succeeded in remaining beyond any serious challenge. Thus, the wage board not merely paralysed the organisation to a great extent, it even determined the orientation of thought at both the Federation and union level by laying down master definitions of various crucial issues pertaining to wage revision. For example, what constituted 'fair wage'—a very contentious issue, argued at length by the AINEF before the wage board—again failed to incorporate the phenomenon of modernisation in its definition and elaboration. Thus, to the unions below, 'fair wage' and modernisation remained two unconnected issues. However, more of that later.

The Process of Wage Determination and Related Issues

The study of wages has mostly been the study of wage determination. However, in the context of the Bachawat Wage Board, let us see how the process of wage determination influences other issues, particularly the technological set-up, the pattern of industrial relations and bargaining and the structure of unionisation. Conversely, one has to see, again in the same context, how these issues influence the process of wage determination.

The state of wage theory is responsible, to a large extent, for the telling absence in the literature on industrial relations of studies with a focus on the interpenetration of the process of wage determination and the process of industrial relations as well as the structure of unionisation against the background of technology. The market theorists' version of wage setting has been built upon the bedrock assumption of maximising behaviour. In such a scenario, economic agents actively seek to promote their own best interests and the influence of competitive market forces is the key point. For an analysis of wage dispersion, differences in human-capital investment and other characteristics of the job, as well as the costs of acquiring various types of information, are held to be sufficient as an explanation. The institutionalist version, as different from market theory, of course argues that in place of supply and demand, analytic importance should be attached to unions and large corporations, and the details of labour market behaviour are an asset to the institutionalist viewpoint. Yet here, too, a coherent theory is singularly absent, and the details are just like many trees without making up a forest. Wage administrators do have a deep knowledge of the pragmatic, as opposed to the abstract and, moreover, wage administration has drawn, apart from economics, on psychology, sociology and industrial engineering. Yet, due to the lack of a coherent theory, they have very little developed analytic ground (Annable, 1984). Thus, while in the process of wage board deliberations, the wage administrator's viewpoint reigned supreme in Justice Bachawat's questions and comments, and sometimes in the arguments of the AINEF also, no coherent relationships were ever established between new technology and wages. Not surprisingly, the argument of employers—the INS

(Indian Newspaper Society)—reflected the dominant market argument. The questions raised by Justice Bachawat related to the infrastructure of wage determination, and to the issue of 'clubbing' (the Times of India group had been showing in the post-Palekar period, new printing centres as separate companies for printing while publishing the same newspaper). Questions were further addressed relating to the cost of production, tariffs and revenue, the financial position of the industry showing the 'capacity to pay,' new placements and position, the wage policy structure (including various allowances and retirement benefits) and the impact of modernisation on the industry.

I had remarked earlier that the Federation's version of 'what constituted fair wage' included considerations emanating from new technology in its wage board submissions, but those considerations were not the bedrock on which the submissions were built. On the other hand, it reflected the ideas propagated by the wage administrators, namely, that fair wage should conform to the locally accepted wage, that it should conform to the rising fortunes of the industry, that it should reflect the international pattern of wage fixation in the newspaper industry and, finally, in order to work satisfactorily, it should be conducive to job satisfaction, above all it should be *just*. Thus, what constituted just would imply the above conditions, plus a sense of satisfaction. The economic yardstick of *minimum* wages was obviously not enough to deter mine what constituted fair wage, though that yardstick was used as an argument.[17] It is again interesting to note that in the wage board discourse on wages—fair wage, living wage and minimum wage—technology as a determinant is absent.

Being a union guided by Left ideology, the Federation was certainly aware of the basic Marxist perspective on wages, as its submissions reveal. Quoting Marx from the section on 'Wages' in *Capital* (Vol. 1), it argued:

> If history took a long time to get to the bottom of the mystery of wages, nothing, on the other hand, is more easy to understand than the necessity, the raison d'etre, of this phenomenon.

[17] *Submissions filed by the All India Newspaper Employees Federation Before the Wage for Non Journalist Newspapers and News Agency Employees* (hereafter referred to as *Submissions*), Vol. 2, New Delhi, n.d., pp. 390–406.

In its function of means of payment, money realises subsequently the value or price of the article supplied, i.e., in this particular case, the value or price of the labour supplied . . . .

Moreover, the actual movement of wages presents phenomena which seem to prove that not the value of labour-power is paid, but the value of its function, of labour itself. We may reduce these phenomena to two great classes: (1) change of wages with the changing length of the working day one might as well conclude that not the value of the machine is paid, but that of its working, because it costs more to hire a machine for a week than for a day. (2) The individual difference in the wages of different labourers who do the same kind of work. We find this individual differences, but are not deceived by it, in the system of slavery, where frankly and openly, without any circumlocation, labour power itself is sold. Only in the slave system, the advantage of a labour-power above the average, and the disadvantage of a labour-power below the average, affects the slave owner; in the wage labour system it affects the labourer himself, because his labour-power is, in the one case, sold by himself, in the other by a third person.[18]

The AINEF did not rest with only citing Marx. It attempted to give a fundamental answer to what constituted fair wage, by quoting Engels:

A fair day's wages, under normal conditions, is the sum required to procure to the labourer the means of existence necessary, according to the standard of life of his station and country, to keep himself in working order and to propagate his race.

But let us inquire out of what fund does capital pay these very fair wages? Out of capital, of course. Labour is, besides the earth, the only source of wealth; capital itself is nothing but the stored up produce of labour, so that the wages of labour are paid out of his own produce. According to what we may call common fairness, the wages of the labourer ought to consist in the produce of his labour. But that would not be fair according to political economy. On the contrary, the produce of the workman's labour goes to the capitalist and the workman gets

[18] Ibid., pp. 379–81.

out of it no more than the bare necessities of life. And thus the end of this uncommonly 'fair' race of competition is that the produce of the labour of those who do work gets unavoidably accumulated in the hands of those that do not work, and becomes in their hands the most powerful means to enslave the very man who produced it. A fair day's wages for a fair day's work! A good deal might be said about the fair day's work too, the fairness of which is perfectly on par with that of wages. But that we must leave for another occasion. From what has been stated it is pretty clear that the old watchword has lived its day and will hardly hold water nowadays. The fairness of political economy such as it truly lays down the laws which rule actual society, that fairness is all on one side—on that of Capital. Let, then, the old motto be buried forever and replaced by another:

Possession of the Means of Work—Raw Material, Factories, Machinery—by the Working People Themselves.[19]

This citation of Marx and Engels in the wage board submissions raises interesting questions. The AINEF leadership, mostly belonging to the two communist parties,[20] was clearly aware of the classical Marxist views on wage and the views of Marx and Engels on the issue of 'fair wage'. This should have automatically led them to posit the wage question against the background of technology and necessary labour time. But the prevalent legal discourse on wage adjudication almost dictated that such a leadership too should fall in line. Hence the next paragraph, 8.42, immediately after the citation starts with a climb down: 'In India, however, in any wage adjudication, reference must be made to some of the Articles of the Constitution of India.'

Then follows a rambling presentation of some Articles, the 42nd Amendment Act, references to the Fourth Pay Commission, the Fair Wages Committee, as well as the verdict of the Supreme Court in the Standard Vacuum Refining Company case.[21] The

[19] Ibid., pp. 381–83.
[20] The AINEF President, the late S.Y. Kolhatkar, was a veteran leader of the CPI(M), particularly of Maharashtra and K.V. Kapur, the General Secretary, an important trade union functionary of the CPI.
[21] *Submissions*, Vol. 1, pp. 384–401.

notable point is that nowhere in the said Supreme Court judgement or reports of the Fair Wages Committee and the Pay Commissions is wage linked to technology and upgrading of the work
environment accepted as the natural accompaniment of revision of
wages taking place against the background of revision of technology.
The relation between wage determination and technology still
remains reified in the minds of the union leadership brought up on
communist politics and the reification owes not a little to the
structure of industrial relations prevalent in India. Probably
another reason could have been the very nature of foreign led
computerisation of the Indian newspaper industry.[22] Domestic led
growth and a wide diffusion of new technology to medium and
small newspapers would have meant a reskilling of labour on a
wide scale. But that not being the case, the question of automatically
linking wage to technology did not arise with much force, nor were
the employers compelled to accept the linkage as natural on an all-
India scale.

We may venture into thinking along other lines. In the tradition
of party-led unionism, serious industrial studies have been few and
far between in union literature. Studies on the labour process as
well as on changes in the work organisation under the impact of
technological change have been totally absent, as opposed to the
mushroom growth of studies done in the West under the influence
of industrial unionism, syndicalism and new syndicalism. Union
studies on the work organisation not being familiar ground, the
AINEF can hardly be expected to posit the wage question against
the background of new technology and the changing work organisation. Indeed, one can find in AINEF literature (for example, in
its Silver Jubilee Souvenir) a large amount of space being devoted to
declarations of peace, disarmament and secularism, but hardly
anything on work organisation in the industry or on changing

---

[22] It is true that far from being a fossilised two sector economy, newer and newer
areas are being conquered by the largely imported new technology in India and
thus the diffusion cannot be said to be nil. In fact, one school of thought has begun
arguing that contrary to the dependency theory, some critical developing countries
are attaining negotiating strength vis-à-vis multinationals. International technological change has added to the bargaining power of developing countries as a
corollary, and is prompting an evolution of the trade union movement in our
country and other similar countries. See, in this connection, for a clear formulation
of the 'bargaining' school, as opposed to the 'dependency' school, Joseph M.
Grieco (1984).

technology. Combatting new technology by challenging its unilateral introduction by the management and proposing counter measures for modernisation was a line sneeringly described as syndicalism or company unionism by the traditional communist led unionism in India, and rejected outright. In a way, the submissions of the AINEF were patterned definitively from the outset.

In this context, what the AINEF failed to grasp was that the wage board, the Award, and company based agreements on the basis of the Award were in the nature of a capital-labour 'accord' that the bosses wanted to achieve. In the broad range of unionised newspaper offices, accommodation was needed to facilitate accumulation.[23] Thus a set standard for wage negotiation, bargaining and productivity deals and a tightening of the work organisation were absolutely necessary. The wage board's functional role was thus set against the background of new technology. It signified further that unionisation and mechanisation that appeared as a simultaneous process would no longer be necessarily so, and modernisation would now try to promote deunionisation. The reasons are not very difficult to seek: the earlier structure of centralised union leadership, so long motivated by wage bargaining, was becoming inadequate in the face of new technology; ironically, while the centralised union leadership was busy in wage bargaining, the local unions were left rudderless and defenceless against the onslaught of modernisation. The problems thrown up by modernisation were also 'new'. It called for a new type of response, which was not forthcoming. Thus modernisation promoted the tendency towards deunionisation. The more the wage accord was facilitated and other issues remained unattended, the less the union structure remained relevant. A new arrangement of division of labour, a spate of issues involving social security, an antiquated union structure, new work norms—all these meant that the employers' strategy on wage determination would be able to go through the wage board, accept higher wages to an unavoidable extent, and then operate plants with a relatively skilled, small, non-union, low cost labour force. A 1980 technology, after being introduced in an industry, would not be satisfied with Taylorisation. Production technology demanded something more. Ironically, the

---

[23] On the connection between accommodation and accumulation see, for example, Segal and Philips (1988: 208–13).

AINEF fell into that trap. We shall now go into the details and see that one of the most significant victories of the newspaper owners during the entire wage board period was its success in directing the debate over social security away from the issue of wage entitlement and putting forth an unquestioned assumption that the two are delinkable. And whenever social security questions came up in the wake of modernisation, these were viewed as necessary or conducive to productivity and that mysterious thing, 'job satisfaction'. Thus, all said and done, wage and social security remained delinked.

I have argued earlier that being forced to agree to an adjudicated process of wage settlement was not all that much of a setback for the bosses, for precisely at that time they were engaged in introducing new technology, and wage revision became an integral tool for labour control by the management. So too became the question of social security. We know that the modern management bible asks you to resort less and less to direct supervision. Close supervision of a large workforce can be very costly for the firm as well as unproductive, for if vigilance is too much, 'as is now invariably the case with hired labourers, the slightest relaxation of vigilance is an opportunity eagerly seized for eluding the performance of their contract'.[24] Moreover, it is not guaranteed that the foreman or the supervisor will be an efficient conduit of information about worker behaviour and performance. The management knows that new technology removes much of the need for close supervision and it understands that a contingent contract, stipulating piece-rate or an alloted quota of work, is also effective, simply because even more than large scale assembly work, under new technology management requires more labour cooperation, more team effort, and again more satisfaction. And, again, neither close supervision, nor contingent contract, can save the company from collective worker absence, particularly in cases where the requirement is firm-specific human capital. Thus, the stress is now more on indirect methods of control. Industrial relations become 'human relations,' a shift from what McGregor (1960) has termed 'Theory X' to 'Theory Y'. One of the most eloquent advocates of

---

[24] This wisdom is not exactly new, for the quote comes from John Stuart Mill (1909: 111).

the efficacy of this shift argued that when the employer is confronted with the poverty of his power, he too may turn to human 'relations'. Finding little common ground with the employees regarding the legitimate boundaries of his authority, he may want to find what other motivations there are and discover the answer in some of the findings of human relations research (Simon, 1957). Since a significant portion of industrial relations research began to be directed at identifying the causes of employees' dissatisfaction, particularly after the celebrated Hawthorne study, it was natural for employers to look to issues of social security as consistent with a management style that relied on indirect labour control, called Theory Y by McGregor. New technology has made much of scientific management—with its stress on close supervision, as much as possible piece rate, time and motion studies and strict selection criteria—inadequate and obsolete. Modernisation requires modernisation in labour control techniques too, which would be built upon formal assumptions like:

(a) The expenditure of physical and mental effort in work is as natural as play or rest.
(b) External control and the threat of punishment are not the only means for bringing about effort towards organisational objectives. Man will exercise self-direction and self-control in the service of objectives to which he is committed.
(c) Commitment to objectives is a function of the rewards associated with their achievement.
(d) The average human being learns, under proper conditions, not only to accept but to seek responsibility.
(e) The capacity to exercise a relatively high degree of imagination, ingenuity and creativity in the solution of organisational problems is widely, not narrowly, distributed in the population (Annable, 1984: 49–50).

Thus, the wage board was not opposed to the AINEF raising social security issues before it, nor were the employers fanatically resistant. What was needed for the Federation, therefore, was to link the process of wage settlement with the process of settling social security measures and to treat wage as really 'compensation' in the widest sense of the term—compensation for intensification of work, compensation for job insecurity, compensation for a high price rise market, compensation for surplus hours worked, compensation for an intensive work environment, for having to assume increasing operational responsibilities, mental strain, physical efforts and, finally, compensation for the unilateral introduction of new technology by the bosses whereupon the workers have to cooperate in industrial restructuring and the necessary accumulation process. In other words, wage settlement would no longer remain just an economic issue to be settled through collective bargaining; it would become the contending point in power—the centrality of the wage question in industrial relations would again appear after assuming a new form. The AINEF failed to apprehend this new form of centrality while confronting the wage board phenomenon.

In the Federation's wage board submissions, social security demands can be found broadly in three places: in the first volume of *Submissions*, the AINEF places its charter of demands involving various allowances, leave, working hours, and so on; in the third volume, these demands are explained; finally, in the second volume of *Rejoinder and Supplementary Memorandum*, the AINEF elaborates its views on 'Modern Technology and its Impact on Working Conditions'.[25] Though the last item is in the *Rejoinder and Supplementary Memorandum*, this is the basis on which the AINEF had argued earlier in its main submissions. However, the point remains, why was the 'main' question incorporated and itemised in the 'supplementary'?

In the revision of wages, the AINEF demanded basic pay, dearness allowance, house rent allowance, night shift allowance, city compensatory allowance, medical allowance, leave travel allowance, education allowance, pension scheme, local conveyance allowance, and raised the issues of working hours and leave. As we shall now see, first by comprehending the social security provisions only in the form of allowances and, secondly, by not making the provisions integral to wage determination, the AINEF fell prey to that managerial strategy which saw social security grants as a part of Theory Y in terms of Hawthorne results. 'Wage as compensation' was thus severely narrowed, the tension over wage revision was lessened and the whole process was emasculated, for social security provisions would not be intended as 'compensation' (nor

[25] *Submissions*, Vol. 1, p. 42; Vol. 3, pp. 631–916; *Rejoinder and Supplementary Memorandum* (hereafter *Rejoinder*), Vol. 2, 1990, pp. 408–556.

can all damages to working capacity be compensated), and they would be geared to producing 'job satisfaction' only.

The Palekar Award fixed basic wages, dearness allowance, house rent allowance and night shift allowance, while the Shinde Wage Board had earlier recommended, in addition to wage scales, dearness allowance and gratuity. It may be seen that the critical issues arising against the background of modernisation involved health, specifically occupational health and security, pension, shorter working hours as well as the placement problem under the new set-up. All these implied, further, that 'wage' be redefined.

If 'minimum wage' implied the minimum for reproducing labour power, and if that involved the concept of 'need-based wage', it meant that the local wage level, the industry-wise wage level, the minimum nutritional requirement and the rise in the consumer price index be taken as the bedrock of calculation. From this, 'fair wage' would be just a logical extension, implying that the worker would justly require recreational and more human facilities. But modernisation meant that this close circle of conceptualisation around the *minimum*, the *need based* and the *fair* be broken and the internality of labour relations be stressed more throughly. After all, factors like nutritional basis rose out of the poverty studies of the sixties and such a discussion involved a neoclassical dimension. The nutrition requirement or the consumer price index certainly implied the requirement of the reproduction of labour power. But it restricted, at the same time, the legitimacy and gamut of *compensation* and delivered very few punches on the structure of class relations within the factory. By taking *extraneous* factors as the basis of wage determination, it left the *internal* ones immune to attack; but modernisation precisely demanded that the internal structure be subjected to a thorough critique and the process of restructuring work flow not be spared. All this meant that issues like pension, occupational health and security and shorter working hours be turned into integral parts of the wage question and the assumption of undisturbed class relations within the plant also be challenged.

New Technology, New Issues

Let us consider the example of occupational health and security in this context. As we have seen, the AINEF had demanded a medical allowance. Either the workers were enjoying ESI (Employees' State Insurance Scheme) facilities in different newspaper companies or, if their pay was above the limit, they were often getting a paltry medical allowance—in the *Statesman*, for instance, Rs 75 per year or Rs 6 a month! Now, even if this sum was revised upwards or the company paid the worker's ESI contribution, how would that tackle the problem of occupational health and security? The AINEF itself had argued about the detrimental effect of continuous night shifts on newspaper employees and working journalists, and about other occupational hazards involved in night shift work by quoting extensively from an ILO publication entitled *Night Work*.[26] It argued about the effects of night work on biological and psychological rhythms. According to this publication:

> In the pathology of night workers, there are some distinguishing characteristics: a delay in the appearance of effects, some of which are permanent (hence the need, in studies on the subject, to take all the necessary methodological precautions); the presence of indirect effects, including, for example, the indirect effect on nervous and digestive disorders, of the direct effect of insufficient and disturbed sleep; a wide variety of individual reactions depending on family, material and social situations, from which a 'typology of the shift worker' and a 'typology of shift work' can be derived.[27]

The AINEF, therefore, observed in its submissions:

> These observations should lead to a search for new forms of organisation of night work involving a reduction of working time so as to achieve a better reconciliation of work with social and family responsibilities.
> The desirable rearrangements could not be made, however, at the individual level alone. The solution should bring about reforms extending beyond the range of the undertaking, and this would necessitate the adoption of a concerted social policy in this area. 'Thus the organisation of night work must be

[26] *Submissions*, Vol. 3, pp. 834–62.
[27] Ibid., pp. 837–38.

regarded as one of the forms of overall distribution of working time, which must be thought out again as a whole and lead to a redefinition of long-established patterns.[28]

However, the most damning indictment came during the submission of the *Rejoinder and Supplementary Memorandum.* The relevant section is a massive 148 page memorandum on the impact of modern technology on working conditions. I shall discuss the question of occupational health and safety later. But it is necessary to note that this memorandum is one of the most brilliant expositions of the issue by a trade union—a remarkable attempt to integrate the question into the problem of wage revision. In this memorandum, the AINEF countered the assertion of the bosses that 'there can hardly be any complaints about hazards after the introduction of new technology' and compensation for damage to health is not possible because, 'as a result of the cost of modernisation, the employers' paying capacity has been eroded'.[29] It substantiated its argument by quoting the Third International Graphics Conference: 'It is true, the introduction of mechanisation and automation make it possible to abolish certain manual, physically heavy and unhealthy jobs, but may imply, at the same time, a more tense mental activity, resulting in increased nervous tension and greater fatigue.'[30]

We have already seen that throughout the eighties the AINEF was keeping itself abreast of developments in knowledge about occupational health and safety under new technology.[31] In the *Rejoinder*, studies on the effect of new technology on the eyes, nerves, spine, the reproductive organs of women, the brain, and so on, were reported in detail. The computer, the visual display system, the position of the chair, the air-conditioning system, chemicals and the increasing stress of night work were discussed. Thus, the AINEF was clear on one point: that damage to health due to occupational factors cannot be compensated in a *real way*; it cannot be cured but can only be prevented. Thus, a medical allowance would in no way, nor for that matter would other medical facilities, help in the reproduction of the physical capacity

[28] Ibid., p. 855.
[29] *Rejoinder*, Vol 2, p. 408.
[30] Ibid., pp. 411–12.
[31] Circular dated 30 April 1985 is important in this regard.

expended during working hours. Health cannot be reproduced, as Engels (1980: 120–33) had argued almost a hundred and fifty years ago, and thus the occupational health and safety system must constantly be supervised. Trade unions can make ergonomics an issue in the power struggle with the bosses. They can thus demand constant monitoring facilities, guarantees against retrenchment or the loss of pay due to weakened physical capacity, a totally restructured ESI system, guaranteed rest periods during working hours at regular intervals, and so on. Though the AINEF mentioned some of these factors, yet the thrust was on medical allowance. While it argued that 'it is no more a question of doubt that the health of the employee is primarily a concern of his employer,'[32] the stress was on allowance, and the quantum of medical aid. The Second Pay Commission had said that the nature of treatment and the class of treatment should not depend upon the status of the employee but upon the nature of the illness itself. The AINEF drew the attention of the wage board to this observation of the Second Pay Commission and then concluded by saying:

> Newspaper employers should also give medical assistance by way of medical allowance to their employees on the following terms:[33]

Class VII	Rs 30 p.m.
Class VI	Rs 40 p.m.
Class V	Rs 50 p.m.
Class IV	Rs 60 p.m.
Class III	Rs 70 p.m.
Class II	Rs 80 p.m.
Class I	Rs 90 p.m.
Class IA	Rs 105 p.m.
Class IB	Rs 120 p.m.
Class IC	Rs 135 p.m.

The argument was thus a case of a mountain producing a mouse! The employers, as proved later in various agreements, willingly swapped health provisions with allowances. This was a serious comedown for, in the first place, the workers previously under the

[32] *Submissions*, Vol. 3, p. 872.
[33] Ibid., p. 873.

ESI system now desired to opt out and switch to the allowance system. Second, the workers thus lost a moral argument against the capitalist work organisation. This was a classic instance where social security provisions, instead of being a fight against modernisation and an integral part of redefining the wage question, became, through the 'allowance' entity, a part of managerial strategy to ensure job satisfaction and worker-compliance to modernisation.

The definition of wage conceived in terms of 'job satisfaction' was thus a trap laid for the Federation. The philosophy of 'social welfarism' was another such device to divert attention from modernisation and restructuring of the industry. In India, I have already argued, the presence of the State in industrial relations created certain conditions in the process of unionisation and industrial struggle. Added to this was the factor of the ideology of 'social welfarism' which acted as a legitimate tool for the State to make its entry. When dealing with the problem of wage fixation, the Supreme Court made the famous declaration known to all labour jurists and industrial relations experts in our country:

It is well known that the problem of wage structure with which industrial adjudication is concerned in a modern democratic state involves, in the ultimate analysis, to some extent ethical and social considerations. The advent of the doctrine of a welfare state is based on notions of progressive social philosophy which have rendered the old doctrine of laissez fair obsolete. In the nineteenth century the relations between employers and employees were usually governed by the economic principle of supply and demand and the employers thought that they were entitled to hire labour on their terms and to dismiss the same at their choice, subject to the specific terms of contract between them, if any. The theory of 'hire and fire' as well as the theory of 'supply and demand' which were allowed free scope under the doctrine of laissez fair no longer hold the field. In constructing a wage structure in a given case, industrial adjudication does not take into account, to some extent, considerations of right and wrong, propriety and impropriety, fairness and unfairness. As the social conscience of the general community becomes more alive and active, as the welfare policy of the state takes a more dynamic form, as the national economy progresses from stage to stage and as under the growing strength of the trade union movement collective bargaining enters the field, wage structure ceases to be a purely arithmetical problem. Considerations of the financial position of the employer and the state of the national economy have their say and the requirements of a workman living in a civilised and progressive society come to be recognised. It is in that sense, and no doubt to a limited extent, that the social philosophy of the age supplies the background for the decision of industrial disputes as to wage structure.[34]

In observing thus, the Court literally took a leaf out of Barbara Wootton's argument (1955) that the social and ethical implications of the arithmetic and economics of wages cannot be ignored today.

In short, then, this predominant philosophy of social welfarism engulfed the union movement, and wage was stripped of the 'compensation' argument. The Industrial Disputes Act, 1947, had defined wages as 'all remuneration capable of being expressed in terms of money which would, if the terms of employment, expressed or implied, were fulfilled, be payable to a workman in respect of his employment or work done in such employment.'

The Minimum Wages Act, 1948, also defined wages in similar terms.[35] Thus, what was needed was to challenge this conceptualisation of wage in the arguments before the wage board. Instead, the AINEF thought that by buttressing the 'social welfarist' dimension, it could push the press barons into a tight corner. Naturally it failed, for it could not link the integral relations between wages, modernisation, social security and compensation. The AINEF could have, on the contrary, argued that modernisation, irrespective of anyone's desire or explicit stipulation, was going to change the terms of employment, and hence the terms of wages had to be redevised. But, probably, this would have been too raw an argument which could have antagonised Justice Bachawat, and hence the Federation, even while walking on the borderline of that strategy, skirted the question ultimately. Thus 'Why Wage Revision?'[36] in the Bachawat *Submissions* makes interesting reading for the way it has ordered the listing of causes and omitted the paramount one, namely modernisation. As the AINEF saw the question,

[34] Standard Vacuum Refrigerating Co. v/s Workmen, *LLJ*-1-1961, p. 232.
[35] Clause IX, 1948.
[36] 'Why Wage Revision?' in *Submissions*, Vol. I, pp. 43–61.

revision was needed since 'the concept of a living wage is not a static concept,'[37] the region-industry standard continuously gets updated, prices rise and 'the addition of dearness allowance does not sufficiently make up the gap between wages and the cost of living,'[38] the 'concept of need-based minimum wage has to be translated into reality,'[39] wage-related elements (like allowances, bonus and social security) and fringe benefits assume importance for 'economic and practical' reasons, to ensure labour-capital cooperation; and, finally, since the Working Journalists Act in Section 8 provides that 'the Central Government may in the manner hereinafter provided (a) fix rates of wages in respect of working journalists; and (b) revise from time-to-time, at such intervals as it may think fit, the rates of wage.[40] Thus modernisation, the paramount factor in the redetermination of wages, remains unmentioned though, as I shall show, the shadow of modernisation always hovered over the functioning of the wage board and the Federation was aware of it.

Strangely then, while arguing on the extent of jurisdiction of the wage board, the AINEF had strongly supported taking a broad view of the Working Journalists Act (which had defined newspaper employees as 'any working journalist, including any other person employed to do any work in, or in relation to, any newspaper establishment'[41]), it did not basically question the terms of reference of the board, set up by the government. Also, it did not argue that 'conditions of service' as envisaged in the Act of 1955, have to be reconsidered, that pension has to be made integral to wage, or that social security provisions should perforce be included in the adjudicating process.

The Bachawat Wage Board was constituted under Section 13(c) of the Working Journalists Act by the Ministry of Labour, Government of India, vide its order No. D.O. 528(E) dated 17 July 1985, and issued Notice on behalf of the Board on 6 August 1986. Thus, the AINEF got an entire year to construct its basic thesis on wages. Yet it was reticent in questioning the entire ground on

---

[37] Ibid., pp. 44, 47.
[38] Ibid., p. 50.
[39] Ibid., p. 52.
[40] Ibid., p. 56.
[41] Section 2(C) of the Working Journalists and Other Newspaper Employees (Conditions of Service) and Miscellaneous Provisions Act, 1955; *Submissions*, Vol. 1, ch. 3.

wh: :h the board was constituted and to prove its inadequacy. However, it was vaguely aware of this need, which can be gathered from these excerpts:

1.12 It is over two years now that the AINEF framed and submitted its Charter of Demands. Several changes have taken place in the newspaper industry. The industry, during these two years, has resorted to heavy modernisation and automation in all fields. The work of human labour, which was being hitherto done by human beings, has been, to a great extent, taken over by satellite cameras which have replaced composing by human hands.

1.13 These changes are not entirely reflected in the Charter of Demands submitted by the AINEF. The AINEF elsewhere in this statement has dealt with the impact of modernisation both on wages and manpower; suffice it to say here that these changes which have taken place during the last two years will have to be taken into consideration and, to that extent, the Charter of Demands dated 24 July 1984 stands amended.

1.14 Automation and modernisation have not only changed the face of the industry but have also changed the qualities of some of the occupations due to sophisticated software and hardware, and the advanced technology has improved the skill of labour. These factors will have to be taken into consideration as *added factors to the case of revision of the wages of the newspaper employees* (emphasis added).[42]

We shall see, again and again, how this half-hearted effort to integrate the wage question with modernisation cost the Federation dearly. The management triumphed even while agreeing to 'substantial' wage increases in some cases, for it succeeded in achieving a good trade-off silently and, in the power struggle inside the plant, the worker stood defeated. We shall again see that the very structure of unionism was responsible for this defeat.

The AINEF, in its submissions on the financial position of the newspaper industry and the state of the industry in the pre- and

[42] *Submissions,* Vol. 1, p. 5.

post-Palekar Award period, argued quoting the Supreme Court judgement in the Ahmedabad Mills owners case that, for the purpose of wage fixation, the gross profit has to be taken into account because agents' commission, depreciation or R & D are ultimately geared to realising profit, wages payable to employees form the primary responsibility and all other liabilities come after wages.[43] It referred to the other Supreme Court judgements in the Gramaphone Company case, the Indian Link Chain case, Unichem Laboratories Limited and quoted the Court:

> When an Industrial Tribunal is considering the question of wage structure and gratuity which, in our opinion, stands more or less on the same footing as wage structure, it has to look at the profits made without considering the provision for taxation in the shape of income tax and reserves. The provision for income tax and for reserves must, in our opinion, take second place as compared to the provision for wage structure and gratuity, which stands on the same footing as provident fund which is also a retiral benefit. Payment towards provident fund and gratuity is an expense to be met by an employer like any other. The financial position shows that the burden of payment of gratuity and provident fund can be met without undue strain on the financial position of the employer, and that burden must be borne by the employer.[44]

This judgement also ends significantly by upholding the 'considerations of social justice'. The AINEF quoted the Court, which had asserted in Unichem Laboratories Ltd. that the Tribunal was justified in computing gross profits without deducting taxation, depreciation and a development rebate. Thus, it is clear that the AINEF was aiming for a strategy that would forestall any managerial attempt to hinder wage revision on the grounds of modernisation expenses. It was further aware that owing to modernisation, the shape of labour cost in relation to the total manufacturing cost was going down. It showed this decline from the summarised financial position of 45 newspapers submitted by the management (INS) to the wage board, in emphatic terms (see Table 4.1).

---

[43] *LLJ*-1-1966, p. 1, cited in *Submissions*, Vol. I, p. 126.
[44] *LLJ*-11-1971, pp. 594–95, cited in ibid., pp. 127–28.

Table 4.1
Labour Cost to Total Manufacturing Cost in Six Companies

	1980	1984	1985
Bennett and Coleman Co. Ltd.	18.87	17.47	15.05
Indian Express, Bombay	17.89	13.00	–
Hindustan Times	15.50	14.69	–
Malayala Manorama	11.01	8.56	–
Mathrubhumi	16.65	14.00	–
Andhra Jyoti	15.07	11.95	–

Source: AINEF *Submissions*, Vol. I, p. v.
Note: Figures are percentages.

Thus, it could argue that wage increase could not significantly alter the process of newspaper modernisation. It had already noted the close association between the growth of big houses and the growth of big press and stated that:

> a perusal of the above compilation of the balance sheets and profit and loss accounts will show that between 1981 and 1984–85, the subscribed capital of the industry in respect of 45 companies has increased from Rs 898 lakh to Rs 1,189 lakh and the reserves have increased from Rs 2,571 lakh to Rs 6,852 lakh. The gross assets during this period increased from Rs 7,215 lakh to Rs 14,901 lakh and gross profits from Rs 1,058 lakh to Rs 2,167 lakh. At the same time, the gross revenue of these companies has increased from Rs 27,998 lakh to Rs 38,375 lakh.[45]

The *Report of the Fact Finding Committee on Newspaper Economics* was also cited by the AINEF during the course of its submissions. All these show that the AINEF was, mostly implicitly but sometimes explicitly also, arguing that modernisation did not reflect the financial burden of the industry and its bad condition, but rather the good condition of the industry, and that hence the industry could afford a wage revision. But, the point remains, why did the AINEF argue that *notwithstanding* modernisation, the industry could afford wage revision and not argue that *because of* modernisation, it should pay more? Once again, this remains an intriguing question.

[45] *Submissions*, Vol. I, p. 252.

It stated, in clear terms, that borrowings do not show a weakness in the financial structure of the organisation and it is resorted to not because of non-availability of capital as such, but because it is a part of the system itself. As it showed from the Report of the Fact Finding Committee, the wealthiest newspapers were the most indebted and paid a lot as interest. 1984–85 was the period when they went in for large scale modernisation. A few examples are cited in Table 4.2.

Table 4.2
Borrowings of Nine Major Companies, 1984–85 (in Lakh Rupees)

Newspaper	Subscribed Capital	Loans	Interest Paid
Bennett and Coleman Co. Ltd	199.33	1,793.02	214.27
Indian Express, Bombay	86.50	792.06	141.50
Indian Express, Madurai	4.04	490.10	75.18
Hindustan Times Ltd	21.38	966.55	65.98
Kasturi & Sons Ltd	44.00	899.86	107.38
The Statesman	79.33	441.96	65.48
Mathrubhumi	6.27	254.56	35.36
Ananda Bazar Patrika Ltd	17.00	544.41	60.40
Malayala Manorama Co. Ltd, Kottayam	37.00	62.51	73.70

Source: AINEF, *Submissions*, Vol. I, pp. 256–58.

The AINEF also countered the management's argument to the effect that borrowings could have been occasioned by wage rise or a rise in newsprint cost—the two factors most cited by the INS. In fact, one of the most absorbing parts of the entire submissions is the deep analysis of the financial position of the industry, and the dissection of the financial statements of 45 newspaper companies.[46] It argued that interest paid on the borrowings utilised for the purpose of capital expenditure cannot be considered as a revenue expenditure, and thus modernisation and expenditure incurred on it implied capacity to pay.

It may be seen that the growth of paid-up capital was rather tardy. Loans increased, as did reserves and revenue. In any case,

[46] Apart from the submissions, this was reflected elsewhere also. See, for example, the lengthy *Letter of AINEF to All Units*, dated 8 November 1989.

Table 4.3

Financial Position of 45 Newspaper Establishments, 1981–85

(in Lakh Rupees)

Item	1981	1985
Subscribed capital	898.19	1,189.39
Reserves	2,571.09	6,852.15
Loans	6,068.25	9,913.92
Current assets	7,623.38	9,582.96
Current liability	5,278.46	7,141.20
Gross assets	7,215.10	14,901.89
Advertisement revenue	10,711.79	19,366.28
Circulation revenue	9,334.92	16,316.66
Other revenue	1,458.93	1,632.47
Gross revenue	27,998.38	38,375.10
Gross profit	1,058.28	2,167.85
Losses	56.89	115.05
Interest paid	886.50	1,268.52

Source: AINEF, *Submissions*, Vol. I, p. 262.

the way the modernisation of the Indian newspaper industry proceeded through the decade, the AINEF argued, showed that the
industry could pay the worker, as 'the obvious inference is that old
reputed establishments can command other resources for their
working capital'.[47]

The period of modernisation was examined by the Federation in
other ways also, as evidence of the industry's capacity to pay more.
It showed that the industry had prospered by comparing the state
of the industry before and after the Palekar Award. It increased
the selling price of the newspaper substantially. In the case of *Desh*
of Calcutta, the rise was 400 per cent (from 1 January 1979 to 30
November 1986), the *Times of India*, New Delhi 186 per cent;
Jugantar 200 per cent; *Kerala Kaumudi* 309 per cent; the average
rise being 180 per cent. This rise from 1981 to 1985 was much more
than the rise during 1965–1978, though it was half the earlier
period. Yet the rise in circulation, though steady, was not that
spectacular. However, the rise in circulation revenue was phenomenal and in every other way (display and classified advertisement
rates and advertisement revenue) the increase was again noticeable.
The AINEF concluded:

[47] *Submissions*, Vol. I, p. 263.

It will be seen that the number of newspaper establishments [which] derived income from advertisements below 25 per cent were 112 in 1977, while those which derived income from advertisements between 50 per cent and 74 per cent were hardly 26, and above 75 per cent was nil. Whereas the position is, in 1983, that more than 26 newspapers derived income from advertisements above 75 per cent and 144 (as against 26) papers derived income between 50 per cent and 74 per cent while hardly 50 newspapers secured income below 25 per cent and 49 per cent.[48]

The observations of the Fact Finding Committee on Newspaper Economics appointed by the government also seemed to support the arguments of the AINEF. The Committee had expressed aloud its doubt that quite a few major newspaper concerns have been earning profits in considerable excess of the normal rate of return which the government generally allows in price fixation and losses suffered by the newspaper undertakings were generally insignificant.[49]

Basically then, the AINEF's submission was that the newspaper industry was better off in the post-Palekar period. Indeed, it argued that its growth was more in the period between the Palekar Award and the Bachawat Board than between the Shinde Award and the Palekar Tribunal. But this raises two very pertinent questions on the mode of argument of the AINEF. If, indeed, as the submissions ran, modernisation coincided not with a crisis period of the industry but a growth period, which was the case, should the AINEF not have reckoned with the possibility that this expansion might immediately be followed by a crashing out of some independent newspapers by more monopolisation, more borrowing, more indebtedness, liquidity shortage and, above all, job shrinkage and that, hence, the likely future had to be covered by adequate social security provisions? In other words, the crucial task was, once again, to link modernisation with a new set of trade union demands and a new way to challenge the existing power structure in the industry. But the second question is more important. If, as the Federation argued, after the Palekar Award, wage increase was accompanied by heavy modernisation and a price increase in newspapers and advertisement rates, was this trend not likely to be

[48] Ibid., p. 308.
[49] *Report of the Fact Finding Committee on Newspaper Economics, 1975,* ch. xiv, paras 14.16, 14.17.

repeated in the post-Bachawat period immediately after the Awarc of wage revision? And, hence, should the Federation not have thought of articulating demands for countering the possibility that would offset wage increase? Pension, reduction of working hours and other likely issues were vital for such a strategy. For example, the AINEF could have argued for a total ban on non-compliance to the Press Council's directive regarding the news-advertisement ratio (60:40), so that it could be 'more advertisements if only more news'; in other words, more newspapers—more jobs. Or it could have said that wage revision should not be separated from verdicts of Press Commissions; it should be part of a comprehensive deal. It is certain that both the government and the wage board would have objected to this way of arguing, and would have been aghast at this attempt to flout the rules of the game. Once again the terms of reference would have been questioned and the authors of the game—modernisation - wage increase-job shrinkage-state neutrality-state welfarism—would have been in great discomfort.

However, in this context, when we are discussing possible alternative lines of argument, it must be kept in mind that the way in which the AINEF analysed the state of the newspaper industry is itself valuable, for it shows how labour views the relation between two very important processes—the labour process and the process of valorisation. It is important to note that this relationship has, till now, not received enough attention. The entire Bachawat submissions of the Federation may be regarded as an attempt by the labour movement in the newspaper industry to view the said relationship from its own perspective.

We know that Pigou (1933: 450–60) had argued that there is a range of indeterminacy in wage determination. But, while he tried to show that management's lower limit and the sticking point vary with the elasticity of labour demand, he could produce no satisfactory explanation of union behaviour. It has now been generally agreed that by comparison with the voluminous literature on the theories of the firm and the consumer, the union received little attention. One reason cited has been that while the behaviour of the firm and consumer can be interpreted as 'maximising', that of the union cannot. The argument further runs that a union has distinct institutional requirements apart from the desires of some of the members and, moreover, the union does not sell labour. Rather, it fixes a price—the wage—at which labour services are sold by individual workers. The argument goes even further:

A realistic model of the trade union is that of an essentially political rather than economic institution. The union leader acts under pressure from many sources: its members, rival leaders in the union, rival unions, its own employer, other employers, the government, and perhaps even the consumers (Kerr, 1977: 207).

But even while attributing to the union a political instead of an economic reason for explaining the element of indeterminacy, such an argument can be faulted on two clear grounds, as can be evinced from the Federation's behaviour at the wage board. First, it overlooks the necessity of unionised labour in the production process and the determinants of its bargaining power. Second, it overlooks the factor of the structure of industrial relations also, the arbitrary and adjugating role of the State, the specificity of the valorisation process and modernisation, the general political climate, ideas regarding 'need based,' 'minimum' and 'fair wage' and, finally, power struggle between labour and capital inside the factory as well as in the industry. We have seen, through the preceding discussion, that wage determination is a political process also, particularly under the shadow of new technology, automation and rationalisation. This is a political process not because the union is always involved in multiple pressures and is playing a game with the management as well as with the followers,[50] but because the process is essentially political. It is from this specific political angle that the Federation's views on the principles of wage fixation and basic wage structure assume importance.

The Federation had criticised Justice Shinde's Award of wage fixation on the basis of the newspaper for which the employee worked, as it had not taken into account the fact that newspapers often belonged to a group, chain or multiple unit. This tendency gained particularly after the introduction of new technology, where the engineering department, binding department, stores, offset rotary machine section, process department and, in some cases, even the composing section worked for all the newspapers belonging to a multiple unit.[51] The Federation was thus clearly aware of the particular nature of the accumulation process in the newspaper industry and now demanded what has been popularly termed as

[50] See, for an example of such a view, Ross (1968). See also Ross (1960)

[51] *Submissions*, Vol. II, pp. 338–39.

'bunching' in the wage board arguments in regard to the classification of newspapers for determining its revenue and paying capacity. This, in itself, was a revolutionary demand, for can anyone imagine workers demanding a standardised wage, say, in all the units of one Birla company? The Indian Express group objected to the Bachawat Award upholding the AINEF's demand for 'bunching,' which sparked off the Indian Express strike in New Delhi in December 1989.

The Shinde Wage Board ultimately became the subject matter of adjudication under Section 10 of the Industrial Disputes Act. Justice B.N. Banerji was entrusted with the adjudication. The National Tribunal headed by Justice Banerjee had agreed that 'all are employees under the Limited Companies and not under particular newspapers. There is little justification why all should not equally share in the opulence of the employer company.' (*Submissions*: Vol. 2: 345) The AINEF now extended this argument and submitted that the formation of separate companies was a hoax to shield the process of accumulation, and in the background of modernisation that would accentuate chain ownership and COUs, it squarely declared:

The real objection is to the fixation of a uniform scale of wages for the employees in the group. It is true that if after classifying the group on the basis of its gross revenue, a scale of wages is devised which that particular class has the capacity to pay, the employees must be paid those wages. What the employers do not relish is the fact that thereby they pay the same uniform wage to those who produce a successful paper and those who produce an unsuccessful paper. The Times of India Group produces, e.g., the daily *Times of India* which brings in enormous revenues and the daily *Economic Times* which brings in comparatively less revenue. Would it be right, it is asked, to pay equal wages to those who work on the *Times of India* and those who work on the *Economic Times* even assuming the Group has the capacity to pay? It is contended that this only makes unequals equal. The objection has really no substance. Whether a paper is more successful or less successful, the people employed on them work full-time and with the same care and efficiency . . . .
It may be assumed, without any cavil, that the persons who

have been selected and appointed by the Management to produce the *Times of India*, on the one hand, and the *Economic Times*, on the other, are doing the best for the success of their paper, and that alone is sufficient to earn for them the best that the establishment can pay. It must be remembered that we are still in the realm of 'minimum wage' and the goal of 'living wage' is far away. Therefore, if a uniform fair wage should be given to the same occupational categories, which is the accepted principle in wage fixation, the commercial success or otherwise of the product is irrelevant.[52]

What is immediately notable is that in arguing for 'bunching,' the AINEF is not merely raising the issue of minimum wage. It is hitting at the accumulation method directly. But, again, it does not link a critique of the valorisation process with a critique of the labour process. But even from the AINEF's own submissions, it is clear that new technology demands multiple editions and chain-linked publications, and 'bunching' clearly hits at the managerial strategy that would argue for unequal wages for employees working for different units of the same chain. A critique of the valorisation process demanded that it be coupled with a critique of the labour process in the wage board submission through demands regarding newer norms of placement, norms of reskilling programmes, norms of authorisation of modernisation programmes, norms of a working day, of night shift, occupational health and safety, and so on. Sadly, a combined critique was lacking. Once again we find the same half-hearted attempt to combine the issue of modernisation with wage revision. As we have seen, the AINEF placed the issue of modernisation in the same chapter, Chapter 8, dealing with 'Principles of Wages Fixation and Basic Wage Structures'. It noted the increase in the skill of employees, the potential reduction of staff strength, profitability of the organisation and increased efficiency thereof,[53] it quoted extensively from Juan Rada's *The Impact of Micro-Electronics* (1980) to show that 'the introduction of new technology can be a valuable opportunity to improve simultaneously productivity and conditions of work [and] technological and managerial options are opening increasing possibilities for the design

[52] Ibid., pp. 346–47.
[53] Ibid., p. 511.

of work which takes both human factors and production efficiency into account.'[54] It raised the question of occupational health and safety, amongst other issues. The AINEF's high consciousness about the phenomenon of modernisation can be further evinced from two other points raised by it: first, it noted ruefully, referring to the ILO, which 'while talking about collective bargaining in respect of modernisation, had in mind the change in service conditions as a result of modernisation,' that 'in the newspaper industry ever since the management has resorted to heavy mechanisation and automation, there has been no collective bargaining. Practically everywhere automation was brought about unilaterally by the newspaper employers.'[55] However, the AINEF should have looked inward and asked itself why such a thing happened and was its own wage board oriented nature not to blame for that?

Second, it brought the Fair Wages Committee Report to support it, as the Committee in the chapter dealing with wage differentials had held that the following factors should be taken into account:

   (*i*) degree of skill
  (*ii*) strain of work
 (*iii*) experience involved
  (*iv*) training required
   (*v*) responsibility undertaken
  (*vi*) mental and physical requirements
 (*vii*) disagreeableness of the task
(*viii*) hazards attendant on the work; and
  (*ix*) fatigue involved.[56]

But the problem remained that the Federation had conducted no scientific study involving these factors, and hence could not integrate these factors in its wage claims. It had not even conducted a pilot study. It had, of course, relevant publications of the ILO and WHO and other documents as supporting evidence. But the judicial process requires, first, primary evidence and assertions. Even a casual perusal of the factors cited by the Fair Wages Committee shows the notion of compensation involved in the process. But

[54] Ibid., p. 525.
[55] Ibid., p. 540.
[56] Ibid., p. 538.

when the Federation did not know how much to be compensated, how could it claim what was to be the compensation? And in order to arrive at how much was to be compensated, it required a critical study of the labour process—in other words, how labour was reacting to nature and other given materials of production, to each other, how it was being made to work and, finally, how much it was being compelled to work 'extra,' i.e., beyond 'reasonable' limits, thus generating imperatives of compensation. But the Federation lacked substantive evidence of required skill, strain, experience, training, fatigue, hazards, requirements, and so on.

The problem was further compounded by the lack of attention to another factor. The labour process involves the process of superintendence also as it involves processes like group work, assembly lines, and so on. The AINEF realised that modernisation would result in a new work flow, and reskilling in every case would not be the same. Thus, wage differentials would accrue from that. If PTS operators gained much, the orderlies or drivers would not gain to that extent. In the absence of any well-worked out rationale, in each individual newspaper establishment, there would be disputes among the workers regarding placements, and the management could then turn the very act of negotiating a wage revision agreement on the basis of the Bachawat Award against the workers and the union. Thus the exposition on modernisation was only grafted on to the main body of the argument, it was not integrated. Hence, para 8.155 sounded half empty, as it contended: 'In terms of wages, it means that the rates of wages for every kind of work done with the application of modern technology must be higher as compared to what was given under the old technology.'[57]

Yet, in spite of all the loopholes in the AINEF's submissions, the way it fought for a minimum wage and argued about the minimum standards required for food and housing, clothing, fuel and lighting, health and efficiency, medical facilities, obligations to children, recreation and social obligations and, finally, other amenities, and insisted on strict compliance with the stipulations of the Factory Act, 1948, that guides the printing and allied trades in India, showed that the entire process of wage determination was a process of class struggle as well. The *Submissions* of the AINEF to the wage board bore the print of that.

[57] Ibid., p. 529–30.

As is well known to anyone acquainted with the struggle of the newspaper employees, pension has been one of their most insistent demands throughout the decade of the eighties. Besides the unrest in *Malayala/Manorama* and *Jugantar*, the most important struggle was in Ananda Bazar Patrika Ltd in 1984. It is no wonder then that one of the most important demands placed before the wage board by the Federation was related to pension.[58] But typical of its halfway response to modernisation, the Federation was able to raise the issue of pension succinctly and sharply, but failed to connect the issue with modernisation, and thereby lost a chance to emphasise its imperative.

The Federation argued that newspaper employees had been granted only two retirement benefits—gratuity and provident fund—and both were inadequate. The provident fund benefit was, in fact more inadequate for, as the Federation noted, 50 per cent of provident fund savings were from the employee himself and, in many cases, this portion was already withdrawn by the employee for marriage, long-term sickness or house purchase. Hence, pension can be the 'only real retirement benefit which an employee is entitled to and should be given.'[59] The Federation argued; 'It is, therefore, urged that the Wage Boards should frame pension on the identical terms as those provided by the Fourth Pay Commission.'[60] Yet, it was never argued that modernisation has made pension vital and pension means not merely retirement benefits, but job security too in the context of workers' struggle against reduction in manpower level, 'golden handshake,' redundancy, retrenchment and other forms of rationalisation.

The Report of the Expert Group on Pension Scheme for Journalists as Well As Non-Journalist Employees of the Newspaper Establishments (1989) significantly noted the position of the employees, employers and the government. The employees obviously argued that the proposed pension scheme should not be at the expense of any previous or current scheme intended for all the members of the employees' provident fund, and that benefit in the form of pension should be available for past service and cover employees irrespective of age and other retirement benefits. The position of employers was that they 'may not be able to bear any additional

[58] *Submissions*, Vol. III, pp. 893–906.
[59] Ibid., p. 901.
[60] Ibid., p. 906.

liability towards a pension scheme' after the 'heavy cost of the likely revision of the wage structure as may be decided by the Bachawat Boards'. The government's position was equally forthright. Para 10 of the Report informs that:

> The Government's representative clarified that the retirement pension may not be allowed in addition to the contributory provident fund because similar demands may be received from the employees of Public Sector Undertakings and other institutions. The government had in fact considered such demands and was of the view that this additional retirement benefit would have serious cost implications. The government was therefore not in favour of this proposal.

The government also 'clarified that apart from this, it would not be feasible for the government to make any contribution to meet part of the cost of the pension scheme for journalists.'

The afore-mentioned Report of the Expert Group mooted the idea of triple terminal benefits, and of converting the existing Employees' Family Pension Scheme and Employees' Deposit Linked Insurance Scheme into a pension scheme. Here too the government's response was lukewarm. In its words, 'The Government may have to examine whether 11.6 per cent of the government's contribution to the Employees' Pension Scheme can be paid to the new fund set up for working journalists and non-journalist employees of newspaper establishments' (para. 12.2).

Thus, who would be financing the scheme and who could successfully avoid the burden remained the crucial problem for the bosses and the State. New technology and the consequent imperatives for terminal benefits remained very much a distant shadow, and were totally avoided in the deliberations of the Expert Committee. This is not be surprising if one looks at the composition of the Committee. Only 2 members represented the employees out of 8, the Chairman being the Chairman of LIC and the other five members coming from the General Insurance Corporation, Press Commission, Ministry of Finance, Bureau of Public Enterprises and the Council of Indian Employers (CCIE) representing employers in newspaper establishments. The Committee was set up by the Ministry of Labour, vide their order of 24 May 1988 following the assurance of

N.D. Tiwari, then Minister of Finance during his budget speech for 1988–89, that a bill should be considered by Parliament to provide a reasonable pension scheme for working journalists.

Significantly, again, the terms of reference (para. 3) did not include the task of assessing the need for a suitable and comprehensive terminal benefit scheme, following the introduction of new technology. No doubt the recommendations remained a hotchpotch, and as yet a non-starter. But, more significantly, the Federation also avoided any reference to modernisation while arguing about pension. The INS had submitted that pension was not wage and, therefore, the wage boards could not recommend any pension for journalists and non-journalist employees. The Federation got busy in refuting the contention, and argued in detail showing Court judgements as well as the precedence of Pakistan that 'pension is a wage as defined under the Act'—the Industrial Disputes Act (para. 8.6). But this was basically a defensive exercise for, by taking an aggressive stance, the owners succeeded in pushing the imperatives consequent upon modernisation to the background and avoiding any talk about their own obligations. The Federation continued to argue that if a workman fulfilled the terms of employment, he would become entitled to remuneration in the post-employment period. In its words:

> To deny a workman's pension on the ground that it is not a wage, because it becomes payable only after the fulfilment of the term of employment, is putting a narrow construction to the provision of the Act (para. 8.7).
>
> The right and correct construction would be that the pension is payable or to be paid to a workman having fulfilled the term of employment for a particular period and, to that extent, it may be considered as a deferred remuneration, which becomes payable only after a particular period (para. 8.9).

Thus the argument revolved round establishing pension as 'wage'. This being basically a *defensive* exercise, the *offensive* strategy of establishing the owner's onus for providing pension against the backdrop of modernisation was not pursued by the Federation.

The Federation had argued extensively on the industry's 'capacity to pay' revised wages, allowances and pension. But as its *Written Submissions on Tentative Proposals Made on the Direction of Hon'ble Wage Boards During Their Hearing in Delhi From January 10 to 19, 1989* shows, even when it was given an opportunity by the wage board to submit its opinion on tentative proposals made by the board, it did not link modernisation with the issue, nor did it tell the board that the greatest lacuna in the tentative proposals was that the board had not viewed the entire question in the perspective of modernisation. It was content with cryptically remarking that revision should have been greater:

> The burden imposed by the tentative proposal ranges between 13 per cent and 23 per cent. Even without going into the correctness of the burden shown by the newspaper establishments in their statements, it may be stated that a burden ranging from 13 to 23 per cent is grossly inadequate and a substantial improvement should be made in the tentative proposals.
>
> It is submitted that wage revision is normally expected at the end of every three years. Though the Supreme Court, in the case of the French Motor Car case, has observed that it need not be time-bound, but if the economic situation changes rapidly, wage revision becomes imminent.
>
> Wage revision of 15 per cent is to take place once in three years. Keeping this in mind, newspaper employees are entitled to a 45 per cent rise over the Palekar Award, which came into force nine years back. As against this 45 per cent, several top newspapers like the *Hindustan Times* and *Indian Express* have themselves shown wage rise as a result of the tentative proposals ranging between 13 and 19 per cent. These facts prove beyond doubt that the newspaper employers are in a position to bear substantially larger additional burdens on account of wages over the tentative proposals. There is, therefore, a case for improving the tentative proposals substantially.[61]

It is surprising that objections to the tentative proposals simply rested on a Supreme Court judgement, not on substantive grounds. Or was the AINEF led into *really* believing that the wage rise was enough, implying enough compensation (to many it was certainly unexpected as far as the extent of revision was concerned), which

[61] *Written Submissions of the AINEF on Tentative Proposals Made on the Direction of Hon'ble Wage Boards During Their Hearing From January 10 to 19, 1989* (23 January 1989), pp. 73–74.

is why it ended with a perfunctory objection? This possible per-
functoriness is all the more surprising if one goes through the list of
new machines and new designations and compares them with the
earlier ones.[62] It will show the amount of deskilling and needed
reskilling, and this will also strengthen our observation that only a
conceptualisation of *compensation* could have effectively utilised
the issue of wage revision in the new work process. I shall present
these in a table for convenience as well as show how the arguments
for wage revision fell short of fully grappling with the phenomenon
of modernisation (see Table 4.4[a]).

In fact, arguing along these lines, the Federation could have
gone further and shown that with reskilling and the revised work
flow, workers now were assuming much more operational and
sometimes even managerial responsibility, and hence they needed
to be paid more. In composing, processing and printing—the three
main areas—workers were becoming operators and hence placement would now be a real ticklish question.

It would not merely be a question of revision of post, but an
appreciation of the new role of workers at each stage of production.[63] Certain new jobs have also emanated from automation and
are done manually, not directly related to the working of the
machines. Some examples are given in Table 4.4(b).

After the placement plan was suggested by the management in
the *Statesman*, it was found that while some departments gained
due to reskilling (like lino operators and rotary men), some others,
indeed a large number, lost through the process of deskilling. As
expected, grievances mounted, a mad scramble ensued, the union
was accused of caring for 'skilled' labour only, union following
dwindled and it became evident that the Federation's line of
thinking fell short of reality at the plant level.

These dynamics were lost on the Federation. Instead, it merely
argued that,

> after ensuring a fixed minimum rise that may be decided by
> these wage boards, employees should be stepped up in the
> revised wage scales to the next step and thereafter one, two or
> three fitment increments should be given for every five years of

[62] Ibid., pp. 76–78.

[63] This was one of the reasons why union leadership in many newspapers collapsed
so quickly during the turmoil over modernisation.

service in the establishment instead of post, as has been suggested in the proposals.[64]

That the relation of technology and the work process with job evaluation and fitment was too uncomfortably close to be ignored was admitted by the wage board also, as it had to appoint a one man committee to submit a report on job description, evaluation and upgradation.

Dilsukh Ram, independent member of both the wage boards for working journalists and non-journalist newspaper employees, was asked to undertake the job study. The terms of reference set by the boards for the placement of jobs also clearly show the shadow of new technology over the institutionalised process of wage settlement:

(a) all jobs which have been newly created as a result of application/introduction of new technology/modernisation since the publication of the Palekar Tribunal Award;

(b) jobs of which upgradation on account of higher skill, occupational hazards, etc., have been demanded by the employees in their submission to the wage boards.

The questions put to the INS by Dilsukh Ram also show the same connection: questions like the nature of technological change, whether new categories and groups of employees have come into existence consequent on modernisation and, if so, what have been the scales of pay and other benefits allowed to them, the nature of training and retraining, and so on.[65] The AINEF, in fact, caught the thread but, as I have continuously shown, it did so only partially. In a very interesting demand regarding groupings, the Federation argued that 'a super group, a group higher than Group I of the Palekar Award, should be created to accommodate the following categories which have sprung into existence on account of the introduction of new technology in printing'.[66]

Who would form the new group? The AINEF went on to list them, with which the Wage Board partly complied on the basis of the opinion of Dilsukh Ram:

[64] *Written Submissions of the AINEF on Tentative Proposals, 1989*, p. 71.
[65] *Dilsukh Ram Committee Report on Job Description, Evaluation, Upgradation, etc.*, submitted to the Bachawat Wage Boards (1 August 1989), pp. 5–19.
[66] Ibid., p. 93.

Table 4.4(a)

New Machines, New Designations, Old Machines, Old Posts

Name of the Machine and Function	Designation of the Person who Works on the New Machine	Designation of the Worker on a Corresponding Existing Machine	Period of Training Required for Existing Hands to Switch Over to New Machines	Period of Training Required for New Hands
(1)	(2)	(3)	(4)	(5)
1. Phototypesetting machine sets the matter for printing through computer terminals	PTS Operator, VDT Operator, Terminal Operator, EKB Operator, Keyboard Operator	Lino Operator, Mono Operator, Ludlow Operator	6 months	1 year
2. Processor processes the matter set by PTS machines and develops the bromide	Processor Operator, PTS Assistant	None	6 months	6 months
3. Cameras (computerised) prepare photographic negatives of the paste-up pages for making plates	Camera Operator	Camera Operator (highly skilled)	6 months	2 years
4. Scanner processes the colour transparencies, separates the colours and prepares negatives for plate-making	Scanner Operator	Camera Operator (highly skilled)	6 months	2 years
5. Ultraplus platemaker (exposer) exposes the negatives on	Plate maker/Offset Rotaryman	Plate Maker Colour	6 months	2 years

6.	Autoneg (processor) develops the photo-sensitive plates exposed by (5) for printing (5 and 6 are combined and are done by the same)	Plate maker/Offset Rotaryman	Plate Maker Colour	6 months	2 years
7.	Offset rotary prints the newspaper in black and white and colour	Offset Machineman/Rotaryman	Rotaryman	6 months	2 years
8.	Electronic teleprinters transmit and receive messages/news stories	Teleprinter Operator	Teleprinter Operator	6 months	2 years
9.	Computers	(a) Computer Operator	–	6 months	2 years
		(b) Computer Programmer	–	6 months	2 years
10.	Central Computer Unit	(a) Electronics Engineer and Computer Programmer	None	–	9 months to 1 year
		(b) Systems man, Controller			

Table 4.4(b)
New Designations and Corresponding Old Ones

New Designation	Corresponding Old Designation	Period of Training Required for Old Hands to Switch Over to New Jobs, and for New Hands
Paste-up Man		
Pastes the bromides, photographs, ads and headings as per lay-out	An identical job was done by the compositor and make-up man but the new job requires higher skill	For a skilled compositor, 6 months training is required; 2 years for a new hand
Process Assistant		
Retouches the negatives prepared by camera/ scanner and removes the blemishes left by the camera	An identical job was done by the Colour Retoucher	
Artist		
Together with Paster, the Artist is required to give finishing touches to the final page as well as design the full page. This is a job for a fully qualified artist. The volume and dimension has increased	Similar work was mentioned in the Working Journalists grouping	A 3–5 year diploma course or equivalent training required

1. P T S Operator
2. P T S Engineer (mechanic)
3. Offset Printing Foreman
4. Printer (composing Supervisor)
5. Supervisor
6. Camera Operator (process and offset)
7. Colour Separation Scanner
8. Senior Printer
9. P T S Controller
10. Display Advertisement Operator

11. Key Board Operator
12. VDT Operator
13. Electronic Key Board Operator
14. Terminal Operator
15. Computer Operator
16. Scanner

It may be seen that most of the forementioned designations (barring 3, 4 and 5), for which the super group was claimed, belong to pre-press section work. While the Federation rightly pointed out the shift in the work process from hot metal to cold, and argued that a 'differential has to be made on the basis of the *skill* involved in both the jobs'[67] (emphasis in original), it failed to note that such a formula for wage restructuring might create problems for the union at the plant and company level wage agreement. Since the benefits would mostly accrue to the skilled workers at the pre-printing stage, this would surely create tension among the workers, particularly those belonging to the printing stage and other employees too. As the experience of the *Statesman* revealed, the management deftly handled the issue, a prestigious stratum of workers was created, there was a rift among the workers and, with the PTS operators, (formerly the lino operators) forming the bulk of union activists, the workers of the printing section often harboured a grudge against the union. All in all, it became clear that the union had failed to enable the entire work force enjoy the benefits of modernisation to a more or less equal degree. In short, the Federation's perspective was once again myopic. Having failed to place the issue of modernisation at the heart of wage revision, it now erred doubly. It isolated the issue of skill, so the workers faced a potential fracture. As proved by later events, the management was only too pleased to play up the issue of *skill*. The whole issue was mystified and the entire question of modernisation of work conditions, worker's life and social security measures was successfully shelved behind other issues. The Federation failed to go beyond the mystification of *skill* of a certain stratum of workers. What the Indian newspaper industry witnessed was exactly the opposite of 'new syndicalism,' championed by a section of labour theoreticians, like Serge Mallet and Alan Touraine, to whom technological change, automation and a consequent

[67] *Submissions*, Vol. 2, p. 615; see also *Dilsukh Ram Committee Report*, p. 97.

growth of skilled labour *per se* signified a growth in class consciousness![68]

Let us go back to Dilsukh Ram's Report. The Report noted that *reskilling* was not something over which the workers had to get excited, for behind every incident of reskilling, there was a process of *deskilling* to a much greater degree. For example, under a traditional printing process, a much higher level of skill was required, and training was for a minimum of 3 years, as against 3–4 months for phototypesetting key board/VDT (or similar job) operators.[69] This was truer in the case of blockmakers, photo engravers and etchers, where an entire generation of skill would become extinct. The result with regard to cylinder press operators, proof readers, and so on, would be the same. Indeed, the employers themselves admitted that new technology jobs were doing away with old skills and argued that, in various newspaper establishments, employers had already given higher wages and recognition to these designations, employees had already accepted them, and now this should be officially accepted by the board too. The INS itself argued that the required skill in new jobs was less than in the earlier case.[70] Here, again, the Federation only selectively stressed skill and not compensation for deskilling. As always, 'reward' and 'compensation' confounded the workers with ideological obfuscation!

Yet, the growing shadow of new technology over the institutionalised process of wage settlement was so obvious that the Dilsukh Ram Committee had to note that new jobs had come into existence in both printing and the administrative sections, that this preceded a great amount of deskilling and reskilling, that new technology meant a whole new range of occupational health and safety issues, and suggested that a new grouping be created to accommodate new jobs.[71] Though this tackled the issue of new technology to some extent, we have seen, it failed to challenge straightaway the unilateral introduction of automation in the newspaper industry. It will be worthwhile to quote at length what

[68] See, in this context, Touraine (1965) and the critique of 'new syndicalism' by Nichols and Beyon (1977).
[69] *Dilsukh Ram Committee Report*, p. 17; see also *Report of the Second Tripartite Technical Meeting for the Printing and Allied Trades*, ILO (Geneva, 1981), pp. 7–8.
[70] *Dilsukh Ram Committee Report*, pp. 18–19.
[71] Ibid., pp. 328–39.

Dilsukh Ram added in his own handwriting at the end of the 327 page typed Report:

> With the advent of computerised phototypesetting, the working environment has undergone a change. It is stated with great satisfaction that the phototypesetting operator sits in air-conditioned comfort with no fumes and dust, and operates with effortless ease. The picture is not as rosy as it is made out to be. Technological advances have had an impact on the working conditions. They have given rise to physiological, psychological and sociological problems and they have to be studied in their entirety and remedial measures taken . . . . There is an inter-relationship between work, performance and stress . . . .[72]
>
> As stated earlier, automation has affected the factory side and gradually but surely 'light is putting an end to lead'. A whole new era of chemicals has come into existence with its effects on those who handle them. This should be an area for study as they affect the health of workers.[73]
>
> From the material furnished it is seen that the work load has increased and productivity has also increased. This is demonstrated by the number of copies printed and increase in circulation figures.[74]

After suggesting new grades for new technology jobs, Dilsukh Ram then added at the end of his handwritten note these very important lines:

> I, therefore, suggest the following working conditions for VDT operators, etc:
> 1. Those working on VDTs should not work for more than 4 hours a day.
> 2. That they should not work for more than one hour at a stretch. There have to be rest pauses. There should be a rest pause of 15 minutes.
> 3. That the eyes of those engaged in VDT operation should be first tested before they enter upon their work.
> 4. There should be periodic eye tests to ensure that the operators do not suffer from any disability.

[72] Ibid., pp. 329–30.
[73] Ibid., p. 332.
[74] Ibid., p. 336.

5. The special problems of women workers should be kept in view before they operate VDTs.[75]

Needless to say, while these suggestions were important (they would improve working conditions and, more importantly, they admitted the necessary link between wage revision and improvement in working conditions), they failed to meet the challenge of the unilateral introduction of new technology adequately. Thus they remained only halfway suggestions, for the power situation within the plant was not going to be altered by them. I have shown earlier that this confrontation by organised workers to new technology was bound to be halfway, for having argued at length and at times brilliantly on the effects of new technology on the work process,[76] the Federation failed to integrate the exposition into its basic strategy for wage revision. Thus, the Federation could not advance beyond conceiving of 'allowances' and the power structure remained undisturbed as the basic labour process was maintained without much change.

Discourse Constraints

We can understand the halfway nature of the response from a study of the discourse constraints. Whether true in other cases or not, in legal discourse, one of the binding factors would be the precedents, the earlier structure, the division and the definition of

---

[75] Ibid., p. 339.

[76] See, in this connection, an 89 page note submitted before the Wage Boards for Journalists and Non-Journalists entitled *Advantages and Disadvantages of Modern Technology* by the AINEF on 28 December 1987. It can be reasonably claimed to be one of the clearest expositions of new technology by a trade union body. The discerning observer may read in this perspective Vol. 3 of *Submissions*, which deals mainly with allowances. An example of the halfway confrontation can be found from ch. XIII dealing with *Night Shift Allowance*. The demand for night shift allowance is built, once again, on the health hazard and on arguing then for rationalisation of the work hour, roster, etc.; it goes on to claim that night shift allowance should be granted handsomely. See also *Rejoinder and Supplementary Memorandum of AINEF*, Vol. 2, ch. VII, titled 'Modern Technology and Its Impact on Working Conditions,' pp. 408–550.

what constitutes the substantive, the peripheral and the circumstantial. In legal discourse, furthermore, the assumption regarding juridical neutrality is inherent and the challenge mounted against this perceived neutrality is necessarily subversive. All these limited the Federation's challenge to new technology. Briefly we can note:

1. The Federation had to base its arguments on Supreme Court judgements. This meant that the shibboleth of 'welfare state,' 'social justice,' 'fair wage,' etc., had to be the ground on which the Federation could construct its arguments.
2. The Federation had to make the Fair Wages Committee Report its main plank. Thus, the phenomenon of modernisation could only be used as a side element of the strategy and not the main one. Even when the Federation got the chance to make a rejoinder to the employers' arguments and submissions, it stubbornly clung to the Fair Wages Committee Report. It quoted para 15 of the said Report, which said:

    While the lower limit of fair wage must obviously be the minimum wage, the upper limit is equally set by what may broadly be called the capacity of the industry to pay. This will depend not only on the present economic position of the industry, but on its future prospects. Between these two limits, actual wages will depend on a consideration of the following factors and in the light of the factors given below:

    (*i*) the productivity of labour;
    (*ii*) the prevailing rate of wages in the same or similar occupations, in the same or neighbouring localities;
    (*iii*) the level of national income and its distribution; and
    (*iv*) the place of the industry in the economy of the country.[77]
    It is obvious that in the conception of the Fair Wages Committee, technology, power relations and trade union struggles enter in a very roundabout way. On the basis of such a conception, the Federation could go only

[77] Para 15 of the Fair Wages Committee Report quoted in *Rejoinder and Supplementary Memorandum*, filed by AINEF, Vol. 1, pp. 85–86.

halfway in devising a strategy to countenance modernisation in the wage revision struggle, and particularly in
the wage settlement process.[78]

3. The domination of the 'allowance' concept also ruled over
conceptualising the issues of social security and occupational
health and safety.

4. Finally, the Federation could only negotiate and manoeuvre
within the given arena of wage settlement. The institutional
process has its own dynamics. As shown earlier, in the prevailing structure of industrial relations, the Federation could
not hope to do much. It could not ignore the process, and it
had to mobilise professional knowledge. It could, at best,
hope that by using the extant form of legal discourse on wage
settlement and mobilising knowledge, it would be able to not
merely effect revision to an appreciable extent but, in the
course of that revision, a change in power relations also. It
could not help if, in the process, union power below was
weakened or a unilateral introduction of new technology by
the bosses got legitimacy through wage board agreements at
the plant or company level.

In short, the discourse constraints show that the Federation
acted as only a child of its time. It would have perhaps been
utopian to think of more and expect that the dominating triad of

[78] Like the compulsive heritage of the *Fair Wages Committee Report,* on another
issue where the AINEF had no other option than to construct its argument on given
ground was the question of *capacity to pay.* The Federation ripped apart the
financial statements of 60 major newspapers submitted by the INS to the wage
board and showed that the industry had the capacity to pay. On the question of
deducting depreciation, tax and development reserves, it argued admirably and
showed 'in deciding the capacity to pay for incremental wage burdens, gross profits
as determined by the Supreme Court in the cases of Ahmedabad Mill Owners' case,
Indian Link Chain and Unichem Laboratories alone will have to be taken into
consideration before deducting depreciation, transfer to statutory reserves, taxation and any investment allowance'. It had to further argue against the observation
of the Cement Wage Board. Here, too, the discourse constraint is evident. For the
point is not that gross profit before the forementioned deduction has to be the
basis, but more than the gross profit, the debt burden showing the capacity to pay
back, the development reserve, depreciation reserve as research and development
expenditure that should go to the wage fund! See the arguments of the Federation
in *Surrejoinder and Replies to Questions Posed and Clarifications—Replies Sought
by the Wage Boards,* Vol. 1, pp. 13–21.

technology, bosses and the structure of industrial relations would be vanquished by a spirited and professional attack by the workers. Class power could not be expected to be so easily vanquished. In a way, the Federation's warning was fundamental—the 'investor's approach cannot be accepted in the approach to settle the wage problems'.[79]

New Technology, the Labour Process and Wage Settlement

If one ponders over the discourse constraints which set the absolute limits to the AINEF's arguments and submissions, one becomes almost willing to conclude that given the fundamentals, the trade union movement in the newspaper industry made the best of the wage revision case under the shadow of automation. This is clear from both the language of the judge and the judged. The Bachawat Award, after all, went beyond the framework of thinking embedded in the Palekar Tribunal Award. Likewise, the thinking of the Federation also went further. This progress could be ascribed to a paramount reason: the advent of new technology. We have already shown that the wage revision proceedings taking place in the context of new technology have been, in fact, a combination of two processes: the labour process and the valorisation process. The overarching role of new technology in the institutionalised process of wage settlement has to be seen from that perspective. How far the union desired to go is important or, for that matter, how far it went. But equally important would be to see how far it could go for, basically, I will argue, the crucial determining element remained the interaction between the two processes. We have seen that the Federation challenged the valorisation process in the industry by contesting the bosses' contention about industry's capacity to pay. It challenged, in an indirect way, the labour process also, by contesting the given elements of the work flow and by claiming the importance of new technology jobs. But, in its thinking and strategy, the two were not combined. As the challenge was translated only in terms of wages, and particularly allowances, the challenge to the labour process petered out. That

[79] Ibid., p. 217.

being so, one can safely surmise that the employers could renew with vigour the valorisation process.

The advent of new technology and the progress of the industry from the Palekar to the post-Palekar period showed what Marx had said long ago: that the unity of the labour process and the process of valorisation constitute the capitalist process of production. By definition, the labour process would be a relation between a man and his instrument of labour, and the way in which this relationship is organised. If the specificity of the capitalist labour process is that the three constituent elements of the labour process in general (human labour, raw material and the instrument of labour) combine to produce not mere use value, but surplus value, then one can note how in this valorisation process, the specific labour process becomes extremely important. The Bachawat Wage Board proceedings show that the labour process is never beyond challenge from labour, and the challenge is on two fronts: first, it challenges the continuous effort on the part of capital to render control over the labour process more and more efficient; second, it challenges the process of valorisation and, consequently, the process of capital accumulation. This challenge from labour is itself a constituent part of the capitalist labour process. The Bachawat proceedings have further pointed to one error in the otherwise very remarkable and fundamental analysis by Braverman—an error pointed out by Sweezy years ago.[80] Braverman had not included labour struggle in his analysis of the labour process under monopoly capital. Labour studies today have to view the labour struggle against the background of the interaction of the two processes. The wage board proceedings gain significance from that perspective.

The problem now takes a complicated turn. For the question now arises, how are we to look at the phenomenon of the lengthening shadow of new technology over the institutionalised process of wage settlement? If drawing a picture of the relative movements of wages and profit during the post-Palekar era was enough, the task would have been easier. But behind the relative movements of profit and wages stand the twin factors of the valorisation process and the labour process. As we have seen, the labour process itself entails labour as an active agency and not just a passive agency of

---

[80] Paul Sweezy's Introduction in Braverman (1974); see, in this connection, Marx (1976), Vol. 1, ch. 7.

capital. Thus, the relative movements of profit and wage will not tell us much about the dynamics of the labour process. Finally, to what degree can labour be an active agency in the labour process, implying how much labour can alter the objectivity of the process, particularly in view of managerial control techniques and theories, is itself a debatable point. We know that a large part of Braverman's exposition depends on his 'deskilling' thesis. The wage board proceedings witnessed the ceremonial announcement of the 'deskilling' of an entire generation of workers and the demise of monopolisable skills (lino operation, block making and proof reading) among a certain strata of collective workers. Along with deskilling, the control of work and worker by the management assumes new hierarchical work relations. The study of wage board submissions assumes a complexity and significance, for it reflects the said 'deskilling' as well as the creation of a new hierarchy on the basis of new technology jobs, and who knows whether the new hierarchy consisting of new technology jobs created out of wage settlement will not act as a newer control technique, or a newer fountain of challenge to the work regime? As the *Statesman* experience subsequent to the wage board award showed, the Federation could not be sure of the possibility of the latter.[81]

The industry had definitely prospered during the post-Palekar phase. It went in for modernisation, took huge sums as loans and yet did not sink. If this was a clear reflection of the valorisation process, this process itself entailed the imperative of an adjustment in the labour process, which means capital had to involve as well as control labour in the modernisation agenda. This, in turn, signified labour as an active agency which did not accept the compliance unquestioningly. It protested, though the protest was later absorbed by the management. The wage board was the arena where the complexity of the situation was evident or, more appropriately, the complex forces with their interrelationships built up the arena.

---

[81] I shall recount the story elsewhere. It is sufficient to know at this point that there was a scramble among the workers as to who would be promoted to the new technology ranks, there was intense pressure upon the SEU (the Statesman Employees' Union) from the aspirants, the new management got elbow room, the union could satisfy none and, finally, when a managerial attack came on the union in the form of suspension of the union President, the workers who had thought they had been deprived of the gains of new technology oriented reordering of wages and posts, did not rally for long behind the union.

162 ■ *Workers and Automation*

The INS submitted facts about the state of the industry to the wage board. Class IB newspapers had shown a rise in gross profit from 1979 to 1985 by 30.35 per cent; Class IA, 182.14 per cent; Class I 184.09 per cent; Class II 241.57 per cent; Class III 267.85 per cent; Class IV 270 per cent; Class V, 66.6 per cent; Class VI 125 per cent; and Class VII 500 per cent.[82] Thus, progress had been registered in every class of newspapers. The consolidated position would be more revealing. (Table 4.5).

Table 4.5
Consolidated Position in the Post-Palekar Period
(in Lakh Rupees)

	1979	1985	Percentage Rise
Gross block	5,125	14,909	190.91
Net worth	2,354	5,068	115.29
Borrowings	3,494	11,391	226.01
Total finance	5,850	16,457	181.31
Gross revenue	16,884	47,580	181.80
Newsprint cost	7,949	25,368	219.13
Revenue (net of newsprint cost)	8,933	22,209	148.61
Interest	472	1,708	261.86
Depreciation	244	1,433	487.29
Gross profit	1,401	3,319	136.90

Source: *INS Submissions*, Vol. 2, Annexure 6.
Note: Gross profit arrived at before depreciation and tax, but after payment of interest.

The process was equally evident simply judging gross revenue. The Federation's reaction to industry's growth was in the form of an argument to the effect that only gross revenue could be the basis of classification of the newspaper industry for the purpose of wages. Justice Palekar and Justice Bachawat had both accepted the contention. Justice Palekar had noted that the growth of paid-up capital may be tardy. He, in fact, cited the example of Bennett and Coleman, which was content in 1978 with a capital of Rs 41.85 lakh when its gross revenue was above Rs 38 crore, gross block above Rs 6 crore and gross profit more than Rs 2.5 crore.[83] With

[82] *INS Submissions*, Vol. 2, Annexure 6.
[83] *AINEF Submissions*, Vol. 1, p. 328.

respect to selling price, circulation, circulation revenue, advertisement revenue, gross revenue and, finally, gross profit, the going was so good for the newspaper industry that its position changed phenomenally after the Palekar Award. Thus, the number of publications also shot up (see Table 4.6).

Table 4.6
Number of Newspapers (1976–83)

Year	Dailies	Periodicals	Total
1976	875	12,445	13,320
1979	1,087	16,981	17,168
1980	1,173	16,967	18,140
1981	1,264	17,880	19,144
1982	1,334	18.603	19,937
1983	1.423	19,335	20,758

Source: *RNI (Registrar of Newspapers) Annual Reports, 1977–85.*

The total circulation also increased (see Table 4.7).

Table 4.7
Newspaper Circulation from 1978 to 1983 (in Thousands)

Year	Dailies	Weeklies	Others	Total
1978	11,242	11,143	18,195	40,850
1979	13,033	12,924	20,432	46,449
1980	14,531	14,303	22,087	50,921
1981	15,255	15,320	20,527	51,102
1982	14,847	14,387	20,860	50,094
1983	16,731	15,372	23,288	55,391

Source: *ABC (Audit Bureau of Circulation) Reports, 1979–85.*
Note: 'Others' include tri-weeklies and bi-weeklies too.

Circulation revenue increased disproportionate to the increase in circulation, mainly because of the rise in selling price (Table 4.8). In the case of *Hindustan Times* this revenue rise was 165.80 per cent, *Statesman,* Calcutta 68.78 per cent, Bennett and Coleman 73.80 per cent and *Indian Express,* Bombay 118.26 per cent, from 1978 to 1984.[84] Similarly, advertisement revenue also increased,

[84] Ibid., pp. 304–5.

Table 4.8
Rise in Selling Price of Select Newspapers (1976–83)

Name of Newspaper	Percentage Increase
Times of India, Bombay	150.0
Indian Express, Delhi	185.7
Ananda Bazar Patrika, Calcutta	233.3
Prajavani, Bangalore	100.0
Statesman, Calcutta	125.0
Femina, Bombay	167.0
Manorama, Allahabad	150.0

Source: AINEF, *Submissions*, Vol. I, pp. 284–86.

the percentage rise from 1981–82 to 1983–84, on an average, being 70 per cent. Some select newspapers showed a percentage rise of 200 per cent or more between 1978–79 and 1983–84, like *Matrubhumi* 225.78 per cent, *Indian Express*, Madurai 228.74 per cent, *Hindustan Times*, New Delhi 316.90 per cent, and Sandesh Ltd. of Ahmedabad a staggering 544.15 per cent.[85]

In short, evidence abounds to show that the Bachawat Wage Board was instituted at a time of newspaper growth and growth-financed modernisation, and the wage claims of the workers were raised against such a background. Wages certainly rose after the Award, though not to the extent that gross revenue rose or gross profit rose. The Federation marshalled an array of statistics to prove that the industry had grown, had the 'capacity to pay' and argued that the 'investor's approach was impermissible'. But the impression gets strengthened, the more one goes through the voluminous literature of the wage board, that the Federation was only half-aware that the valorisation process was going to be accompanied by a suitable labour process also, implying and involving suitable changes in the work process. We have shown that the Federation resisted certain changes, and advocated certain changes itself to counter new work conditions. But it did not help. Nor could it have done much even if it were fully aware for, after all, the structure of industrial relations built upon the interacting twin processes of valorisation and labour is a given reality—a sort of boundary within which labour acts.

[85] Ibid., pp. 321–23.

In my view, the arguments of the Federation, the Award of the Board, the subsequent concurrence of the employers to the Award, the *real life* implementation of the Award in the plants, the struggle of labour as well as the use of new managerial techniques to control it, the setting up of new productivity norms through the intensification of production, cutting of overtime and vacancies through the natural reduction of the labour force through retirement and new superintending posts are evidence that show that neither is labour an inert component of the labour process, nor is it an autonomous agency that can defy at will the materiality of the interacting twin processes: the valorisation process and the labour process. Neither picture of the worker is true. Even though, through modernisation and the wage board, the plants have been by and large automated, the worker has been far from being a docile servant, dominated by the management in a highly 'Taylorised' work setting. But the reverse is also true, as the board proceedings and subsequent events show. The workers' skill, intelligence and professional knowledge have not been enough to circumvent the economic reality of new technology and, more importantly, the consequences of an automated plant on the power structure in the factory.[86] From a 'Taylorised' plant based on assembly line techniques to a 'continuous process plant,' the transition has involved a shift from 'batch worker' to 'process worker'. The arguments and consciousness reflected in the Palekar and Bachawat proceedings testify to that. This transition has involved struggles and, if the overall boundaries of capital could not be transgressed and if wage and other demands were absorbed by capital in the process of transition, we cannot take that as sufficient evidence for saying in Michael Burawoy's (1979) words, that this is all a 'manufacturing of consent,' that the wage board manufactured consent and nothing more!

One last word. It is too early to say how the shift, mentioned in the foregoing, will influence the behaviour of the worker and his union. This is a time of transition: both the Palekar and the Bachawat proceedings reflected this. But if change has been emphasised, we must be cautious and not overemphasise it. While referring to the discourse constraints, I had shown how the Federation had no

---

[86] For a study of the twin themes of capital accumulation and worker struggle in interaction with each other at the level of enterprise, see Datta (1990), pp. 13–18, 73–78, 94–137, 268–78. See also Burawoy (1978); Thompson (1983); Gorz (1976).

option but to continue thinking and arguing from within the same framework, even while trying to break out of it. It is clear that knowledge alone cannot rescue the modern worker in newspaper printing, for the power structure depends on many other factors besides knowledge. Where the whole conditions of production of surplus value depended on maintaining the power structure inside the factory, the challenge emanating mainly in the form of wage revision was bound to be limited. As I have argued, the new issues demanded newer forms of articulation. A wage board oriented organisation was hardly suitable for that. This was, it may be contended, a very fundamental question, for the old structure of industrial relations, old form of trade union organisation and old ways of conceptualisation and articulation would by nature make possible only a half genesis of the new response to new technology. The element of continuity thus should cause hardly any surprise.

We have seen that there was some structural change in the work process, which resulted in changes in the occupational order which, in turn, resulted in upward mobility to a limited extent. But this upward mobility dissatisfied a larger section than it was able to satisfy. We further saw that the State could once again become a coordinating device for generating profit. Finally, we saw class conflict securely locked in a new framework that would not question the basic rules of the bargaining game. But could we say that an 'overarching consensus' has again been achieved? Contrary to what some think,[87] elements of an ideological response born of new technology will become more and more active in the mortal conflicts of power around division of labour. In other words, the lengthening shadow of new technology over the institutionalised process of wage settlement[88] shows that the

[87] The deideologisation of the union is an argument that flows naturally from a functionalist perspective which views a union as an interest group only. The first name to come to mind would obviously be Lipset.

[88] Apart from an analysis of the position of the industry in the Bachawat period, as compared to the Palekar period, which I have looked into a little, it will be interesting to note that the recommendations of the Palekar Tribunals did not contain any single major reference to technology. The point is not that new technology had not become so much a reality in 1979–80, but that the tribunals never felt that technology had anything to do with the institutionalised process of wage settlement, or that the work environment must be taken into account in determining remuneration for work. Thus, the Palekar Report spoke of minimum, need-based, fair, living and other norms of wage, spoke of adjudication of industrial tribunals, wage boards, commissions and even judicial intervention by the

dominant area of enquiry still remains power and division of labour.[89]

I shall show subsequently how the transition from 'assembly' to 'process' production was characterised by a transition in labour relations from 'fordism' to 'post-fordism'—in other words, a shift from a managerial strategy based on pay rise, union cooption and acceptance of the crucial role of heavy machine operators to a strategy based on union bashing, union disruption through the creation of new technology posts, a new hierarchy for control and superintendence, making shop floor stoppage of work, even strikes, increasingly ineffective and, finally, rendering the working class ideologically and organisationally defenceless by placing the onus upon workers to explain why they should oppose 'modernisation' and 'progress,' thereby forcing them to accept modernisation. The technological shift was, thus, a shift to a new strategy for dominating the workers.

To understand this shift, however, we have to see first, in little more detail, how knowledge played a crucial part in the mode of domination that lay at the heart of the introduction of new technology. We have to see how both the politics of resistance and domination remained characterised by a distinct type of knowledge, indeed distinct ways of acquiring knowledge. The State, the bosses and the workers all made vigorous attempts to know the industry caught in the process of technical change. In the end, however, knowledge was found to be a critical factor in the process of subjugating the workers to a new technological regime.

High Courts and Supreme Court. But not a single word on technology and conditions of work could be found there. See *Recommendations of the Tribunals for Working Journalists* (New Delhi, 1980), pp. 49–67. Once again, in ch. x where the *Recommendations* discuss *Revision of Pay Scales and Wages,* technology and work conditions are conspicuously absent. Then again, the Palekar Report does not stretch the concept of 'wage' in view of work conditions in the industry and sticks to the traditional view (ch. II, sec. IV, chs. VII and X). This, we have seen, was soon challenged in the Bachawat deliberations. Finally, a look at the groupings of non-journalist newspaper employees as recommended by Palekar (ch. II, sec. III, pp. 4–6) will also show the marked difference caused by new technology later reflected in the Bachawat proceedings.

[89] Rueschemeyer (1986), ch. 5.

5

Knowing the Industry: The Story of Some Agencies

I shall now talk about knowledge. We shall see how knowledge played a crucial role in the struggle for power both in the plant as well as in the industry.

Robin Stryker, in a recent essay, has shown how, apart from general social factors, political-institutional and organisational factors impede or accentuate the process of knowing the industry and the economy, and how the State—regulatory agencies—has to use social science to know the conditions so that appropriate decisions can be appropriately implemented (Stryker, 1990). This point in the present context can be argued further. It can be shown that class struggles in the Indian newspaper industry did not merely affect the process of valorisation or the process of labour, but the process of knowledge also. In short, it can be argued that even the process of knowing the industry was a product of new technology, and the consequent turmoil in industrial relations.

We have already seen that the Federation tried to respond to the introduction of new technology by acquiring more knowledge about technology, and using that as an input in its wage board deliberations. But more knowledge did not necessarily mean more power, for what was being contested before the wage board was not merely a revision of wage, but power too. Even the process of knowing, whether by the union or by the regulatory agency, was conditioned by the ensemble of relations in which new technology had appeared in the industry. What one would know and how one would know, too, depended on circumstances. The fetish around new technology had helped the employers to cover the realities of power. This fetish crept into the process of knowing too.

New technology appeared in the Indian newspaper industry around the end of the seventies, and the *Hindu* was one of the first to introduce it. The Hindu management was farsighted in another respect. It knew that in the wake of this introduction, several problems would arise—legal, technical and managerial—in the newspaper industry. It sensed an immediate need for consultancy services for the management in various newspapers. Thus the Research Institute for Newspaper Development was set up in Madras, in 1979. It was actually a brainchild of the Hindu management. The Institute started bringing out a monthly journal for the dissemination of information regarding new technology, named *RIND Survey*, from January 1980 onwards. The Institute was subsequently amalgamated with the Press Institute of India. A rural press project was also started, and training courses began to be held for managers and operators. Managers were instructed on how to achieve the shift from the old hot metal process to the 'cold' one in the least painful way, with the least wastage of money and material. In its opening issue, the journal declared:

> It is unfortunate that the Press, which urges such efforts [for research and training] on the part of everyone else, has itself taken a very long time indeed to found an institution which could help the industry to keep itself informed, to provide much needed research, and organise training . . . .
>
> RIND is either a member of, or in close touch with, leading research and training institutions all over the world. As such, it has access to information on development, activities and experience of newspapers and similar institutes. It expects to furnish essential and basic information to its readers through this Bulletin.[1]

The journal took upon itself the task of disseminating updated information on photocomputerisation technology and the experiences of foreign publishing magnates, particularly in the newspaper industry around the world. It reported on the proceedings of various symposia on new technology and the economic use of

[1] 'Ourselves', *RIND Survey* (hereafter *RS*), No. 1, January 1980.

newsprint.[2] It gleefully recorded that even after the suspension of the publication of the London *Times* for over eleven months, its demand did not slacken and sales picked up quickly once the strike over new technology was resolved.[3] It described the various print exhibitions, like Print '80 and Chicago, and constantly advised production managers and superintendents on improvements in offset printing. One important aspect of its contents has been the planning for rural press through small presses handled by a few computers and offset machines.[4] It reported on All India Printers' Meets, on how dailies in other Asian countries have converted to phototypesetting and on how desk-top publishing is becoming increasingly popular, practical and viable throughout the world.[5]

Apart from managerial and technical information, sparse information was sometimes provided on VDT health hazards,[6] on why journalists should know about the management of newspapers,[7] and on how to build up newspaper readership. Aspects like advertisement layout, the spread of ink, improvement of camera work, text typography, the elegance of font and newsprint waste control, however, remained the dominant themes in the bulletin. As the eighties progressed and personal computers entered the newsroom, the PC 'revolution' began to be most frequently reported as republished items of various foreign print journals, like *Presstime*, *Printing World* and *Graphic Arts Monthly*.[8] In any case, one thing was clear. Handling labour problems in the wake of new technology, how to achieve a cut in the manning level, and the linkages with international monopoly giants in communication business through the adoption of new technology were never touched upon in the journal. A content analysis would have shown what was included and what was excluded from the journal. Technical problems were most important, managerial problems second and financial problems third—these were the issues to be addressed. The others were merely insignificant.

[2] *RS*, No. 2, February 1980.
[3] *RS*, No. 5, June 1980.
[4] *RS*, No. 9, September 1980; see 'A Charter for the Rural Press,' 'Management of Rural Press,' *RS*, No. 3, March 1983; *RS*, No. 10, October 1984.
[5] *RS*, No. 3, March 1982.
[6] *RS*, No. 6, June 1982.
[7] *RS*, No. 6, June 1983.
[8] *RS*, No. 9, November 1988.

The Ananda Bazar Patrika management organised a print exhibition towards the end of the seventies in Calcutta. The exhibition was a success in terms of the number of visitors. A print exhibition was held by the All India Master Printers Association in 1991 and colourful literature on new technology was distributed. In special supplements, the various newspaper managements brought out literature on new print technology like in the *Hindu, Desh* and the *Times of India.* The Indian Newspaper Society (INS) took care to inform the public of the huge cost incurred for introducing new technology in the perspective of wage revision demands made by the unions.

In the earlier days of hot metal printing, the management never thought of disseminating information as part of its marketing strategy. But now, information on new technology was collected and distributed as part of the overall selling of the industry's identity. New technology was not merely introduced and adopted; people—the lay readers—were to be told about this too. The brand identity of the product, i.e., the journal, of course, aimed at covering what the *RIND Survey* had deliberately kept out— the impact of new technology on the labour process. Thus, in the structure of knowledge gathered and disseminated by the owners, the absence of material on the labour process remained significant. Equally obvious is the fact that trade unions took upon themselves the task of knowing the industry and the new technology to be introduced in the interest of their own struggle.

The Statesman Employees' Union study on modernisation, called *A Working Paper On the Press Tycoons' Modernising Onslaught On Newspaper Workers,* came at the initial phase of such an imperative.[9] This working paper came out in 1982, when the management of the *Statesman* had placed the idea of modernisation before the union and had started talking vociferously on it with the employees. Within a year a Bengali daily, *Aajkal,* came out with electronic photocomputerised technology. The *Hindu* had already effected the transition, and the *Hindustan Times* was in the midst of it. The panic among the employees was due more to the fact that nobody knew anything substantial about the new technology, no union leader could authoritatively comment on the

---

[9] *A Working Paper on the Press Tycoons' Modernizing Onslaught On Newspaepr Workers,* The Statesman Employees' Union, Calcutta, 1982.

assertion of the management that there would be no retrenchment consequent to modernisation, the strike at the *Economic Times*, Calcutta, had been ruthlessly crushed and, in banking as well as the insurance industry, the union leadership had either capitulated or the results of anti-automation movements had not been very encouraging. The feeling among the Statesman Employees' Union leadership was that, before confronting the management on the issue of introducing new technology, it must acquire adequate knowledge about it. It must inform the workers of the *inevitability* of a cut in the manpower level consequent upon modernisation, irrespective of managerial assurances. It must also link the advent of new technology in India from outside with deliberate State policy and with the IMF loan then being negotiated. There was much confusion on how to counter modernisation. By accepting compensatory pay increase? By linking modernisation with an agreement on no retrenchment? By refusing any written agreement while controlling its pace of introduction? Or by simply disallowing the introduction? No instruction or advice from the Federation leadership was forthcoming. The Statesman Union's *Working Paper* is a product of such circumstances—panic, anger, confusion and an inherent tendency to struggle. But, above all, it was the outcome of the feeling among union militants that in order to tackle new technology, one has to *know* it.

Thus, the *Working Paper* has two parts. The substantive account narrates how new technology has come about in the course of the evolution of printing technology, the technical changes, its political economy and the possible motives of the management behind introducing it. However, the annexures form a more substantive part. The second part, the annexures, makes a concrete case study of the *Statesman* itself and, by mapping out the comparative workflow charts under hot metal and the soon to be introduced cold technology, it aimed to show how a drop in the manning level was inevitable, both department-wise and on the whole. The annexures created a sensation in union circles throughout the industry. It was debated whether, by showing the possible ways to reduce staff, a strategic mistake had been committed or not. In any case, the *Working Paper* was the first such attempt. Information here served two purposes: enlightening the rank and file members about the harsh reality of modernisation and informing the Federation leadership of the possible scenario and urging it to brace itself for a stormy future and upheaval in the industry.

In the *Statesman*, as a consequence, the management had to slow-pedal modernisation and devise a circuitous route to implement it. Modernisation was certainly delayed. But notwithstanding the *Working Paper*, the management was able to use new technology as a union bashing technique to emasculate the union movement there. As regards the intended second effect, the outcome was equally instructive.

Initially, the Federation leadership was enthused at the Statesman Union's study. It lauded the effort in its own resolutions, started a study on an all-India scale and, in 1983, a booklet on the all-India scenario on modernisation in the newspaper industry was brought out (NCNNAEO, 1983). It was distributed among the various union affiliates of the Federation.

But, strangely, the Federation's own response and its recommendation of the Statesman Union's *Working Paper* did not provoke or lead to any other concrete study by a union with respect to its own enterprise. The Federation, thereafter, sent questionnaires to the unions, though most of them remained unanswered. We shall return to this point later. The Federation's own study led to some resolutions in various conferences but, as the wage board deliberations proved, the lack of concrete studies by unions in various plants was a severe handicap in mounting substantive arguments on various aspects of modernisation. But, more importantly, that these two documents failed to be a catalyst indicated something else. It proved that while there was a lack of strategy in the Federation leadership's thinking on modernisation, the unions could not be enthused with simply two informative booklets. Knowledge is no substitute for strategic thinking on how to combat increased managerial power. Dissemination of information had to come as part of an overall strategy of the struggle for power. The fundamental problem with these two documents was that they did not situate technology in the context of power. The concern for retrenchment, perhaps justifiably, was paramount. The documents also did not reflect the concern that, with help of new technology, the management could marginalise the union and initiate a process of deunionisation. The Federation leadership also did not realise that a powerless union leadership would not fight against a reduction in the staff level or for various social security measures. It did not realise that, above all, the *frontier of control* was the key to struggle over all fundamental issues at stake in modernisation: job, social security and work satisfaction. Acquisition of knowledge did not necessarily mean power though, to have power over a thing, one had to know it!

The next step that the Federation took was to frame a questionnaire for the unions. This questionnaire mainly stressed information regarding any possible new technology agreement in the plant and the provisions thereof. While this was naturally the first worry of any trade union, the questionnaire was remarkable in its failure to ask its member affiliates anything on the possible impact of new technology on the labour process. Moreover, the circular did not ask its union affiliates to collect from the individual members of the union necessary data on the possible adverse impact on health, stresses and strains, attitude to new technology, and to newer forms of supervision. Again, very few, if any, cared to reply. This again told upon the Federation's concrete arguments before the wage board, as well as its capacity to confront the management concretely on these issues. Leadership suffered at both levels—at the level of the Federation for not getting feedback from union affiliates, and at the level of the unions for not getting feedback from individual members. The Federation leadership dismissed the non-response towards the questionnaire from below and took it to be customary.[10] No one thought of the reason why the unions. feeling powerless before new technology, felt discouraged about sending replies or what could be learnt from this direct correspondence between the awareness of power and awareness of the need for information and knowledge.

I have already indicated how the AINEF took it as its special responsibility to inform its members of the current literature on new technology, and particularly on its possible effects on occupational health and security.[11] From the ILO, WHO and graphics industry sources, news items were culled and circulated. Being a member of the International Graphical Federation (IGF) and the International Federation of Journalists (IFG), the Federation could recirculate the necessary circulars. Among the important topics

[10] Talk with K.L. Kapur, General Secretary of the AINEF, New Delhi, on 12 January 1990.

[11] AINEF circular no. 29/89, 12 December 1989. Similar circulars deal with 'Safety in the Use of Chemicals at Work—ILO Convention 170,' circular 23/90, 18 December 1990; and on organisation of work, circular 11/91, 11 March 1991; circular 13/91, 1 April 1991 reports on suggestions of Federations of Workers in Media and Related Trades in Japan concerning VDTs.

covered in its circulars, there was a summary of a joint IGF/IFJ Conference at Geneva (10–11 November 1986) on New Technology and Media Concentration: International Capital Links in the Media Sector and Demarcation Lines between Editorial and Technical Departments. Again, a summary of the International Trade Union Guidelines on Visual Display Units was similarly circulated. The circulars of the Standing Committee of Trade Unions of the Graphics Industry based in Berlin were similarly reported to the unions. On possible health damage due to uninterrupted work on VDUs, continuous night shift work, and the spray of chemicals in printing, the Federation took care to inform the members. And, as the wage board submissions showed, the Federation had developed an inventory of literature on these issues. My own visits to various plants have shown that the union officials at the grassroots level acknowledge the value of these circulars in enabling them to have knowledge of new technology, though it is difficult to say with certainty how and to what extent this knowledge was converted to practical use by the union movement.

The Federation collected copies of agreements in the newspaper industry in countries in East Asia and tried to learn how the trade union movements in those countries were trying to tackle the social consequences of new technology. Representatives were sent to conferences in these countries and their speeches and reports were circulated.

However, the pattern of the news items circulated reveals what we have been trying to suggest, namely, that the Federation leadership had no clear idea of what to particularly concentrate on in its exposure of new technology, and what to achieve through these circulars. Thus, the Federation rarely tried to find out how new technology was aiding particular labour regimes in Malaysia, Singapore and Korea in the context of new industrialisation; how new technology has affected forms of labour supervision in the media industry; and, more importantly, what was the fate of the agreements (the copies of which the Federation had collected and distributed)—in other words, the aftermath of new technology agreements. Apart from this absence of purpose, there was another ambiguity. When the Federation leadership reported on conferences, did it want unions led by it to follow similar guidelines and find out the state of affairs, frame its demands accordingly, and fight on similar charters? While the *Submissions* certainly show traces of such an influence, the fact of ambiguity cannot be negated. I shall give an example.

The ILO held the Third Tripartite Technical Meeting for Printing and Allied Trades. Its report was circulated to the members.[12] This report described broadly the nature of new technologies for typesetting, printing, binding, finishing, despatch and so on. It discussed the consequent changes in the structure of the industry and the employed labour force. Then it discussed the major parameters of working time (normal hours of work, annual leave with pay, other types of leave and retirement age). Then came the organisation of working time (normal hours, overtime working hours and compensatory time off). Shift work also came under discussion. The organisation and content of work was also analysed (like the use of workers' skills and potential, responsibilities entrusted, cooperation amongst workers, interest in work and occupational hazards inherent in work). Finally, the report discussed decentralisation of production.

This report had an obvious influence on the final arguments of the Federation before the wage board. However, as I have shown earlier, these aspects were emasculated and reduced to one aspect only—the financial aspect.

The workers' response to the need for acquiring knowledge about new technology and the industry thus remained structured. As we have seen, the leadership of the union exhorted, and the rank and file remained passive. The Federation sent circulars, and the circulars often remained unanswered. One union took the initiative; the initiative was lauded, but it was not taken up, followed and spread. The drive for the accumulation of knowledge and the union response at the plant level remained separate and were not integrated. This begets the question: why did this happen?

The first obvious line of enquiry is who are the people who took the initiative? K.L. Kapur, the General Secretary, is not a worker. Associated with the *Hindustan Times* for long, he works as a full-time Secretary. S.Y. Kolhatkar, the President, was a veteran communist leader of Maharashtra. The Statesman Employees' Union's leadership also consisted of members who were longtime political activists. Madan Phadnis has been a full-time busy lawyer well versed in labour laws, and acts as the legal consultant. He is the Vice-President of the Federation . Now, these and other such people may be

---

[12] Circular no. 11/91, 11 March 1991.

called the intellectuals, comprising the intellectual stratum amongst the newspaper employees. Obviously, the realisation among these people regarding the need for knowledge may often remain, though connected, at variance with the response at the shop-floor level. Structurally, the organisation may not force a two way communication since, for an agenda predominantly dominated by 'old' issues and wage bargaining, a two way communication is often not needed. It is an *extra*—desirable but not essential. But, more importantly, the reason seems to be that the new discourse of knowledge of the industry arises within the old discourse constraints and, hence, such disjunctions are bound to appear at the initial stage. Factors like the structure of the organisation, the implications of 'outsiders' in the union, and the structure of old union discourse all contributed to the disjunction and prevented a combination of the two levels—the drive for accumulation of knowledge in the movement and the workers' response at the plant level.

Thus, the Federation did not advise, instruct or train its union affiliates to fight for a better work organisation at the plant level. Nor did it frame its own charter at the national level, itself incorporating the aspects raised in the circular. It remained hamstrung by the absence of concrete information on these issues at the plant level. Thus information from abroad remained non-usable. The Federation itself admitted, in a reply to a questionnaire of the ILO concerning printing and allied trades, that no substantive consultation is done by the management in printing plants in India, the reskilling programme is shoddy, collective bargaining rarely touches upon the organisation of work, and occupational health and safety levels are dangerously low.[13] Yet the Federation leadership rarely thought of how these aspects could be concretely formulated plant-wise in the country. In brief, one can say that the phenomenon of knowing the industry by the Federation had been ascribed from the beginning with a limited character. The dominating factor in ascribing such a limitation has been, to borrow an old term, trade union consciousness. Even worse, it was a union consciousness of an old type that gathered knowledge in only one particular way, and did not know how to unmask the impact of new technology upon the labour process in a concrete way, how to articulate the consequent relevant issues at the *plant* level, or how to link the increasing information on new technology with the *concrete* fight

[13] Circular no. 17/90, 9 November 1990.

for a change in organisation of work. In short, knowledge and power or knowledge and the effective capacity of workers to fight remained unconnected.

The most thorough spurt in knowing the industry, however, came with the institution of the wage board. Wage boards have been successively instituted by the Government of India, under the Working Journalists and Other Newspaper Employees (Conditions of Service) and Miscellaneous Provisions Act, 1955 for the purpose of fixing and revising the rates of wage in respect to both journalist and non-journalist employees. To revise wages, the wage board had to know the conditions of the industry and the changes thereof. For submissions to the board, both the employers, with their primary forum the INS (Indian Newspaper Society), and the various organisations of employees, including the AINEF, had to know and submit necessary information before the board. Clearly, we find a connection here. The state of industry provokes a struggle for revision of wages. The state of struggle, in turn, influences the state of knowledge. It has been the same elsewhere too. For example, in England commotions in Fleet Street and ongoing technological change led to the formation of the Royal Commission for Newspaper Industry, popularly know as the McGregor Commission, whose two volume reports have become essential today for knowing the British newspaper industry. In our country too, after the turmoil in the textile industry, both the Union government and the Uttar Pradesh government appointed committees and brought out reports on the state of the industry. However, in all these cases, the main agent was the State. The unions, in their demands and struggles, have followed the lead given by the State for knowing the industry. Almost without exception, the bosses have been averse to handing over information regarding the industry, displaying an unexceptionally conservative attitude towards information and knowledge, barring of course the minimum that they want for their own purpose. For example, the Palekar Tribunal, after sending 3,516 questionnaires, received replies from only 70 newspaper establishments covering 219 newspapers[14] and lamented: 'The response, as on previous occasions, was not very encouraging, indicating thereby the general apathy

---

[14] *Recommendations of the (Palekar) Tribunals for Working Journalists and Non-Journalist Newspaper Employees*, 12 August 1980, Government of India, p. 1.

and indifference of the newspaper proprietors concerned to place factual data and material to assist the Board.'[15]

The Palekar Tribunal, after examining the state of the newspaper industry, came to the conclusion that 'the newspaper industry is one of those industries which have prospects of continuous development in the foreseeable future'[16] and declared with glee:

> After examining the general condition of the industry at present and comparing it with its condition in 1967, I feel no doubt that the newspaper industry has a great future. It has been continuously growing. The profits are rising. Rise in circulation, in spite of repeated hikes in the sale price of the paper and advertisement rates . . . . Luckily for the industry, it is the sort of consumer industry which by creating addicts, ensures its own perpetuation. Newspaper proprietors have come to recognise that special talents are necessary for launching a successful paper, and have started hiring talents for that purpose after gauging the tastes and interests of the reading public. Subjects like sports, the cinema, drama and the like which some years ago were hardly noticed by 'respectable' journals are being given pride of place. New fields are opening up. Physical and social sciences, agriculture, horticulture, etc. are being paid greater and greater attention. I have, therefore, no doubt that in a developing economy like ours throwing up a variety of subjects and problems in which the reading public is interested, and with a steadily growing body of educated employed, the demand for newspapers is bound to rise continuously. The only constraint had been the availability of newsprint. Luckily, the position has eased now and is expected to be easier with indigenous production, for which factories are being set up.[17]

This long quotation calls for an explanation. It can be seen that Justice Palekar does not include anything relating to conditions of work in the industry in his report on the 'State of the Industry' from which the quote has been taken. Nor does he refer even once to the question of technology, though it was in the late seventies that new technology first appeared in the industry. New technology

---

[15] Ibid., p. 1.
[16] Ibid., ch. VIII, para. 8.1.
[17] Ibid., para. 8.8.

would be the chief factor in fulfilling Justice Palekar's hopes. Yet it did not strike the Tribunal that to know the state of the industry in the context of wage revision, conditions of work and the organisation of work had also to be investigated.

The Bachawat Wage Board marks a radical departure in this respect. This wage board, apart from knowing standard information on the state of the industry (like circulation figures, the state of profitability, tax burden on the industry, the share of newsprint cost and manpower level), emphatically tried to link the two hitherto unattended aspects: *organisation of work* and *conditions of work*. I have already indicated how the advent of new technology and, in that context, the articulation of new demands by the Federation marked the times of the Bachawat Wage Board. It is no wonder that, in spite of a certain narrowness in the terms of reference, the board had to direct its investigations according to these considerations.

The conclusions of the Fact Finding Committee on Newspaper Economics, the Annual Reports of the Registrar of Newspapers and the Press Commission Report were marshalled by the Federation in its submissions to the Bachawat Wage Board, apart from the substantive evidence drawn from the Fair Wages Committee and the secondary arguments drawn from external sources like ILO and WHO literature. In fact, the collection and collation of these reports marks the long way in knowing the state of the industry, including the working conditions and organisation of work. Though the context was wage revision, the Federation's arguments impelled the Board to take cognisance of the work environment under the new technology regime, and we know that the Board had to appoint a one man committee to look into the state of technical change in the industry and the consequent effects on occupational safety and health. Dilsukh Ram, who was the lone member, did a detailed study, asked for the views of both employers' and employees' organisations, and came out with recommendations. More than the recommendations, the study by Dilsukh Ram was significant because it was the first time that a systematic effort was made to assess the impact of automation on all the three aspects of the industry: the printing section or the factory side, the administrative section and the journalist section.[18] Dilsukh Ram

[18] See Annexure II of the *Submissions Made by the All India Newspaper Employees Federation and Indian Journalists Union Before The Expert Committee for Newspaper Employees*, 7 September 1990.

took note of the process of adoption of machines, new jobs which had come into existence, as well as the changes in the work environment. It is from the Dilsukh Ram Committee Report that one can now have a fair idea of the process of deskilling and reskilling in the industry, the new process of work supervision, the emerging factor of added stresses and strains and, the extent of danger to occupational health and safety. Thus, knowledge of the work organisation and work environment has become possible today with the massive report submitted by Dilsukh Ram to the wage board. We can see, once again, the critical factors behind this: the struggle over wages and other working conditions, the intervention of the State, and the changing regime of technology. In other words, knowledge of conditions of production emanates from the interpenetration of two processes at a given critical juncture: the process of valorisation and the process of labour.

The focus on working conditions in the proceedings of the wage board forced the government to take a detailed look into the forementioned factors in the context of the country's newspaper industry. Accordingly, the Ministry of Labour set up an Expert Committee to look into the issues of safety, health and hygiene, as well as medical allowance, leave travel concession and overtime allowance in respect of newspaper employees. The committee (known as the Ishwari Prasad Committee) sent a questionnaire to the unions for relevant information.[19] It also wanted individual survey records of the personnel working in the visual display unit for occupational health surveys.

However, the report and recommendations of the Expert Committee were like a mountain producing a mouse. The recommendations included implementation-monitoring machinery at the level of Chief Inspector of Factories, designing of work stations and its improvement with a view to reducing visual and other physical and mental discomforts in the PTS room, regular medical examinations, care against repetitive strain injuries, caution in the use of various hazardous chemicals, responsibility of employers as regards dust, fume and maximum noise level, strict maintenance of top standards regarding the manufacture of VDTs, and a forum for consultation and information exchange in the form of a safety committee.[20]

---

[19] *Quesionnaire Sent by Expert Committee for Newspaper Employees* (hereafter *Questionnaire*), New Delhi, Ministry of Labour, 18 July 1990.

[20] AINEF circular no. 10/91, 11 March 1991.

But these were mere platitudes. The Committee was probably daunted by the employers' boycott of its deliberations, and it avoided any reference to placing responsibility on the employers— the responsibility for maintaining the proposed norms in the industry. For example, the Committee avoided the question of reduction in work hours and a shorter active period of work for VDT operators. The AINEF detected the conciliatory tone of the Committee and, in a letter to the government, wrote tersely:

> . . . the committee, we apprehend, has succumbed to the pressure tactics and blackmail methods resorted to by the employers, particularly their organisation, Indian Newspaper Society, which have successfully sabotaged the task entrusted to the Committee. We would not hesitate to state that the employers have been amply rewarded for their negative attitude in not cooperating with the Committee. It is a well known fact that they boycotted the Committee right from the beginning and their tactics have paid them rich dividends.[21]

The story of the Expert Committee is highly instructive from two angles. It nullified the recommendation of the Bachawat Wage Board which, in paragraph 10.13 of its report, had recommended the appointment of such an expert committee. But the Committee, instead of consisting of expert personnel on equipment, health and industrial engineering, became a body of bureaucrats with the government appointing its officers on it.[22] Thus, the intervention of a State agency and the accumulation of knowledge regarding working conditions in an industry may be a response to workers' struggle, but it can carry, at the same time, the stamp of authority of the employers. The report itself becomes a renewed control by the bosses over the work process. The process of accumulation of knowledge here is distinctly the process of control too. From the Federation's point of view, it proved that such knowledge is necessary for power. But, given the class relations and power relations, that is never a sufficient condition of power. More importantly,

[21] AINEF circular no. 12/91, 21 March 1991; IJU (Indian Journalists Union) circular no. 3/91, n.d.
[22] A renewed suggestions was made by the AINEF for setting up a real expert committee in its Central Working Committee Meeting in Bombay on 7 April 1991, vide *Resolution On the Expert Committee Report.*

another question emerges. Why is it that there is always a huge gap between such reports and the consequent recommendations? The report embodies knowledge and the recommendations as the practical aspect of it; in other words, they represent the aspect of control and the relevance of knowledge to power. It is another thing if the AINEF had thought that its own huge submissions and the formation of an Expert Committee with its report on the state of the industry would alter the scenario in a positive way! Indeed, as the whole episode of the Expert Committee showed, recommendations always remain a secondary part of such an enquiry. The enquiry and the resultant information about the industry are always occasioned by a restructuring of the industry. It is at such a critical juncture that all the forces locked in industrial relations—the bosses, unions, the state—start feeling the need for information and knowledge. Such knowledge, as I have been arguing, rarely changes the 'frontier of control' in the plant or in the industry. Yet precisely through the whole ceremony of acquiring knowledge and coming out with (inevitably soft) recommendations, the workers are again disciplined. It is not merely knowledge that helps to control; even its discursive mode has the inbuilt function of control!

The fore-mentioned contention may be exemplified. The main questionnaire issued by the Expert Committee contained items on the state of technology, safety, health and hygiene, safety organisation, medical care, leave travel concession, overtime allowance and some financial data. But the questions excluded any information on control, supervision, compulsive arrangements, stress and strain. For example, compulsive overtime due to the deliberate and gradual reduction in the level of manpower, the appointment and placement of workers on a temporary basis and for the whole company (in the case of a common ownership unit) instead of for a single definite paper, the overall milieu of insecurity, the absence of any regular medical check-up system which, as a result, does not yield any information on occupational illness, do not enter into the information pool that is to be collected through the questionnaire. Indeed, the onus of furnishing information is placed on the employees and not on the bosses, and the latter could thus conveniently boycott its proceedings. We are debarred from any information on shop floor movement restrictions imposed by the management, and the consequent stresses and strains. The annexure for financial data is also a stereotype. When furnished it can duplicate only the financial statements submitted elsewhere, which contain information on paid-up capital, gross block and development rebate.[23] But the type of financial information needed for the purpose of the Expert Committee, conveniently excluded from the boundaries of the questionnaire, would have been increase of overtime expense over the years and a department-wise breakdown, the growth or otherwise of the productivity of the worker over the years, the wage differentials within a plant, and the amount of medical expenses incurred on an average by employees outside the ESI limit (Employees State Insurance). However, even with such information the problem would have remained. For example, in many plants, operators working on VDTs would not like to furnish information on their state of health lest it give the management an opportunity to show who is ill equipped to work among the workforce. A union may be less enthused to furnish information, lest the management consider such an act unfriendly and the cooperative state of bargaining may consequently break down. In other words, the Expert Committee was to have gone down to the plant level to see things for itself and the policy pressure on the bosses was to have come from above.

Take Question 5.3.4 of the Questionnaire. It states:

> Please indicate the various steps taken to ensure that the conditions at the place of work and of rest as also in the canteen in the establishment are hygienic, and hygienic sense is inculcated amongst the workers. Please give suggestions if any.

Now, whoever is familiar with factories (and newspaper plants are no exception) knows that maintaining a facility of a canteen has always been a demand of the workers. The management invariably wants to do away with subsidised canteen facilities in lieu of a tiffin allowance. The maintenance of canteen cleanliness is the lowest priority of the management. The canteen is often run on contract. Thus, why is the onus of 'hygienic sense' placed on the workers when it has to be *inculcated*? Should the question not have been aimed at securing information on room space, drinking water facilities, amount of expenditure, capacity to serve a certain number of workers at a time, and inspection of canteen arrangements by a safety officer?

[23] Sections 5 and 6 of the *Questionnaire* are interesting for their bureaucratic approach, op. cit.

Take again Question 5.4.7. It states:

(*a*) Does the establishment have a Plant Medical Officer?
(*b*) Is there a regular medical check-up for employees of the Plant?
(*c*) If so, what are the categories of persons covered and the frequency of medical check-ups?
(*d*) What are the first-aid and medical aid arrangements in the establishment?

But even if there is a plant medical officer, is he/she trained in occupational health and safety? Again, even if there is a check up, is it for detecting the hazards emanating from the work environment? The question does not seem to have any inkling even that what the workers need is not general diagnosis and therapy, but occupational diagnosis and appropriate therapy. It is common knowledge that workers may find a doctor for ordinary stomach trouble but rarely anyone, for say, pneumoconiosis or mental fatigue.

Now, let us look at Questions 5.4.8 and 5.4.9:

Are the workers conscious of the hazards associated with the chemicals they handle?
What is the attitude of workers to safety in general? Negative/Indifferent/Interested/Positive.

Why does the question not ask if the management has prepared a chemicals directory and told the workers of the hazards? Similarly, what should be the fundamental point: 'attitude of the workers to safety' or 'attitude of the management to safety'? Is there not an implicit assumption that occupational accidents do happen due to negligence of the workers and also due to their ignorance of basic safety rules?

Finally, Question 5.5.1:

Does the establishment employ qualified safety officers? What duties do they perform?

What does the Expert Committee imply by *qualified safety officers*? Work safety is an issue that is still being formulated, and that too primarily due to class struggle. Safety indicates industrial engineering, knowledge of occupational health and safety, and a progressive human resource development policy. All these denote ergonomics, an area around which labour is increasingly fighting against capital, and the thrust of which has been to situate the question as the *responsibility of capital*, to shift the onus from the agenda of labour to the agenda of management.[24] In this way, even a questionnaire meant for individual survey records of personnel working in VDTs can be scrutinised to find the inbuilt bias against labour.

It can be seen, then, that the process of accumulation of knowledge is a process of power too. New technology, industrial relations and the need for information are all connected by that strong thread—the question of power and the subjugation of the worker to the boss.

Market information leads to more control over the market; similarly, organisational information leads to more organisation. Thus, the State had reason to secure more information about the industry in the throes of turmoil over change in technology and wage claims, through regulatory agencies like wage boards, expert committees, press commissions and Registrar of Newspapers. It must not be presumed that employers did not have the sense to realise the functional role of knowledge. The publication of the *RIND Survey* is proof of such realisation. Yet they were not willing to make their knowledge public. Their knowledge of changing work conditions at the plant level was deliberately kept confined within the circle. Even regulatory agencies were frowned upon. Market segmentation, the high degree of competition and the characteristic perishability of the product all told upon the behaviour of the industry. To secure control over new technology, workers, particularly compositors who were the first to be retrained, wanted diffusion of information about the industry, technology and the generation of machines. To secure the same control, employers wanted restrictions upon access to information. The State regulatory agencies wanted to build up a pool of informa-

---

[24] See *Report of the Expert Committee for Newspaper Employees* (New Delhi, Ministry of Labour, January 1991), pp. 81–97. Indeed, the recommendations of the Expert Committee skirted the crucial question of responsibility. As often happens with such expert committees, the accumulation of knowledge about working conditions in the industry by the Committee remained unconnected with the question of responsibility for its recommendations. The recommendations thus remain 'soft'.

tion for the same control, with no view to improvement-oriented recommendations but the regulation of industrial relations. The role of knowledge in the behaviour of agencies and, conversely, the role of the behaviour of agencies in building up knowledge have remained, uptil now, a neglected area in labour process studies.[25]

We have shown that the whole phenomenon of knowing the industry arose at a time when the newspaper industry in the country was being redesigned, and corporate structure really became the ruling structure in the industry. In such a context, the bosses wanted only *institutionalised* knowledge about the engineering, financial, journalist and personnel management aspects of the industry. Just as corporate America saw the rise of the discipline of modern management, where engineers became managers,[26] here too knowledge of the industry had to take a certain *form*. By merely rationalising firm behaviour and acutely judging inter-firm studies, we cannot gain an understanding of the process whereby managements of the *Hindu, Deccan Herald, Times of India, Ananda Bazar Patrika* and *Hindustan Times* trained their technical and managerial personnel, built up their own inventory of information on the industry, and yet remained unenthused about such knowledge becoming public through the intervention of State regulatory agencies. Such a process intrinsically excluded public debate over corporate structure and corporate technology, especially a debate in which labour would be involved. It was well understood that such a debate would imply, sooner or later, the influence of such public discussion over the frontier of control. Hence, the *form* of such knowledge of the industry remained structured in a particular way. Marx had said: 'The specific economic form . . . in which unpaid surplus labour is pumped out of direct producers determines the relationship of rulers and ruled, as it grows directly out of production itself and, in turn, reacts upon it as a determining element' (1976: 791).

We have seen that knowledge of the process of valorisation and

---

[25] See, for example, the neglect of this aspect in an otherwise incisive study by Partha Sarathi Banerjee (1988). I am indebted to Partha Sarathi Banerjee for drawing my attention to two papers by Zeitlin (1979) and Giffin (1984). Banerjee's own questionnaire is instructive when compared to that of the Expert Committee.

[26] Noble (1977), ch. 10, 'Modern Management and the Expansion of Engineering'.

labour remains an integral part of the two processes and is a part of
what Marx had called, 'relationship of the rulers and the ruled'. In
an era of scientific management and its aftermath, it had become
imperative for the management to acquire, pool, store and process
information. It is this structure of the process of acquiring knowledge that dictates the nature of knowledge, what should be within
its corpus, what should remain excluded, amongst whom to disseminate, and again whom to opt out. Social science has served,
willy nilly, for the most part, such a project of power.

A decade after the advent of new technology in the newspaper
industry, much light has been thrown on the industry. But how
much of this knowledge has ascribed to the labour process a
central place in the enquiry? How much, again, has this knowledge
helped labour in its fight against capital, in its agenda on the
frontier of control?

Wage boards and the devious role of knowledge, however, were
only a part of the strategy of capital for maintaining the frontier of
control, and instituting new modes for controlling labour. But to
fully comprehend the strategy and the shift in the mode of control,
let us look beyond wage boards and institutions of knowledge,
where strikes, protests, plant level conflicts and the day-to-day
functioning of the Federation formed the real stuff of politics—the
politics of resistance against such a transition.

6

New Technology at the Shop Floor Level: The Story of Deunionisation in Some Indian Newspapers

We have seen how new technology exercised a decisive impact on the institutionalised process of wage settlement, and the structure of industrial relations became a critical factor in the whole process. This was, however, analysed from the perspective of a total wage settlement. But the dynamics of power—domination/resistance–as affected by technology, cannot be fully understood unless the analysis is shifted from industry to the plant and shop floor level, where the impact of technology has been no less decisive. Indeed, it new technology was not reciprocally potent at the shop floor level, it could not have served so much at the industry level too over the institutionalised process of wage settlement for the entire industry. The weapon of new technology was effectively used with surprising rapidity and recurrence by the management for deunionising the worker. One union leader, describing his experience of deunionisation, called it 'the most crushing assault'.[1]

Our discussion on wage boards suggests that while new technology changed the structure of industrial relations and the pattern of work conditions within the factory, and altered the power scenario,

---

[1] An office-bearer of the Statesman Employees' Union (SEU), Calcutta, described it thus in an internal communication to an associated union while writing of his experience regarding the aggressive policy of the new management; SEU's letter (12 April 1990).

the union leaders continued struggling for wage revision at the industry level, disregarding this process below. New Technology affected the work process, but wage bargaining at the top continued as if no fundamental change was occurring below. All these reduced the strength of the collective worker. Here a dialectical opposite can be suggested. At the plant and shop floor level, workers certainly adopted day-to-day forms of resistance. But bereft of any idea of the magnitude of assault by new technology on the entire industry, these everyday forms of resistance crumbled quickly. New technology reduced worker's power within the factory. The fundamental form this assault assumed was the tendency toward deunionisation. The study of deunionisation in some newspapers of the country will, I believe, show how new technology altered the balance of power at the plant level while having already reduced the effectivity of workers at an industry level.

New Technology and the Tendency Towards Deunionisation

As already shown, deunionisation started at a time when the newspaper industry in India could boast that it 'never had it so good.' Managers were overjoyed that the sales, earning and profit were all increasing and modernisation, in spite of putting pressure on resources, had not yet resulted in an established company crashing out of the market although there were some exceptions, like the Amrita Bazar Patrika group. Business was excellent, and from 'high' to 'low' there was a general agreement that wage could and should be revised. Revision since the Palekar Award was overdue, and thus the attention of the workers both at the Federation and at the plant-union level naturally became focused on questions of wage revision. It was hard to comprehend that while unions and the Federation were gaining increasing voice over the question of wage revision, the possibilities for coordinated and centralised control by the management over the industry could co-exist with this growing voice of the workers at the plant level. It was also difficult for the workers to comprehend that this insistent demand for wage revision would accentuate the tendency towards increasing modernisation, and thus towards centralised control for effecting increasing modernisation. With labour costs running high and sales not picking up appreciably, the buyer of labour services could not pay the worker more than the value of his/her contribution to production, with the total wage bill getting increasingly larger. Therefore, unless there was rise in man-hour productivity to offset it, an increase in the price of labour was going to cause the employer to either employ fewer units of labour or create conditions for such centralised control as would make the desired rise in man-hour productivity possible. Thus, this queer economics was going to make increased managerial control an inevitability along with wage increase.[2] The thrust towards deunionisation was now equally inevitable.

We can once again go back to the structure of industrial relations and bargaining in order to understand why the deunionisation drive of the management in the industry faced less resistance than expected. We know that public attention is focused on collective bargaining mainly at the time contracts expire, and day-to-day interaction during the life of the contract goes unnoticed. Here, as wage board deliberations were the principal form of settlement, the way the terms of settlement influenced day-to-day interaction went unnoticed. This affected, at a more fundamental level, the fate of unionisation (for example, its fate at the plant level). Ultimately, it is the threat to strike that gives weight to union demands. Of course, without unions employers would be constrained by labour market conditions and considerations of the morale of employees. But unions today have become an integral part of labour market considerations and, without explicitly threatening to strike, a union can influence the behaviour of employers by simply articulating the issues. It is this potential role of the union which is curbed through a process where wage settlements are determined at the top and collective bargaining is restricted by and large to that level, while conditions below change gradually but surely under the impact.

---

[2] This was exactly the Indian Express management's argument in its correspondence with the Indian Express Workers Union of Hyderabad, and the argument of the INS also before the Wage Board. It is surprising to find how the bosses all over the world think along the same lines. See, for example, the *Statement of the United States Chamber of Commerce* before the United States Congress, House Select Sub-Committee on Labour (Committee on Education and Labour), titled 'The Shorter Workweek,' reprinted in Wortman (1970), pp. 240–47.

Some writers have noted this phenomenon, but studies on unionisation have rarely focused on the structure of bargaining and the labour-management relationship in the light of their consequent impact on the structure of unionisation itself. With the union at the Federation level not attending to problems of coordination of bargaining at the industry and company level, a certain amount of tension is inevitable. With bargaining (implying here wage board deliberations) becoming highly centralised, complaints and cases of neglect of local interests and company specificities can become real. The economic incentive to take 'wages and the issue of work conditions out of competition,' through local manoeuverability, became real, as in the case of the *Hindu* and other papers. And, once again, the lack of coordination between centralised deliberations and the local form of resistance compromised the strength of unionisation in the newspaper industry.[3]

One further point is worth noting while introducing the story of deunionisation in the newspaper industry. Apparently, the unions would have remained comfortable had they not introduced new demands in their day-to-day resistance at the plant level, and even to some extent at the industry level. Ironically, they could not have remained without voicing new demands, even if they had wanted to. The more the introduction of new technology and the legitimation of new working conditions proceeded through centralised delibertions and took on an increasingly impersonal character, the more the unions felt compelled to resist at the plant level, often realising that such resistance may not succeed. This accelerated the tendency toward deunionisation through newer forms of aggression by the management, as well as due to the union's inability to cope with the new reality.

A long-standing debate in the literature on union pay determination has revolved round the degree of union perception of the trade-off between wages and employment. Arthur Ross has argued that unions do not perceive such a trade-off, and are basically 'political' entities. John T. Dunlop's position has been that unions do perceive such a trade-off and are 'economic' organisations.[4] But, as we shall see in the story of unionisation in the newspaper industry, this division has been largely schematic. Particularly with

---

[3] This question has been noted, though very inadequately, by Mitchell (1980), pp. 22–23.

[4] For a discussion on the debate, see Mitchell (1972), pp. 46–61.

the introduction of new technology assuming the form of an offensive against labour, could the unions behave as exclusively 'economic' or exclusively 'political' organisations? The unions found, as is abundantly clear from the AINEF submissions to the Bachawat Wage Board, that contrary to the prevalent view of economists that a wage employment trade-off is axiomatic (that is, if pay was increased over what it otherwise would have been, employment would be lower than it otherwise would have been), this was not directly observable. The introduction of new technology could signify an employer's capacity to pay; the introduction of a new work system could mean, in many instances, a reduction in the worker's position in the plant at the shop-floor level. This would mean an encroachment on workers' 'equity interests' (property rights) in their jobs which would give rise to a host of reciprocal and compensatory workers' demands and a new round of labour-management conflict. The concept of 'property rights' in jobs has little meaning in the formal industrial relations system in India, particularly in the private sector. But this has always had a rich significance for unionists.

> If employers behave in ways that injure workers' interests, their behaviour is not viewed as passively sliding up a demand curve but rather as a Bad Thing. Such Bad Things are the direct targets of union demand for manning requirements, work rules, restrictions on subcontracting, and other practices. Economists would say such union efforts are attempts to make labour demand inelastic, but unions see themselves as simply requiring equitable treatment (Mitchell, 1980: 67–68).

In other words, union perception has rarely treated the issue of technology as a question of 'trade-off'. New demands have arisen, which are neither excessively 'economic,' nor exclusively 'political'. But as I shall show in the course of this chapter, such a union perception has often been confined to the plant level (and is 'spontaneous') while, at the wage board level, a 'trade-off' was attempted, if not a trade-off between wages and employment, certainly a trade-off between wages and increasing modernisation. Thus, in many cases union resistance below weakened and crumbled in precisely the period which was witnessing a rise in wages in the newspaper industry.

The industrial relations scene in many countries witnessed the emergence of new technology agreements between the management and labour, as trade union concern mounted from the mid-seventies at some of the potentially negative effects of technological change. In India too, new technology agreements began to be concluded. The wage board deliberations were of the nature of negotiations for new technology agreements and wage revisions. Justice Bachawat and all the parties knew that such negotiations were taking place under the shadow of the introduction of new technology. But, at the company and plant level, in many cases, new technology agreements had been concluded prior to Bachawat or during the deliberations, as at Ananda Bazar Patrika Ltd and the *Statesman* at Calcutta, the *Hindu* at Madras, *Deccan Herald* at Bangalore and the *Times of India* at Bombay. In many cases the deals were explicit, in others tacit.

A study of deunionisation involves a study of the fate of these new technology agreements. For precisely through the working of these agreements, consent was often manufactured, union power curbed or quietened, further modernisation ensured, work-flow changed and the earlier rhythm of the union movement disturbed and hampered. One line of thinking among leaders of West Bengal newspaper employees was to avoid written agreements in the face of these likely consequences. The Jugantar and Amrita Bazar Patrika Employees Union followed this line and avoided signing such an agreement. But here, too, the agreement was tacit. However, more important, the disastrous consequences here could not be avoided. The consequences were, in fact, most severe. Besides the intrinsic uncertainties in such agreements, the difficulties had been compounded due to, as I have shown, lack of coordination between top and below, in fact due to the lack of any coordinated strategy at all. The growth of unemployment and the effects of new technology on working conditions and on the quality of working life have been the two major concerns behind new technology agreements. The unions had to 'carry out as a high priority a comprehensive study of the employment and social consequences of advances in the new microelectronic technology . . . together with wide ramifications of its applications'.[5]

[5] Trades Union Congress (TUC) to its General Council in UK, cited in Gill (1985), p. 122.

The new technology agreements, not merely in the newspaper industry but elsewhere too, apart from having a compensatory clause on wage revision or other monetary terms, have included the following aspects, all or partially: demands from the unions against any unilateral introduction of new technology, build-up of technical expertise by unions, demands regarding access to information, retraining, reduction of working hours and systematic overtime, control over work, health and safety, employment plans, maintenance and upward revision of wage structure and, finally, a review procedure for monitoring the pace and design of modernisation. New technology agreements have been frowned upon by some discerning observers of industrial relations,[6] the principal arguments being that once these agreements are concluded, the retreat journey begins; a hostile economic and political climate aiding the managerial offensive cannot be tackled through them; and a review of the agreements in practice shows that these can only be the first step towards the establishment of a new standard for regulating technology at the company and work place level, and only if constant vigil is maintained. It has also been noted that during the first rush to introduce technology, there are a spate of agreements. But soon there is a distinct *tailing off* of such agreements, and once a system is introduced in bits and pieces, additions begin, and a further rationalisation of work ensues until the full system is affected, and then further improvisation begins anew. In most cases, the rest of the programme of modernisation remains hidden from the unions, which is informed only of the initial phase. Thus technological change often proceeds unilaterally without any agreement at all. We shall see in this study of deunionisation that these potential weaknesses in new technology agreements became crucial in making the managerial strategy a success.

By a drive towards *deunionisation* I mean the following: the aggressive attitude of the management towards unions and the retreat of the unions in the face of such relentless aggression, particularly in the form of restructuring of plant organisation in the wake of the introduction of new technology; the increasing inability

---

[6] Manwarning (1981). In fact, Manwarning wrote, 'The most striking feature of these agreements is that unions have not secured a reduction in working hours. In fact, none of those presented have seen hours cut . . . . In short, new technology does not guarantee increased earnings, and there remains much which must be bargained for'.

of the unions to come to terms with the new issues and new phenomena consequent upon such restructuring; the decline of the national union and the relative surge of company unionism; and, finally, the mass withdrawal of workers from the old forms of unionisation. In the newspaper industry, the phenomenon was almost inevitable, irrespective of the type of bargaining the union resorted to—cooperative or adversarial. Industrial relations in the Indian newspaper industry saw the triumph of deunionisation— whether the bargaining was cooperative or adversarial became increasingly irrelevant. Among union leaders in south Indian newspapers, particularly the *Hindu* and *Deccan Herald*, there has been a tendency to think that cooperative bargaining saves the day—the same line of thought which had earlier persuaded the All Indian Bank Employees Association (AIBEA) to conclude an agreement on mechanisation in the banking industry. As the General Secretary of the Hindu Office and National Press Employees Union confided to me, when confronted with questions about the proclivity of the union towards cooperative bargaining, 'new technology has come and the invasion is all embracing; hence why create unnecessary rancour? A rigid posture will not in any way help the workers.'[7] But dispensing with a 'rigid posture' in no way helped stop the marginalisation of the union—the critical decisions regarding modernisation continue to be taken unilaterally, just as it is happening in plants where unions are losing one after another, after having resorted to adversarial bargaining.

As we know, *cooperative bargaining* refers to positive-sum or integrative bargaining, in which collective bargaining is seen as a method of problem solving or joint conflict resolution. It assumes that there is an underlying commonality of interests between the parties that outweighs particular conflicts and entails a long-term perspective where both sides trust each other and neither seeks the advantage of short-term shifts in the balance of power in order to weaken decisively the position of its negotiating partner. Conversely, *adversarial bargaining* refers to zero-sum or distributive bargaining where one party's gain is the other's loss. Here the bargaining assumes that there is a pervasive conflict of interests between the parties, and entails a short-term, low trust perspective

---

[7] Talk with union leadership on 5 December 1990.

in which each side's strategies and tactics take into reckoning any change in the balance emanating from fluctuations in business and political cycles (Zeitlin, 1990: 405–6). But then these are only ideal types; the State regulates bargaining in more than one way and the situation becomes complicated when tripartite consultation at the national level bypasses the phenomena of cooperative or adversarial relations at the level of individual firm or plant.

As the example of the *Hindu* suggests, cooperative bargaining often overlaps with neocorporatism. It is true that national level tripartite consultation often encourages cooperative bargaining. But examples show that if the national level tripartite consultation fits with the management's overall design of restructuring, modernisation and aggression against the union, this may provoke adversarial bargaining too. The unions may have no option left. And, with the initiative passing on to the side of the management, the unions often become a helpless spectator in the face of the process of deunionisation. Existing theories of industrial relations provide little guide to explaining the increasing irrelevance of the typology of bargaining in great moments of recession, and modernisation and consequent rationalisation. In the *Statesman*, we shall see, bargaining continued for long. But contrary to what Dunlop has suggested in the case of the United States or Clegg for UK, it did not create a commonality of interests.[8] Rather, the process was used by the management to cut off the withdrawal routes of the union and a decisive blow was struck, suddenly interrupting the process of negotiation.[9] When the the extensive material on new technology agreements and wage board agreements at the plant level is examined, one will be surprised at the extent to which the unions went out to cooperate with the management to implement modernisation plans. Yet deunionisation could not be halted. If cooperative bargaining was encouraged, that too enabled the management to effect the marginalisation of the worker in shopfloor politics. If adversarial bargaining was the norm, then too the management would not be deterred in bypassing the union in its programme of modernisation. In many cases, due to the lack of coordination and being driven to the wall, extreme militancy and 'syndicalist' strategic orientation and behaviour flourished in the

---

[8] Clegg (1979), ch. 6.

[9] For a story of a similar tactic followed by the management of General Motors, see David Noble's seminal study (1986: 280–95).

union's approach. But as the example of the *Statesman* shows, while this emphasised the lack of institutional efficacy and the dysfunctionality or backwardness of the national industrial relations system (particularly in the Indian newspaper industry), this in no way blocked the *secular* tendency towards deunionisation. The national institutional structure and regulations, characterised by the Journalists Act, the setting up of a compulsory wage board at the apex and the office of RIN (Registrar of Newspapers) and the setting up of Press Commissions in no way hampered the secular tendency; at worst, they directly helped it, and at best they added legitimacy to the process by providing a 'neutral' terrain. The peculiar simultaneity and juxtaposition of substantial wage revision concluded at the top and deunionisation below, the macro structure and the micro level developments can hardly be explained by the formal shape of the industrial relations system. For that we have to go back to the politics of modernisation, and the power struggles involved in it. In short, the crux is again power and division of labour.

Deunionisation, thus, remains associated with another concurrent tendency—the decline of the national union.[10] If the Federation was crucial in achieving a revision of wages, it became less important for plant level struggles. And in all the following examples, the national union was irrelevant or only marginally relevant in the struggles erupting there. The vertial structure of the AINEF was overshadowed by horizontal mobilisation. New technology dealt a mortal blow to the earlier union structure. The earlier union structure, with the Federation office performing the necessary task of 'post office' at New Delhi, declined as the crucial issue revolved around the phenomenon that *the union's place within the firm was being negotiated*. As our narrative unfolds, we must remember that the story of industrial relations in Indian newspapers in the eighties is not simply a collection of local stories. For, to understand the local episodes of deunionisation, we must take into account the institutional linkages between local and national structures and the passing away of the managerial strategy from a variant of 'fordism' to 'post fordism'. If, earlier, wage hike, assembly line, the nature of newspaper production and recognition of the union's justified role in running the firm were the elements of

[10] For a similar analysis, see Regalia (1986).

managerial strategy, now wage hike was linked with process production and a marginalisation of the union in determining the justification, viability, nature and programme of modernisation. It has meant, above all, redrawing the boundaries of union politics. The narration is then an argument that the wave of disputes in Calcutta newspapers has provoked a reconfiguration of industrial relations in the industry. It is an argument about the renewed importance of local unions. The failure of local unions, ironically, underscores this importance. It is a caution against the supposed efficacy of the old style, huge, monolithic union structures in countering modernisation. It is an argument also, for the need for coordination of both the levels. In a word, an argument for unionism of a new type.

Deunionisation in Three Calcutta Newspapers

The ABP Strike of 1984

I shall begin with the 72-day strike in the Ananda Bazar Patrika (ABP) group of papers in Calcutta. The ABP group is one of the most powerful newspaper groups. It is a COU commanding 3 dailies and 7 periodicals. A productivity deal entailing automation was concluded with the ABP Employees' Union without any problem a few years before the strike of 1984, hence resistance in the wake of modernisation was least expected. A strike was, thus a total surprise for both the management and the Federation. It shows how the workers never comprehended the phenomenon of automation in all its complexities from the beginning in a conscious way, and resisted only when pushed to the wall. The ABP union was a solid union which held unchallenged sway over the workers, organising and presenting itself as the rival centre of authority. Whatever might have been the agreement, a confrontation with the management was inevitable over what Carter Goodrich (1975) has called the 'frontier of control'. Thus, when the workers felt that they were being pushed to the wall through the managerial imposition of a stricter work-regime, all their hesitation disappeared. With virtually spontaneous solidarity from other newspaper unions, a desperate strike was launched knowing that victory was a remote possibility.

The ABP strike related directly to the demand for social security (pension), which had come up in the wake of automation in the newspaper industry in general and the ABP in particular. The 1979 agreement in the ABP stipulated a productivity deal whereby automation was introduced, financial gain offered to the employees and strict controls imposed on the shop and floor movement of the workers. Though there had been some hesitation in going in for such an agreement, the dominant idea among the union leadership was, if automation was inevitable, why delay settling the issue and accept it later under forced terms? In any case, prior to the agreement, computerisation had already started. The agreement was thus the result of the strategic strength of the management and the tactical delusion of the workers; the latter who were very strong then because automation in the newspaper industry was still largely an untested and uncomprehended phenomenon. This lop-sided balance resulted in a wage increase, but an additional work load, severely curtailed movement within the premises and increased authority of the managerial staff. The delusion was thus to break down soon. The Statesman Employees' Union's strident stand against computerisation and the AINEF's insistence on social security provisions and continuous friction with the management over the 'frontier of control' resulted in rising struggle from 1982 onwards. The strike erupted in 1984. To the union, the demand for pension seemed a defence mechanism against automation, consequent retrenchment or voluntary retirement and the new work regime as well.

The strike commenced inadvertently on 24 April 1984. The workers were away attending a union meeting when some outside labour was engaged to mail the *dak* edition. This was resented by the union, an altercation with the managerial staff and outside labour followed and a scuffle ensued. The workers immediately stopped work. The management did nothing to settled the dispute. As the union viewed it, the 'strike was provoked by the management' and workers' 'involvement was spontaneous'.[11] There was no scope for the legal niceties of giving proper notice or conducting a strike ballot. The suddenness can be properly grasped only when we keep in mind the situation in the wake of technological

[11] Dasgupta (1985). For an account of the strike, see *Anandabazar Patrika Dharmaghater Samiksha* (Calcutta, 1984).

change. The issue of pension was now raised as the first item in the hastily constructed charter of demands and submitted to the management after cease work commenced. This further confirms my reading that protests against automation seldom occur on the issue of new technology per se, but often on other related or consequent issues. Thus, the management is often strategically better placed in an adversarial situation than the union, for while the former is ready with a total restructuration plan when opting for an adversarial form of industrial relations, the latter responds only piecemeal. As a union leader, actively involved in the strike, stated while reviewing the strike:

> The strike was, from the very beginning, on the horns of a dilemma. On the one hand, the bosses had thrown down the gauntlet and the workers could not but take it up. On the other hand, they would thus continuously face the arguments of all legalists that it was not a properly declared strike and a minority group of communists had bulldozed the strike through the rank of the employees . . . . It may even be pondered, in retrospective, who gained through this provocation and whether the workers could have done better had they chosen the ground of struggle according to their own choice and plan (Dasgupta, 1985: 18).

This is a pertinent observation, for, after the strike, the debris of conflict were cleared for unhindered growth on the basis of electronics technology.

During the course of the strike, the issue of pension naturally occasioned reference to the entire question of new technology. Yet pension continued to be raised apart from a discussion on the need to challenge the modernisation strategy of the employers. New technology and the frontier of control had clearly become related issues during the course of the strike. Yet, old forms of unionism and union response viewed the two as delinked and, while persistently referring to the diminishing frontier of control during the strike, challenging the modernisation strategy of the bosses never came on the agenda. This explains why the management remained more firm than the union throughout the 72 days for while, to the management, new technology, concessions on social security issues and the frontier of control were interlinked parts of the same strategy—domination, more profit and a new work regime—to the workers these remained unrelated parts. Thus, the ABP union might have been enraged over the refusal of the managers to grant pension, and might have read in this refusal (and also in the incident of hiring outside workers and such other conflictive incidents) a deliberate attempt to extend the 'frontier of control' on behalf of the bosses. But it never saw the issues as linked. The strike collapsed as the structure of domination was not challenged and, thus, the challenges remained ad hoc and piecemeal. A coherent stretegy could not be worked out. The strike petered out as it failed to mobilise the workers for long. In this tussle over the frontier of control, apart from a coherent strategy to formulate the issues, maintain a line of control, devise ways to resolve the dispute and keep its power uninterrupted, other aspects of the conflict also went against the workers. After the organised attempt by the employers to break the strike after 51 days quite successfully, other sections of the working class led by different central trade unions rallied round the striking workers only after that. Yet, even at the time, the issue remained just one of solidarity with an ongoing struggle for pension. Except for one or two speakers (Arabinda Ghosh of the Centre of Indian Trade Unions in particular), no one raised the overall issue of new technology, the imperatives of social security provisions, the strike breaking capacity of new technology, or the compulsive requirement of maintaining the frontier of control in the face of rationalisation and modernisation. But, ironically, behind the issue of pension and the sudden rush of blood at the incident of temporarily hiring outside workers for a secondary job, these were main questions.

The most crucial thing was, of course, the strike breaking capacity of new technology, which the workers had underestimated during the ABP strike. This was similar to the later strike in the *Times* at London. Earlier, if a handful workers were willing to enter, that would not cause much anxiety in the picket. For either the picket would stop the rank-breaking workers from entering the factory premises, or they knew that a handful of workers could not run the machines. What mattered was that the crucial place in the assembly line operation (here the lino operators)—the heart of the system—had desisted from functioning. But automatons do not strike. So after 51 days, a handful of electricians entered the premises with the help of the police and a high court order and started the automatons. Contrary to the expectation of the striking workers, the move was successful and the papers started coming out. The strike started fizzling out a few days later. New technology thus crucially changes the balance of power within the plant—the line of control moves in favour of the bosses and old style unionism gets more and more ineffective.

The ABP strike is significant in the study of deunionisation in one more way. The strike was preceded by militant unionism of blue collar staff. As always, this was because of the antipathy of the white collar staff, journalists and clerical staff to take a confrontationist attitude towards the management, which led to further antipathy. The strike itself witnessed a total divide between blue and white collar workers and the birth of a joint union, or rather association, of journalists and a section of non-journalist employees, the Jukta Committee. The Jukta Committee was a powerful force arrayed against the workers. The transition from union to association signified not merely a change in nomenclature, but in status, attitude and ethos as well. If automation implied the necessity of forging a commonality of interests between blue collar and white collar workers, it meant a decline of old type unionism too. The management understood the phenomenon and put it to its own use, while the union continued ignoring it to its own peril. As things stand today, the Jukta Committee has come to stay. Certainly the patronisation of the employers is a factor. But if the union has to survive and reemerge as the main body of workers, it must appropriate the specific character of the Jukta Committee—the embodiment of the commonality of interests of both white and blue collar employees.

The strike further revealed that whenever the introduction of technology is accompanied by a complex web of socio-political factors, one of the most important variants is always the consciousness of the workers, which is not a static quantity, but is itself a dynamic thing. The old form of unionism never counted this dynamic nature of workers' consciousness. Thus it often failed to confront new technology adequately. Today, the ABP union stands derecognised, and the persecution of striking employees, though stopped, remains a grim reminder of the structure of power within the plant. Shop-floor movement remains severely restricted. The bargaining agent is the Jukta Committee. Out of a total of 800 blue collar staff, roughly 200 still owe loyalty to the old union, as evident from the elections to the employees' cooperative. And it is had to say when and how this tendency towards deunionisation will be reversed and a shift will occur from cooperative to adversarial bargaining.

Bargaining, Attrition and the Decline of the Statesman Employees' Union

The case of the Statesman Employees' Union (SEU) is more significant. The SEU has been one of the premier unions in newspaper organisations in India, and certainly once the strongest newspaper union in Calcutta. Any workers' movement in the *Statesman* (like the strikes of 1966 and 1968) becomes politically notable because of the the *Statesman's* unique position as the mouthpiece of British interest in India. People have regarded the *Statesman* as being by and large, objective in its reporting, rarely resorting to scurrilous or yellow journalism. Its printing skill under the hot-metal system was widely appreciated, block makers were noted for their expertise, and photographic features were a speciality when other newspapers totally lacked photographic coverage. The paper maintained foreign correspondents, again a rarity in those days. And, finally, the workers took pride in the fact that they worked in the *Statesman*, and that the fame of the company was in no small measure due to them. The situation was thus ripe for company unionism as the management also often resorted to a style of benevolent guardianship.

But the Statesman Employees' Union (SEU) was far removed from any idea of company unionism. It was firmly linked with the All India Newspaper Employees' Union (AINEF), was the key organising link of the West Bengal Newspaper Employees' Federation, was a member of the 12 July Committee, was on the platform of several trade union organisations for campaigning on political and democratic issues, and though not formally part of a central trade union organisation, was firmly aligned with Left politics in West Bengal. Given this background, the SEU was not likely to accept the modernisation programme of the management without offering any challenge. The leadership of the union had prepared a note on the likely impact on the work flow consequent upon modernisation and the probable impact on job pattern as well as staff level. The note was printed and distributed among various newspaper employee unions throughout the country and was regarded by the AINEF leadership as the first authentic study on modernisation in the newspaper industry in India. It set the initial attitude of the union towards the managerial agenda. It was one of explicit opposition to the programme. But, more importantly, it questioned the managerial prerogative to unilaterally introduce such a programme, interrogated the financial management of the company and raised the uncomfortable question as to whether this programme was going to benefit the workers and the readers as well. However, being strongly grounded in reality, it understood that modernisation could not be indefinitely prevented or postponed and the company was slipping down in the market as other papers were fast going in for modernisation. Thus, the attitude slowly developed that if modernisation was needed, it had to be jointly planned and programmed by the management and the union. Even specifications of machines and systems were to be jointly decided upon and the hold of the union over the work flow should not be loosened.

The British TUC policy of demanding and advocating counter-modernisation programmes also influenced the union. The SEU had found that after Palekar, the management had been successful almost everywhere in introducing modernisation unilaterally. In a few cases, retrenchment was taking place. The workforce level was going down. Voluntary retirement was being offered. The AINEF was confused about how to provide the lead in facing the issue. In general, unionism in the newspaper industry was going to suffer badly—this is how SEU perceived the situation. This perception determined its response too. Its response was a curious blending of syndicalism, union-control theory and hard thinking on the real concrete tactical problems of the union. However, we shall see that even this could not save the union from decline. Though the union had tried to respond in a new way to the emerging phenomenon of modernisation, the strong burden of old-style unionism proved too much. The managerial strategy triumphed and deunionisation became the impending danger.

According to a note meant for circulation only among the union militants, the workers, in response to the management's proposal for new technology, should say:

> O.K., prove the benefits of modernisation in our life. Guarantee us in advance that there will be no reduction in total work force; show us in advance that our working conditions are going to

improve by cutting the working week; give us now a written agreement that our individual workloads will not increase; until you do that, we will not work under the new technology.[12]

Armed with this attitude, the SEU made a detailed study of the financial status of the company, work conditions on the shopfloor, and a content study of the newspaper and forwarded its own suggestions for modernisation to the management.[13] The note had suggested demands like conditional acceptance of new technology, tabling of the full schedule of the programme of modernisation before the union, a shorter working week, no reduction in the total workforce, no voluntary redundancies, no 'natural wastage,' no blurring of old demarcation lines, occupational health and security, pension, and a shorter work week. It suggested written management guarantees to the effect that the management will not use the new machines to get information on the workspeed or accuracy of individual workers (that is, that they will not use them as electronic time and motion men). All these implied, as the SEU leadership realised, a radical involvement of the union in the implementation of the plan and programme of modernisation. It meant that the union would not obstruct and stop modernisation in a straightforward way anymore. It meant an activist role for the union rather than a mere negative role. But the million dollar question that hung on the union leadership was: Would the workers be able to challenge managerial prerogatives as traditionally determined in this way? Could the *frontier of control* be shifted in favour of the workers through the co-sponsoring of the modernisation programme and by shackling the management in this way? In fact, the history of the period 1986–90 has proved to the contrary. While the union leadership tried to break out of the bind, as its later moves showed, it failed to realise that such an 'activist' role could be assumed only with greater theoretical clarity, a more militant and resolute line, a tactical policy of involving the rank and file workers, and ja firm position of strategic resistance, unless the conditioning demands were met (that is, a policy of quid pro quo). There was a thin line between conditional acceptance and capitulation which the SEU failed to negotiate. I shall recount the story, though very briefly.

[12] Intra-union note on modernisation prepared by the Statesman Employees' Union (hereafter SEU), 1986 (n.d.).
[13] Letter by the SEU to the management, 13 November 1986.

In order to understand the proclivity of the union to assume an 'involved' and 'interventionist' role in the programme of modernisation, and thereby maintain the *line of control*, we have to remember the prevailing conditions in the union movement in the newspaper industry in the early eighties. The militant economism of the AINEF was, as usual, a 'mixture of some economics and a little politics,' and thus the Federation had been singularly unable to provide any sort of guidance to the unions when modernisation appeared on the scene in the late seventies and early eighties. The ABP union had accepted photocomposing without any protest, and the *Jugantar* leadership was struggling to find its feet. The strongest union in the bank industry, the All India Bank Employees Association, had concluded a deal with bankers on mechanisation. The Left political leadership had no worthwhile tactical line on the issue. The pace of automation in big national dailies like the *Hindu* and the *Times of India* was continuing unopposed. In this prevailing mood of despondency, *fait accompli* and resignation, the 'involved' and 'interventionist' tactic emerged. The leadership cared little whether such a tactic would slide into syndicalism, and if syndicalism had been successful anywhere in maintaing the line of control in a big plant in the face of any determined 'modernising' onslaught. Thus, the initial steps of the union (like bringing out the *Working Paper*, submitting a memorandum to members of Parliament on the dangers of modernisation and appeal 'To The Readers And The People'[14] were soon found to be inadequate for assuming an interventionist role. Added to this inadequacy was the increasing pressure of the management. The management would argue, as several of the correspondence letters show, how long the union would resist photocomputerisation, thus affecting the daily's marketability. The old machines, mammoth and truly dinosaurian in appearance, were breaking down and no spare parts were available. After all the company had to survive, and since it was no more a monopoly market for the *Statesman*, it had to modernise itself in order to survive. The union must cooperate.

This was truly a pincer-attack—an economic attack more powerful than any direct coercion and a catch-22 situation in which the union was trapped. If it said 'no,' the paper would suffer and the workers' bargaining strength would deteriorate. If it consented,

---

[14] Issued by SEU, 14 November 1981.

however strong might be the intervention, the management was going to win. This critical situation was the ideal breeding ground for company unionism and syndicalism. Yet, as events soon proved, a syndicalist policy hardly succeeded in keeping the power of the workers intact. The retraining programme was actively co-sponsored by the union, yet retraining remained limited only to the lino operators. The management's strategy visualised modernisation of only the composing department: the 'process' would be left to languish as well as the 'job' department. For if a cut in staff level was to be achieved before all-round modernisation and expansion were effected, a deliberate policy of selective sickness within the various departments of the company was the only route left for the management. Similarly, the union cooperated in bringing out the daily under the process of modernised printing as quickly as possible. It desisted from demanding financial incentives, retraining allowance, commensurate occupational health and security measures, curtailment of the vehicles department by agreeing to the managerial policy of not buying new vehicles (like vans) in place of old vans but leasing them in; and it dropped important demands like pension and reduced work hours when the charter of demands on modernisation was finally submitted to the management and the memorandum of understanding (MOU) was signed. Though managerial expenses were hardly reduced and supervision toned up, the union agreed to the voluntary reduction of overtime allowance and the winding up of peons' quarters at the Delhi office, where a high rise building was to come up with Ansal's, a promoter company, patronage. The union, no doubt, insisted on a comprehensive agreement, the crucial part of which would be an agreed decision on the expansion of the paper, maintenance of the staff level and the future provision of occupational health and security. But if the union had actively started thinking and pursuing a policy of 'co-sponsoring' modernisation, of negotiating each and every clause of the programme, of continuous discussion with the management with its own plan and programme of modernisation that would meet the interests of the employees too, little did it realise that this was a very tricky business—fighting the management on the latter's homeground. Continous discussion, bargaining, suddenly applying the brakes (like halting training programmes to make the management realise that the union meant business), co-sponsoring, and the achievement of some inconsequential gains were thus elements of a policy whose main logic was based on a trial of patience. If the line was bold and innovative, it was too much for a single union to execute. So much for company unionism. Its plus side was also tough and the union failed to hold on to it.

The union leadership had underestimated the management. It negotiated the union into passive agreement. Not only were crucial demands dropped by the union, but the union was 'impressed upon' by the management on the need for financial austerity and peace in the plant to implement the modernisation programme without delay. The management assured the union of its intention to diversify and expand once the intial phase of modernisation was completed. This assurance was even written down in the MOU. But, obviously, as modernisation became a reality, the management reneged upon its assurances. The activist role, envisaged by the union, found its nemesis in a passive position, as well as a *de facto* acceptance of managerial explanations regarding its failure to keep the other side of the bargain, explanations regarding why the circulation was dropping, and advertisement revenue was low, bank loans had to be increasingly resorted to and modernisation must be allowed to proceed without concurrent social security guarantees. The agreement of 1986 proved to be a bitter pill.

Later, the union prestige crumbled quickly. The workers found that the union's decision to assist in the retraining schedule had helped only the bosses; that once the initial changes in the work process had been achieved, nothing substantial could be done to stop the management from going further or from reneging upon the agreement; that workers of other sections were being deprived of the gains of modernisation; that carrying the financial burden of modernisation becomes an obligatory moral load on the workers and it ties their hands; and, finally, union power is curbed as the power of the automatons increase. All these difficulties got compounded in a milieu of plant-wise agreements without the backing of industry-wise agreements. The union could not answer all these questions satisfactorily, and rumblings spread from floor to floor. The management changed its strategy dramatically and a new General Manager was appointed. The Bachawat Wage Board arrears were not cleared. Old machines were summarily disposed of. Shopfloor movement was restricted. Overtime was reduced.

And then, in one fell swoop, the President of the union was suspended(later on dismissed), a chargesheet isssued and an enquiry committee instituted on the alleged ground that the President, a system supervisor, had misused a PTS machine for printing and distributing anti-management propaganda. A strike erupted spontaneously and continued for five days. Yet this was the final nail in the coffin. As we shall see, the story ended with a whimper and union power demonstrably collapsed at the end of the strike.

The workers of departments other than composing were soon arguing about why they should stick their necks out, for it was a matter relating to the composing department and, in any case, they were not going to gain from company modernisation in as much as the compositors would. The union President was informally seen as collaborator of the earlier management, since he had taken on himself the task of impressing upon the workers the need to accept sacrifice in the wake of modernisation. The sudden strong stand of the management unnerved the workers, particularly when modernisation had been effected. The disspirited workers also felt that with modernisation, the loss of union power was a fait accompli, and they would have to learn to live under a stricter work regime. The political leadership of the WBNEF (West Bengal Newspaper Employees' Federation), coming from the CPI(M), was also at a loss on how to tackle the situation: whether to continue the strike or to resume work. The threat of lockout loomed large and the workers understood that the lockout would be like a surgical job, at the end of which the management could begin with a clean slate—fewer workers, more machines and more control.

The management had, time and again, complained of union intervention in essentially 'managerial matters' like the choice and generation of equipment, specific design, designation of post and allotment of work, and had resentfully written to the union: 'It is the accepted principle everywhere that it is management's responsibility to arrange for replacement for the right person in the right job'.[15] It had earlier given a 'clever' offer to the union: accept modernisation or perish! A Hobson's choice had been placed before the union:

---

[15] Management letter to the SEU, 15 November 1986; management letter, 28 November 1986.

Time is fleeting away fast and adverse reactions from our readers as well as from our advertisers have started pouring in, expressing their disappointment and dissatisfaction at our not keeping pace with other leading newspapers by updating our printing technology. It has reached such a pass that it has become a question of now or never.[16]

The union perished by accepting the terms of the choice. For with the strike ridden with self-doubt, bitterness, mutual suspicion, distrust of union leadership and a sense of loss of power, with machines having been installed and automation which could break the strike staring the workers in the face, the union could do nothing. The strike ended unceremoniously after five days without any talk, offer or settlement. A stricter work regime was imposed. The leadership refused to face the electorate in the approaching union election. Detractors now formed the leadership. Even though the situation may change (it has changed a little for the better), the accepted role of the union as a *power* in the plant has been terribly damaged. Deunionisation, thus, has shown one more facet of itself—the loss of union power and prestige.

The accompanying phenomenon of deunionisation, along with new technology, showed the inadequacy of both the explanations as to why the management opts for a new technology: the neo classical economic explanation that a company engages in expensive market research for information on product market opportunities and technical developments only to maximise profitability, with the company thus acquiring a detailed knowledge of available technology and attempting a systematic reduction of the costs of innovation; and the behaviourist explanation that a firm searches for alternatives when it encounters a problem, and this limited search activity ceases when a satisfactory or necessarily optimal solution is found, this implying a much lower level of knowledge of the product and the market process. The history of deunionisation calls for a radical explanation that argues that the purpose of innovation and adoption of new technology is to maintain a higher control over the labour force so as to ensure stability over the condition of reproduction of surplus value. This history also shows the pitfalls of syndicalism and conveys the lesson that perhaps it is too much for a single union, for that matter a single industry, to

[16] Management letter to SEU, 3 February 1983.

match the management in technical skill, behavioural knowledge and political judgement. The situation demands bargaining, but bargaining calls for more knowledge and political determination. But knowledge and political determination imply an understanding of the class nature of technology, the ensemble of social relations around it and the consequent new issues emerging out of it. But this was precisely the requisite which would not be available in older forms of union politics, whether syndicalist or party oriented, which had been based on blue collar bargaining over wages and maintaining adversarial relations over wage related issues.[17]

The irony is that, in both the cases, the harsh reality of deunionisation dawned upon the workers only after the management had effected the technological changeover and had inflicted a crushing blow upon the workers in decisive conflicts. As we have seen, the strike at the ABP was defeated in 1984, and the Jukta Committee was shown to be an emasculated union which could hardly replace the ABP Employees' Union in terms of power, prestige, organisational strength and bargaining weight. Hence, when on 7 November 1989 *Ravivar* (an ABP Hindi weekly publication) was closed down and the employees summarily stripped of all assignments, the workers could only wail and say in despair:

The management is so stubborn in its attitude that it is not ready even to consider any decent scheme for premature retirement. The *Ravivar* people are not limpets. When all efforts for revival of *Ravivar*, for starting a new Hindi publication or the absorption in other departments failed during negotiations for sorting out post-*Ravivar* problems, the staff of *Ravivar* accepted the next best option of premature retirement, a formula which was put forward by a representative of the Jukta Committee itself. But the management took no time rejecting it, and that too without showing any reasons. It also did not put forward any formula of its own.[18]

The appeal was full of anguish and despair. And as for plans to resist and struggle, the appeal could only say: 'Can there not be a

---

[17] See, on this, Dubois (1978), pp. 1–34.
[18] Appeal issued by the Ravivar Sangharsh Samiti, 'This Is How Ananda Bazar Management Treats Its Staff—Murder of "Ravivar" and Other Crimes,' (n.d.).

same policy of dealing with the affected employees when a publication closes down? The *Ravivar* staff is trying to search for some right answer . . . . Remember: next it could be you and your publication.[19]

Deunionisation, thus, not merely implied a decline in union power but a loss of power too. In the *Statesman*, for example, this loss of power could be found in a managerial edict, read in reverse. The occasion was the payment of the Bachawat Wage Board arrears. The General Manager after announcing partial payment of arrears sermonised in the edict:

The payment of Bachawat Wage Board arrears has been possible by the company once again by resorting to heavy borrowings and giving precedence to staff payments over other immediate commitments like purchasing more units for the new Web Offset Press, which is more than necessary. The cost of indigenous newsprint has again increased by Rs 800 per m.t. from 14 October 1990. Only in April–May 1990, there was another hike in price by Rs 910 per m.t. With a 25 per cent increase in petrol and diesel prices, there will be further all-round escalation of costs.

With slender resources at hand, it is a delicate balancing act. With all these additional costs to meet and with many more commitments to keep, the proposed diversification or investment in new publications becomes hazardous.

Without striking a false note, I have every hope that if unnecessary expenditure is limited and even necessary ones are curtailed and narrow self-interests are not given precedence over the institution's welfare, we shall stand a good chance of overcoming our difficulties.

It will not be out of place to emphasise the immediate need to reduce overtime hours further and plan production and non-production work in a manner so as to eliminate it totally.

Disciplinary measures for restoring discipline is only one option, but nothing can be better than members of the staff themselves generating a healthy environment which will discourage promoting sectional and individual interests. Hopefully, there has been some signs of positive thinking on the part of some sections of the staff and a concern for the welfare of the

[19] *Ibid.*

company has also been expressed, but these are only ripples and unless they are transformed into waves, the Augean stables will not be cleared.[20]

Without any significant loss of union power, the announcement of the payment of arrears with the accompanying sting could not have been made in this way. But, apart from the taunting remarks and insults, the more noticeable thing is that the payment of arrears, a normal or routine due for the workers, was announced with conditions and the workers had to swallow it. It announced strictures on overtime, against filling up vacancies, stalled proposed diversifications, cautioned workers of various departments against pursuing 'sectional interests' and, finally, unequivocally stressed the question of who or what constitutes *power* in a plant![21]

Rendering Jugantar and Amrita Bazar Deliberately Sick

The process of how power is constituted and contested became the crucial issue in the wake of modernisation in another old Calcutta newspaper organisation—Jugantar and Amrita Bazar Patrika. The Amrita Bazar Patrika Ltd was an old concern, publishing two national dailies, the *Amrita Bazar Patrika* being the foremost daily in English in colonial days. Run like a family business, which indeed it was, the work atmosphere resembled a bazar rather than a shopfloor run according to Taylorist strictness and efficiency. It had almost no standardised work rule, no regular wage conditions and no regular hierarchical set-up. The machines were old, the supply of raw material like newsprint and ink was always uncertain, and the office as well as the plant was situated in an old north Calcutta area where local hoodlums of the same political persuasion as the owner could always be quickly mobilised to break a strike.

[20] Office Circular issued by General Manager, The Statesman Limited, 20 October 1990.

[21] The question of how power is constituted and contested within the plant in the wake of new technology can be better understood in contrast with a plant where new technology has as yet not been introduced or is not the crucial determinant in labour-management relations, like for example in a public sector unit. See the wage related rules following an agreement, *Hindustan Copper Employees (Travelling Allowance) Rules, 1982, and Medical Treatment Rules, 1982* in Hindustan Copper Limited (a Government of India enterprise).

Yet, in 1948, there was a momentous strike against inconceivable odds (Bhattacharya, 1988). It failed. Though work conditions improved somewhat after that, the overall atmosphere did not change much. It was in this situation that a composite union of journalists and non-journalists gathered strength from the late seventies, negotiated a wage increase after the Palekar Award and secured a nominal pension agreement. Meanwhile, the company started bringing out several editions from other centres like Jamshedpur, Lucknow and Allahabad. It was at this stage that the management declared a lockout. With the intervention of the state government and the bank, the lockout was lifted. But the message had been sent loud and clear. To the workers it implied that the onus was on them to run the plant and accept the necessary sacrifices for that. Indeed, publication again stopped after that. One worker committed suicide. Workers joined work to maintain production. But the union did not press on with the claim that it was itself competent to run the management and revive the sick unit with the assistance of the BIFR (Board for Industrial and Financial Reconstruction). As things stand today the situation is bleak. The plant is under lockout again and the union has been reduced to an extremely passive position. It has to accept retrenchments in the guise of voluntary retirement, drastically reduced wage and other wage-related conditions. Here, again, modernisation, industrial sickness and asset stripping have been a deadly combine in reducing union power.[22] The AINEF and WBNEF have remained helpless spectators before the ongoing process of deunionisation.

Deunionisation and the Question of Power

To cut a long story short, this means that confronted with the modernisation drive in the newspaper industry, the unions failed in all the conventional methods to maintain power and their position in the plant or industry. Securing wage increase, pursuing a policy of company unionism, co-sponsoring modernisation, tagging social security allowances and concentrating on wage board deliberations on a national scale all failed to halt the decline in union

[22] Chief Minister's Statement in West Bengal Assembly, *The Statesman*, 26 February 1991. Both the newspapers have reappeared on the stands from the latter half of 1993, but their stability is as yet uncertain.

power. The process of deunionisation turned out to be the cue for increased managerial power, and the management introduced modernisation within the factory.

I have already referred to the big unions in newspaper organisations in south India. Here unions cooperated with the management and were able to secure some commensurate benefits. But could union power be saved from decline in that way? Did the emasculation of union power not occur there also? When we go into the details, it will be found that deunionisation has been an all-pervasive trend in the Indian newspaper industry in the wake of modernisation.

Almost unanimously, the unions in big south Indian newspapers have professed satisfaction over the implementation of the wage board awards in their respective companies. The major exception has been the *Indian Express* establishments in Hyderabad and elsewhere. But almost unanimously, it seems, the unions have glossed over the reality of the decline in union power. This may be partly because union power there was never as strong, overt or articulate as elsewhere. It may also be that the management there has never been as aggressive as in the *Times of India, Hindustan Times* or *Indian Express*. Yet the fundamental reality of deunionisation cannot be ignored in those cases also.

The Printers (Mysore) Ltd is a COU bringing out one English and one vernacular daily the (*Deccan Herald* and *Prajavani*), one vernacular weekly (*Sudha*), and one vernacular monthly periodical (*Mayura*). It, published two other newspapers, *Evening Herald* and a periodical, *Herald Review*, both of which were subsequently stopped. The dailies have facsimile editions from Gulbarga, Mangalore and Bijapur. Apart from introducing the phototypesetting system in the composing department and installing one web offset rotary machine with four units in the printing department, it has installed an automatic packing machine costing Rs one crore in the mailroom, which has reduced the total number of packers from 25 to 15. The VDUs require two batches of 10 workers for the English daily and three batches of 10 workers for the Kannada daily. The company is involved in the publication of books, mostly school student guides. Computers have been installed in the advertising, accounts and editing departments also. For proofreading, editcomp machines have been installed. They require 25 proofreaders for the *Deccan Herald*, 18 for *Prajavani* and 4 for *Sudha* and *Mayura*. Modernisation was introduced in 1982 without any consultation with the union. Monetary 'compensation' was given, and all the workmen got 2 increments. Though 'compensation' is the word used by the union to describe the unilateral grant of increments, nobody knows in lieu of what this compensation is granted or what this compensation is for. Immediately, there were placement problems. Irritation and conflict ensued after the journalists began to handle the PCs. In 1987–88 there was a 53 day strike over the management's order to suspend 2 workmen, whose designation was rotary cleaner and had refused to jog the bundle. In the wake of the strike, other standing grievances also cropped up. The union demanded the end of the casual system by means of which canteen workers and machine cleaners had been denied permanent status. There were other demands too regarding LTC, pension, upgradation, medical allowance, and so on. The strike ended with the management revoking the suspension order, with the issue being referred to arbitration. The General Secretary, who was also the General Secretary of the Bangalore Newspaper Employees' Union (the federal body of all the newspaper unions in Bangalore), was brought back to Bangalore after a long stint of rotating transfer from one place to another. LTC was not granted, but an interim arrangement was made till the committee appointed to look into the grievances submitted its report. Under this arrangement all journalists and non-journalist employees would receive Rs 140 per month as extra payment. The workers would get an annual medical allowance equal to the monthly basic wage for the last four years. The counters and packers have been placed in grade V, and have received one extra increment over the Bachawat recommendation. Both journalists (totalling 325) and non-journalists (totalling 800) have received additional increments over the Bachawat scale. Senior workmen who have served for 12 years have received one extra increment, and those who have served for 18 years have received 2 increments. Award of pension depends now on the outcome of the expert committee appointed by the government.

The feeling of the union, on the whole, is one of satisfaction at the way it has tackled modernisation, particularly its unilateral introduction by the management. As it sees it, it had no reason to enter into any particular agreement on new technology, contrary to what the ABP union had done. Nor has it entered into any particular agreement on implementation of the Bachawat recommendations. To it, that would have unnecessarily tied its hands from future options. It had submitted a charter of demands some years back, and the management has begun agreeing to them separately, one by one, on its own. And this has given rise to cooperative relations doing away with the earlier adversarial type, and this suits the union too. The whole mood was succinctly summed up by Chenna Basappa Bapuri, the General Secretary, in these telling words:

> We cannot avoid modernisation, but we can adapt suitably to it. We are reasonable, we are strong, we have got unity, very good leadership, we have been submitting demands in a sensible way. The credit goes to the management also, in particular Mr. Harikumar.[23]

Clearly then, to the union, modernisation has not meant a decline in union power. Deunionisation remains an unfounded fear. If the union is sensible, not rash, and fights in a measured manner, there is no reason why its power should decline or an adversarial relation should set in, forcing the management to act drastically. But could it not be true that the union, slowly acquiescing to managerial presumptions and prerogatives, has turned itself into an almost emasculated body, and deunionisation today hides itself behind the framework of cooperative relations?

When the wage board award was implemented in Printers (Mysore) Ltd, it was found that the management had manipulated the dates of appointment of several members of lower grade staff, which affected their upgradation and wage increase. Packers, pinning assistants, typesetting assistants, layout assistants and production assistants have been particularly affected. The gap between the date of joining and the date of appointment has been, in some cases over 10 years and in one extreme case 16 years. Table 6.1 gives an example.

The factory inspector's report of 15 October 1990 spoke of the inumerable work hazards regarding lifts, generator room, offset section, chain block hoists, satellite printing machine, plate making room, retouching room, photocomposing section, firefighting system, air compressors, overcrowding and the canteen and said, 'It

[23] All the information and the statement were given by an official of the Bangalore Newspaper Employees' Union, in a talk with me on 7 December 1990.

Table 6.1
Select Examples from Category-wise Employees: Master Listing
in Printers (Mysore) Ltd

Employee No.	Employee's Name	Designation	Date of Joining	Date of Appointment
016238	Krishna Murthy	Typesetting Assistant	30.7.76	1.9.80
016263	Ramesh, C.	Typesetting Assistant	30.7.76	1.9.79
021726	Palani, V.P.	Packer	01.12.69	1.3.85
021738	Thyagaraj, V.	Pinning Assistant	01.12.73	1.3.85
021740	Ramdass, S.	Pinning Assistant	01.12.76	1.3.85
021757	Subramani, D.	Packer	01.12.76	1.3.85
021763	Gobindaraju, N.	Packer	01.12.77	1.3.85
021787	Raghavaraj, K.	Packer	01.12.77	1.3.85

Source: Category-wise Employees' Master Listing, Printers (Mysore) Ltd., 1990.

was learnt that 137 accidents (all non-fatal) had taken place in the above factory in the past 3 years. Discussed the same and advised that effective steps be taken for the reduction of accidents.'[24]

Apart from the issue of occupational health and safety, which old unionism could not tackle effectively in most cases, even the terms of wage settlement revealed the absence of adversarial relations and the assumed and uncontested existence of managerial rights. Of course there the management has followed the policy of encouraging company unionism—a little of 'give' to ensure some more 'take'. After agreeing to some norms of Bachawat fixation, the company reminded the union that 'it is to be noted that under Bachawat it is not obligatory for a newspaper establishment to employ all in any of the category as mentioned in the Award.'[25] The list of demands submitted by the union in 1985 bore the features of the arguments that would be characterising the AINEF submissions to the wage board. For example, the charter of demands spoke of LTC facilities, increase in medical reimbursements, encashment of privileged leave, voluntary retirement after 10 years, terrycot uniforms for peons, watch and ward and packing staff,

[24] *Report by A.S. Guhadi* (INS/SR-79/90–91/771), 15 October 1990, p. 3.
[25] *Memorandum of Understanding in Printers (Mysore) Ltd, on Bachawat Fixation*, 1990.

washing allowance, house construction loan, rest room for drivers, and so on. These demands certainly called for improvement of work conditions, that itself being a significant step. But, significantly, the charter demanded neither pension nor the joint conduct of the modernisation agenda. Reduction of work hours, and the provision of occupational health and safety were other significant omissions. The management was ready to pay to ensure a cooperative framework. It paid and succeeded.

Let us see how this strategy succeeded. The union had submitted its charter of demands in 1985. The management sat tight. There was a strike as well. The management gave in to one or two minor demands, separately, on an ad hoc basis. Then, when the time came for the Bachawat settlement, the management seized its chance and enforced a comprehensive settlement by fostering a cooperative framework of relations, thus maintaining the essential managerial line of control. The settlement was concluded on 20 August 1990. The experience thus seems pervasive that new technology agreements can remain hidden within wage revision agreements, and a cooperative framework can reinforce the frontier of control within the plant where modernisation is currently being introduced.

It will be worthwhile to quote certain portions of the memorundum of settlement:

3. Productivity

3.1 Both the parties agree and recognise that the newspaper industry should grow at a faster rate in order to meet the needs of the population in the State and the Nation, and also to generate the required resources to meet the urgent need for modernising the industry. The parties commit themselves to work together to attain higher levels of production, productivity and profitability. Further joint efforts would be made continuously in the following areas:

(a) Economic usage of materials for minimising material cost and maximising material productivity.
(b) Improving productivity and reducing operating cost.
(c) Reducing energy consumption.
(d) Improving quality in all operations.

(*e*) Improvement in house-keeping.
(*f*) Necessary improvement in working conditions and health and safety of all the employees.
(*g*) Continuously accepting better working practices, methods.
(*h*) Training all employees in multitrade and in advanced skills.
(*i*) Adoption of advanced technology in day-to-day operations.
(*j*) Improve capacity utilisation of the production units.
(*k*) Effective strengthening of participation and job enrichment.
(*l*) Improving quality of work life, job satisfaction and job enrichment.

3.2 Union agrees to cooperate with the management in restricting/eliminating over stay during lunch/dinner breaks, and also loitering within company's premises and also unnecessary/unauthorised movement in and out of the company premises. The union agrees to abide by and accept and follow periodic directions of the management, in pursuance thereof.

3.3 It is recognised and accepted by both the parties that discipline at all levels has to be maintained. Union, therefore, assures full cooperation for maintaining discipline and optimising production and productivity.[26]

The trade-off here is clear. The management agrees to pay revision, medical facilities, retraining of staff, ensuring, 'job satisfaction' and a little consultation. In return, it extracts union consent for restriction of shopfloor movements, rationalisation, systemic modernisation and increased discipline. The management even concedes to the increase of management's contribution to provident fund to 12 per cent, ad hoc allowance, encashment of privilege leave, enhancement of outstation canteen allowance, and additional increment of senior employees.[27] But, as it is clear, the cooperative framework of bilateral relations under which bargaining takes

---

[26] Clause 3 of the *Memorandum of Settlement, Printers (Mysore) Ltd*, Bangalore, 20 August 1990, pp. 3–4.
[27] *Ibid.*, clause 4.1.

places does not diminish managerial power. Rather, the memorandum buttresses it.

The experience of the *Hindu*, the most modernised newspaper set-up in India, also tells a similar story. The Hindu Office and National Press Employees' Union is satisfied with the cooperative state of relations. It knows that 'everybody is potentially surplus' under modernisation; that 15 minutes of rest at regular intervals after 2 hours of work at the VDT is a necessity which the management does not concede; that 30 per cent of the staff is, unofficially, surplus; that the scanning machine lies idle most of the time; and that facsimile editions will render the outstation employees surplus. But, like Printers (Mysore) Ltd, the Hindu management has also granted several welfare schemes, advanced loans, relaxed stipulations regarding night-shift duty, and granted different allowances like LTC, service recognition, centenary allowance and medical allowance. Also, it has never demanded written agreements. But in the *Hindu*, the workforce level has dropped, a voluntary retirement scheme has come up, and the distinction between the managerial area and the trade union's area is religiously maintained with the solemness and seriousness of Tamil Brahmins![28]

To substantiate my observation that new technology has been a form of managerial aggrandisement throughout India and has given birth to deunionisation, I shall take up another example, again from south India—the *Indian Express* edition of Hyderabad. The Hyderabad edition of *Indian Express* and its vernacular sister edition, *Andhra Prabha*, were started in 1977. The *Indian Express* is technically printed at the *Andhra Prabha* press. The *Andhra Prabha* has an approximate circulation of 25,000 and the *Indian Express* 30,000. The total number of employees is 300, of whom 200 belong to the non-journalist category and 100 are journalists. However, all are compelled to work under appointment to the *Andhra Prabha*. The break-up of the labour force has to be known to understand the true nature of monopoly expansion of big newspapers in India with the help of new technology where, to open up the satellite editions, the establishment needs fewer skilled hands and mostly low grade and middle level non-journalist employees (Table 6.2).

[28] This information comes from talks with an office-bearer of the Hindu Office and National Press Employees' Union, 5 December 1990.

Table 6.2
Section-wise Break-up of Non-Journalist Employees in the
Indian Express/Andhra Prabha, *Hyderabad*

Sl. No.	Category	Number
1.	English PTS	23
2.	English advertisements paste up	5
3.	English news paste up	12
4.	Telugu PTS	20
5.	Telugu advertisements paste up	4
6.	Telugu news paste up	8
7.	Teleprinter section	10
8.	Indian Express rotary	2
9.	Process	19
10.	Rotary	30
11.	Transport	3
12.	Packing	25
13.	Attendants	15
14.	Sweepers	4
15.	Watchmen	7
16.	Casuals	13
	Total	200

Note: The staff from 9 to 16 is common to both the *Indian Express* and *Andhra Prabha.*

Modernisation came about in 1984 with the introduction of phototypesetting computers for both English and Telugu dailies, and the installation of a duplex offset rotary for printing 16 pages. It has a run of 24,000 copies per hour. There are 8 terminals for *Andhra Prabha* and 7 terminals for *Indian Express.* The Hyderabad Andhra Prabha and Indian Express Staff and Workers Union, formed in 1977 and affiliated to both the INTUC (Indian National Trade Union Congress) and the AINEF, led the workers to observe a one-day token strike on 16 November 1990 on a ten-point charter of demands. The demands included issues like permanent status for casual workers, medical check-up facilities, medical allowance, implementation of the interim order of the Supreme Court regarding implementation of the Bachawat Award, and encashment of leave, bonus, and so on. It may be recalled that the Indian Express management had taken the lead in going to the Supreme Court against the Bachawat directive for 'clubbing' whereupon all its editions would be counted as one single establishment, it would be placed in grade 1A, and would have to pay the worker a higher wage scale. In the Delhi edition of *Indian Express*, there had been an eventful 55 day strike in December 1989 and January 1990 against the management's refusal to implement the Bachawat wage scale. In Hyderabad and other smaller centres, the attitude of the managers was more aggressive. There the workers have no medical check-ups or any other medical facilities. PTS operators have complained of back pain, bronchial problems, headaches, watering eyes and eye pain, but to no avail. There was no retrenchment consequent to modernisation, and the surplus staff was shifted to the Vizianagaram edition, which started in 1985. In south India, the *Indian Express* has seven centres of publication—Madras, Hyderabad, Madurai, Cochin, Bangalore, Vijayawada and Vizianagaram. Punitive transfer is common. There has been no new technology agreement at Hyderabad, and the trade union admits that it 'did not have any knowledge of new technology'. There has been no pension scheme and no night allowance scheme. Only an ad hoc payment of Rs 500 per month has been granted, which is not included in the basic pay. In Hyderabad it is still a class V category establishment. Packing people work for 30 days throughout the month. Rotary people work in four batches for an 8 day week shift. And for each 8 day day-shift, they have to do three 8 day night-shifts continuously! When the shift changes from night to day, the worker has to come without any rest. In rotary also, shift duty poses an occupational health problem. S. Balakrishnan, the joint secretary of the union, has been working in such demanding circumstances in the rotary department for 12 years and not even once was a medical check-up arranged by the management.[29]

[29] All the facts about *Indian Express*, Hyderabad, and *Andhra Prabha* are based on the master roll of the employees, the duty roster and the information provided during a talk with an office-bearer of Hyderabad Andhra Prabha and Indian Express Staff and Workers Union on 2 December 1990.

S.G. Franswah, Vice President of the Union, in an affidavit filed on 16 February 1990 before the Supreme Court, argued that jobs pertaining to administration, accounts, press work and the distribution system are carried out by the same staff, though shown to be employed by Andhra Prabha Pvt. Ltd only (para. 6). He testified further that three magazines of the Indian Express are composed and colour pages of the Vijaywada and Vizianagram editions of the dailies are printed at Hyderabad (para. 9). Franswah reported transfers to Bombay as evidence to show that the Hyderabad unit is not a separate company, as claimed by the management, but a member of a Common Ownership Unit (paras. 11, 12, 13).

The case of the *Indian Express* is significant. Apart from showing how aggressive management can become after 'successfully' introducing modernisation, it exemplifies some other aspects of the reality also. It was argued in the beginning of this section that a 'successful' wage settlement at the top (that is, at the industry level) through State mediation is no guarantee for an improvement of work conditions below (that is, at the plant level), for maintaining union power or for checking managerial aggrandisement. Apparently, the case of the *Indian Express* is different from the *Hindu* or Printers (Mysore) Ltd. But, essentially, the story is the same. The management can alter the terms of conflict even over the issue of wage board implementation at the plant level. Particularly in the case of COUs, new, secondary, smaller units will be the place where a big, modern management can impose adverse work conditions, ignore unions, and maintain its line of control. This then, becomes another way in which deunionisation becomes an ominous reality looming large over the workers.

Deunionisation, thus, is a phenomemon that erupts from a situation marked by the interplay of several factors.

1. Labour market structure: the dominant types of jobs in terms of security, regularity and protection, patterns of stratification and segmentation, internal labour markets and the rules governing their operation.
2. The effectiveness of the market: access to jobs, recruitment systems, information and its control, wage bargaining and fixing procedures.
3. Organisation of labour: trade union structure, independence, coverage, economic power and the participation of organised labour in decisions at the enterprise or industry level.

K.L. Kapur, General Secretary of the AINEF, in an affidavit filed in connection with writ Petition 838 of 1990, showed that in 1985 the gross revenue of *Andhra Prabha* was Rs 342 lakh, newsprint cost Rs 98 lakh and other costs were Rs 57 lakh only (para. 9); that it had increased the price of the newspaper from 1 January 1979 to 1 November 1989 more than four times (para. 11); that there is no uniform wage structure at all in the Indian Express, where Arun Shourie, the former editor had been paid in the year ending 30 June 1988 Rs 128,087.20, while a journalist in group 1A was getting, in January 1988, Rs 4,908.60 a month (para. 17)!

4. Role of the State in terms of political economy: legislation and administrative rules concerning wage fixing, conditions of work, definition of employment contracts, worker's rights and the machinery for their enforcement, and the nature of its class support.
5. Production institutions: different types of firms, and mechanisms of control over labour.
6. Finally, reproduction and the reproduction of skills: training, retraining and its relation with the labour market.

In the liberal perspective, the whole scenario assumes a functionalist character and the economic behaviour of these factors determines the degree of cooperation and conflict in labour relations and the state of labour. However, when viewed from the perspective of *division of labour and power*, it will be found that technics and technology introduce uncertain elements in the scenario where a functionalist perspective does not help explain the process. Labour and capital, power and technology, management and the structure of industrial relations—the whole gamut of relationships faces acute tension. Deunionisation is one of the results of such a critical state of relationships. The search for the roots of the phenomenon of deunionisation takes us to the development of power in a plant.[30]

Contrary to the liberal perspective, the management perceives power in a new technological milieu. And it explicitly states that. Deunionisation results not so much from managerial awareness of the need for more profits but more power, for it knows profit flows from power. In modern management theories, new technology has been intimately linked with cybernetics. In one bible which combines cybernetics and management, the message is quite explicit. Some of the features of the energo-cybernetic strategy (EKS), according to the bible, are·

EKS is more a growth and success theory than just a management theory . . . . Optimise intangibles, tangibles are automatically optimised. The objective of EKS is not to increase *profit* but to increase *attractiveness* to the target group (clients,

---

[30] For a liberal statement on the entire problem, see the preface to the work by Gerry Rodgers (1990).

company, boss). You become more useful, you automatically grow. Profit is a natural by-product. Do not try to increase profits (or salary) directly. Do it indirectly by optimising the intangible. (Do I like the job? Do the people like me? Can I learn here?)

EKS is also concerned with power, power in the context of the management of your work and your life, power as a tool, how it can be constructively used, how it is often abused.

Those who strive for power out-compete those who strive for profit.

Excess of power, or power used against the interest of one's environment, destroys one's power.

With increased industrialisation, the ownership of market share gains in power and value while the ownership of production resources loses in power and value.

Power is not visible in balance sheets . . . .

Conventional management looks for internal solutions. EKS looks for external solutions (emphasis in original).[31]

This bible of modern management culture then talks of power. However, it is not as explicit about whom this power is to be used against, nor does it state for what this power has to be acquired. A greater market segment, more financial power, more supervisory power or more effective power for controlling labour? It talks of job satisfaction, which the Indian Express management obviously does not care much about, but which certainly the Hindu or the Deccan Herald management is concerned about. But in both the *Hindu* and the *Indian Express* case, the script of power is well written down. The script often assumes the dramaturgy of modernisation.

It is necessary to dwell on this point. We have seen that 'work-satisfaction' is, supposedly, a crucial problem. In the case of the *Hindu*, the management sees to it that the workers are satisfied, in the case of the *Statesman* and *Indian Express*, 'work-satisfaction' is

[31] 'Some Glimpses of EKS,' statement issued by the EKS Division of the Baroda Productivity Council (n.d.). Interestingly, the EKS course includes a topic, 'The Dynamics of Power,' and explains that the topic will discuss 'power in relation to one's career, power structures in organisations, and power in relation to markets'. The statement claims that the strategy formulated by Wolfgang Mewes is based on observing the lives and work of 25,000 individuals and companies.

irrelevant for the successful implementation of the modernisation programme. Similarly, in the *Hindu* case, the union does not press the management on the modernisation question if the workers are 'satisfied' or 'kept satisfied'; in the *Statesman*, the union adopts an 'obstructionist stand irrespective of satisfaction'. By implication, then, it may seem that deunionisation will result from adversarial relations, while union power will remain in the case of cooperative relations. I have argued that, in both cases, deunionisation remains a distinct possibility. In one case, the collapse of union power is sudden, explicit and abrupt. In the other, the loss of union power is endemic. 'Job satisfaction' may indicate that the worker or the operator is satisfied with the mode of work and is no longer content with the old pattern of adversarial unionism. Nonetheless, it denotes a decline in union politics. Technical competence, knowledge, responsibility, object variety, required interaction and consultation, administrative responsibility, recognition of skill and pay rise are the factors that induce work satisfaction (Mumford, 1973: 307–8). They reflect probably, from the worker's or operator's viewpoint, the pursuit of autonomy also. But whichever way it is seen, this 'satisfaction' never encourages the worker to challenge the frontier of control. Even if these indicate the pursuit of autonomy, it is pursuit in a new form—a definite departure from the recognised ways of workers' power in a plant. In the *Hindu, Deccan Herald* and *Times of India*, these factors are present and acknowledged by the unions. Yet is hard to say how this conclusively tackles the problem of 'expectation' that lies beneath the phenomenon of 'satisfaction'. As one discerning observer noted, analysing the behaviour of a unionised worker:

> . . . the real problems are the actions of management which violate his expectation; the features of management which violate his expectation; the features of employment relationship which degrade and oppress him . . . the social values which deny the legitimacy of his struggle to defend or improve his conditions (Hyman, 1973: 379).

Thus there remain role conflict, the issue of efficacy of consultation within the organisation, and the relation of the state of union democracy to the question of responding to new issues in the wake of modernisation flowing from the interpenetrating relationship between trade unions, shop stewards, work groups and the mass of individual workers. The question of power and control, thus, does not evaporate in a cooperative structure of relations that supposedly ensures 'job satisfaction'. This question remains, and deunionisation refers to this paramount question, and not to the existence of job satisfaction or otherwise.[32] Some perceptive observers of technology have also missed this point, and have either harped on the all-powerful nature of new technology erasing the old relations or have lamented that technology has defeated ideology. Such a line of argument (the latter in particular) will mean that unions are defeated by technology because it is a question of 'technocratic consciousness and the failure of ideology' (Gouldner, 1976: 229). It suggests, further, that the ruling class has been able to create 'belief systems appropriate to its rule'[33] and the formal rationality of organisation has defeated worker's consciousness. I have shown, through the fore-mentioned cases, that this counterposing of ideology and technology is of a specific 'new Left' variety that has mistaken the decline of ideology as the central political problem. The central political problem here, it is worth repeating, is one relating to the labour process, to understanding the response of labour as an integral part of the process and, finally, to understanding the dynamics also, whereby older forms of organisation are rendered antiquated in the wake of newer forms of technology. Precisely because new technology has all these dimensions, the central political problem in labour studies has to be concerned with division of labour and power. Deunionisation, in short, calls for a study with such a perspective in mind.[34]

Let me clarify the point further. One observer of Indian labour politics could not go beyond arguing, along the lines classically expounded by Lipset, that union behaviour is ultimately organisational behaviour, and hence should be understood in terms of organisational theory. In his words:

> Union are interest groups, but interest groups are also organisations.
> Most intra-organisational conflicts in the labour unions in

---

[32] On this question, a useful discussion may be found in Blauner (1967).

[33] Gouldner (1976), p. 231. Another similar line of argument can be found in Benson (1978); see particularly the chapter, 'Working Class and Middle Class Worlds'.

[34] It is surprising how this question is totally ignored in an otherwise valuable collection of relevant studies. See, in particular, Wright and Singlemann (1982).

India are of an inter-elite nature (rather than leaders vs. followers), particularly in blue collar unions.

The most significant environmental forces that affect both the organisational goals and effectiveness of unions in India are the political parties and public policy (Chatterjee, 1980: 87, 89).

Obviously, such a line of thinking is predominantly organisationalist. It excludes labour from the study of labour organisation, and the labour process is excluded as well. In locating significant environmental factors, it is not accidental that only parties and public policy are stressed, and the labour process is excluded. The goals of an organisation, according to traditional theory, would be determined by *legitimating* (or stated) public function and *directing* (or actual) sociological function. Further, the relevance of an organisation remains so long as it can stand internal stress, effectively pursue organisational goals, and relate to the significant environmental factors.[35] Such an organisationalist line of argument will mean that unions collapsed in the newspaper industry because they could not pursue their functions, and both parties and public policy contributed to that decline.

While I do not intend to discount the role of parties and public policy in deunionisation in the newspaper industry, and I have shown earlier the role of public policy in such a phenomenon (Samaddar, 1990), the point to stress here is that a formalist reading of organisational dynamics would have revealed none of the factors pertaining to the labour process that have contributed to the collapse of unionism in the newspaper industry. I have shown how old issues became much less crucial, how retaining the frontier of control inreasingly became the real question, how the old form of unionisation became inadequate—all in the wake of the introduction of new technology. All these further mean that we have to grasp, in Michael Burawoy's significant term, the politics of production (Burawoy, 1985).

Thus, a formalist reading will be unsatisfactory. An analysis of the structure of union politics leads us beyond the formal functional domain to the politics of production, where technology, form of superintendence of labour, concrete conditions for maintaining

---

[35] Rakhahari Chatterjee's arguments are based on Etzioni's organisationalist line of thinking. See Etzioni (1979a, 1979b).

the process of production and the reproduction of surplus value, and the response of labour form the elementary structure. Ironically, wages again become the crucial issue in the struggle over the frontier of control. The radical critics of union politics have repeatedly argued that unions have become too wage oriented in their outlook only to their own detriment. I have shown how not merely new issues arose in the wake of new technology, but that even wage determination itself became a new issue. The AINEF failed not because it harped on *wage*, but because it failed to reconceptualise the wage question according to the imperatives of the new situation.

Here we reach another relevant line of enquiry. We find that the occasion for reconceptualising the wage question arises in the wake of drastic changes in labour conditions. The process of wage settlement and the process of labour are, thus, integrally linked and the form of labour is the result of the combination of two forms. Strangely, however, in studying the wage settlement process, this particularity has often been ignored. For example, John T. Dunlop said with almost a benign innocence:

All wage theory is, in a sense, demand and supply analysis. A wage is a price and the wage structure is a sub-system of prices. Prices and price system are fruitfully to be interpreted in terms of demand and supply. There is no special or peculiar 'demand and supply' theory of wages (Dunlop, 1957: 127).

Indeed, one cannot expect the theme of labour process in arguments about wage determination coming from an American wage administrator. What is striking is the neglect of this question by even Maurice Dobb.

Trade unions are essentially the product of a capitalist wage system, in that they represent the obvious line of defence against the economic weakness in which propertyless wage earners find themselves when acting as unorganized individuals. Their essential function is to overcome this weakness by substituting a *collective bargain* for separate individual bargaining; thereby both raising the supply price at which labour is sold and making the rate of wages uniform over a whole trade . . . . A trade union . . . is an association of a class of persons in a peculiar

234 ■ Workers and Automation

social and economic position, concerned in bargaining over the
sale of labour and the conditions of employment (Dobb. 1956:
160).

Thus, the wage question here is a supply and demand one, and
the formality of the issue does not allow a consideration of the
fundamental question of technology and the labour process. Such
a formalist view does not allow even the consideration of a trade
union as an active agency in the labour process. It is 'an association . . . concerned in bargaining over the sale of labour and the
conditions of employment'. Though 'conditions of employment'
include a wide coverage, yet the formalist tone is undeniable.

Labour Regime and Deunionisation

In this study of deunionisation, we have seen technology as a form
of labour control. Even if technology does not assume this role
directly, the circumstances in which it is introduced invoke the
form and role. As one perceptive observer has noted: 'To think
only in terms of work-relations, job dissatisfaction, embattled
supervisors and union bureaucrats is to ignore the centerpiece of
the game: the awesome power which a company wields over its
employees' (Montgomery, 1989: 156.)

This awesome power stems from a combination of corporate
consolidation and the adoption of new efficiency schemes. The
worker has to face two different systems of control in the factory—
technical and social. The more thoroughly business rationalises
itself, the more extreme becomes the chaos in organised working
class life. The oligopolistic power of the new corporation provides
itself with a new capacity to tackle traditional union responses like
strikes. The union confronts enforced standardisation of methods,
enforced adoption of working conditions and enforced cooperation so that faster work can be assured. This enforcement forms
the backdrop of the rise and supremacy of new technology. Some
have tried to capture this perspective by coining phrases like
'company suzerainty' and 'labour regime'. Inadequate though these
phrases might seem, the defeat of the union movement against the
new order is striking; this is the phenomenon of deunionisation
which has been described as the 'historic reduction of labour
movement to certified trade unionism'. (Montgomery, 1989: 171).

I started by arguing that the phenomenon of deunionisation brought in by new technology means the crumbling or decline of the central structure of the Federation in the face of industrial conflict at the plant level, the decline of the old form of unionism, the fruitless switchover to cooperative bargaining, the increasing tendency towards unilateral decisions by the management, the abortive end to 'new technology agreements,' the restructuring of plant organisations and new forms of labour control and, finally, the reduction of conventional trade unions to mere bargaining agents and non-political entities. All these were evident in the decade of the eighties when new technology was conclusively established in the Indian newspaper industry.

There is no doubt that deunionisation has not been a peaceful affair in the Indian newspaper industry. In fact, it has been a violent and conflict-ridden story. Deunionisation has meant a decline in the union's status, but it has not meant an absence of rank and file workers' militancy. As I have argued, the newspaper workers were defeated because of a lack of synchrony between worker militancy below and the Federation's thrust above. Union defeats were enacted often on the basis of spontaneous resistance at the plants. There have been simplistic attempts to link organisational size with worker discontent and militancy. I have examined the argument that in larger firms, the rates of pay are usually above average and workers may willingly accept a 'trade-off' between high earnings and the more disadvantageous features of such employment. However, as we found in the employment of the *Statesman, ABP* and *Indian Express*, this was not the case. I shall end this section by citing the example of the *Times of India*, Bombay, which will again illustrate the irrelevance of the 'trade-off' argument and substantiate the importance of the issue of labour regime in a study of deunionisation.

The thesis of the deradicalised production worker was framed in a period of stable consumer capitalism. Workload, closures and redundancy were not a serious focus of dispute. Some opinions even more simplistically suggested that recent trends in the organisation and the action of the working class could be discerned solely or predominantly in terms of its changing skill and composition. The story of the *Times of India* shows that new technology, deunionisation and labour struggles are all part of some specific labour regime, the political specificity of which is entirely missed by such arguments.[36] We have to understand that the unevenness of the working class experience relates not merely to unevenness in occupational structure, but to fluidity in political experience, and in knowledge of new technology too. Thus, there may be both convergence and divergence in the relationship between labour response and work structure. To understand the situation of conflicts, their control and forms, institutionalisation, their impact on the internal politics and structure of unions, in short the elements which have characterised the tendency of deunionisation, we have to posit the entire question against the perspective of *labour regime* that characterises the industrialisation scenario. The frequency of occasions of conflict, the structure of union leadership and its access to political resources, and the types of issues and struggles will show the success or otherwise of the labour regime under which new technology is introduced in an industry or in a country. Deunionisation is a specific chapter, a specific epoch. It never means the final taming of labour and its ultimate passivity. It may very well be accompanied by other daily forms of struggle, of the emergence of new issues or new organisations. It signifies, at best, the success of a *labour regime*—a contingent success. To understand the reality of the labour regime, let us see what happened in the *Times of India*, Bombay, first of all.

The Times of India and Allied Publications Employees Union had been the traditional union in *The Times of India* (TOI) and had been one of the pillars of the All India Newspaper Employees Federation. The President of the AINEF, S.Y. Kolhatkar, had been the union leader in the early stages and the movement for instituting wage boards for newspaper employees in the early sixties had been launched by, among other unions, the Times of India and Allied Publications Employees' Union too. The union was not very enthusiastic about new technology and, as the traditional custodian of workers' interests, had been demanding blank social security coverages. However, in 1982, in the wake of the Palekar Award, a separate union was formed by a maverick leader, R.J. Mehta, under his umbrella organisation, Mumbai Mazdur Sabha. This new union entered into an agreement with the management over the implementation of the Palekar Award for wage revision. In 1984, industrial unrest flared up in the Bombay plant

[36] For a good discussion, see Hyman (1978).

over minor issues. There was spontaneous slowdown, a lightening strike and, subsequently an ongoing strike. The Employees' Union sat quietly through the trouble, arguing that it would not like to oppose the workers' movement, though it felt that such unrest would not be in the interests of the workers and would give the management the upper hand. In short, the initiative passed from its hands. The management declared a lockout for 69 days. The strike collapsed. Workers who had joined the strike were allowed to enter the premises only when they pledged a statement of apology. The lifting of the lockout and the entry of employees followed an agreement between R.J. Mehta's union and the management. The members of the Employees' Union did not have to sign the apology letter. However, they were passive and did not consider how much the conclusion of an agreement between a rival union and the management, the signing of an apology letter and the breakdown of the strike would alter its fortunes and affect the frontier of control within the company and plant.

The plant reopened with a plan for modernisation drawn up, and the implementation of the initial phase of modernisation already having started. The Employees' Union could do nothing now. The defeat of the strike heralded modernisation. The consent of the union was not taken. On the contrary, undertakings were secured from the employees regarding 'good conduct'. The bargaining strength of the workers was drastically reduced. The service of seventy employees was terminated without enquiry. All subsequent agreements were concluded with R.J. Mehta's union, thus propping up a blackleg union with official support. The workers were compelled to give frequent undertakings, issue appeal letters and follow the provisions of the management-union agreements.

This foisting of a union on the workers was done with the help of the Maharashtra Recognition of Trade Unions and Prevention of Unfair Labour Practices Act. The Employees' Union challenged the managerial policy, but the Industrial Court sat tight. Now the Bachawat Wage Board Award has given rise to further occasions for such agreements, whereupon workers have been compelled to pay union dues to R.J. Mehta and to his various 'welfare' schemes, diwali subscriptions, and so on, in lieu of pay revision. The management substracts the dues at the time of payment and the workers are obliged to sign copies of the agreement letter individually. Blanket conditions regarding workload, manning, discipline and shopfloor movement were included in the wage revision agreement, 800 workers became potentially surplus and, of them, 250 continued to come to the plant without any assigned work. The management, Mehta's friends and others now gleefully say that Kolhatkar's empire has collapsed (*Kolhatkar ka empire collapse hone laga*)! Only 65 workers still remain loyal to the Employees' Union and the Secretary of the Union, N.A. Sawant, ruefully adds, however, that 200 more voluntarily donate on different occasions to the union fund! Union coordination between the plants in various cities has practically ended. With the Bombay Union, the leading force in the coordination, collapsing, labour resistance at other *TOI* centres has also been effectively curbed.[37]

In short, the frontier of control has moved away in favour of the management, the traditional union (which was also the traditional pillar of workers' resistance) has collapsed, a compliant union has been encouraged, a strict work regime has been enforced, the labour law of the state has helped the management, and the union can now do little else other than wait for a favourable verdict in the ongoing court cases, and finds no way of regaining the initiative; in short, traditional methods and the ethos of unionisation have failed disastrously. Ironically, this is the very period when the All India Federation concentrated all its energies on wage revision and neglected the situation below. Deunionisation, thus, is indicative of a certain labour regime in which new technology has been introduced by the management. The argument that confines itself to changes in the occupational structure only in a discussion on labour response to new technology thus errs on one principal count: it disregards the political specificity of labour response. It

---

[37] This entire account has been constructed on the basis of an interview with N.A. Sawant, General Secretary of the Times of India and Allied Publications Employees' Union (15 March 1991); the declaration issued by Ram S. Taneja, Managing Director of *TOI* in the *Indian Express*, 8 September 1984; the declaration signed by each employee for accepting wage revision, 30 December 1989; Joint Declaration by P.R. Krishnamurthy on behalf of the management and R.J. Mehta for interim relief, 8 Feburary 1990; Notice of Voluntary Retirement Scheme, issued by the Company, 21 March 1989; Charter of demands submitted to Bennett, Coleman and Co. Ltd by Mumbai Mazdoor Sabha, 24 February 1987; Memorandum of Settlement between the management and R.J. Mehta for bonus fixation from 1988–89 to 1992–93, 19 July 1989.

misses the politics involved in the question of the frontier of control and it is oblivious to the existence of labour regimes that accompany modernisation in various countries and situations.

Frederick Deyo has forwarded a comparative typology of labour regimes. There are four dimensions in this typology—severity, level, type and effectiveness. Deyo's discussion was in the context of the political demobilisation of East Asian labour. Though we need not go into the details of Deyo's typology, there is no doubt that he has been perceptive about the types of labour control in the context of new industrialisation in Asia—the repressive and corporatist types.[38] New industrialisation needed the introduction of new technology and has given birth to more effective labour control mechanisms to allow new industrialisation to continue unimpeded. The labour regime, thus, includes factors like the specific type of industrialisation calling for specific types of labour systems, ways of controlling labour movements, the intricate structure of ideology, welfare and labour peace, the political demobilisation of labour, the structural demobilisation of the union movement, the growth of the hyperproletariat and its distance from organised labour, and so on. The labour regime thus reverts back to the notion of labour process as the central question in labour and industrialisation studies. This return is very substantive, as it places the question of the labour process in the broader context of labour control with the help of laws, type of industrialisation, money power and corporate strategies.

We saw in this study that both corporatist and repressive policies helped new technology in the newspaper industry and altered the power balance in the plants. All the realities taken together, like wage board, union baiting and new managerial techniques, indicate that in the Indian newspaper industry—particularly amongst the larger establishments—a specific labour regime exists. This regime is a unique combination of both corporatist and repressive types and has admirably succeeded in demobilising the proletariat and deunionising the newspaper worker. The contested ground was the workplace and the worker lost the contest.

---

[38] Deyo (1989), chap. 4, pp. 106–51. There is growing literature on this topic. See, for example Southhall (1988); Deyo (1989); Dijk and Marcussen (1990); Portes and Walton (1981); Edwards (1979); Hyman and Streeck (1988).

Technology and Power at the Workplace

In this study of new technology at the shopfloor level, which showed the secular tendency of deunionisation in the newspaper industry, we can thus locate the central question—the *question of power at the workplace.*

But this loss of power has not been a mysterious process. As I showed through examples of abortive strikes, deliberate dragging of negotiations, a corporate strategy of taming labour and of coupling the issue of wage revision with new work flow, the sponsoring of a blackleg union, the ready use of partisan labour law and the obsessive concern of the Federation with wage boards to the neglect of the question of renegotiating work conditions at the plant level—this loss of power has followed a discernible route. This process is marked by defeats over maintaining the frontier of control.

The route through which power was lost to the bosses, as we saw, cannot be understood with traditional concepts of unionisation, nor can it be understood with newer ideas of the pacification of labour because of the restructuration of the workforce. These issues become relevant only in the broader and infinitely more important context of labour regime under which new industrialisation and the necessary taming of labour take place. The existence of specific labour regimes is an issue that demands more study.

The traditional concepts and practices of unionisation have largely neglected the question of the labour process and, more specifically, the question of how 'management rights and union interests'[39] are defined in a plant. Conversely, one could say that they failed to understand the contested ground of 'union rights and management interests' too. This has been an area chronically dominated by 'legalistic' thinking. Too often, in both experts' and union officials' circles, the bungling of the ill-fated manager, or the union official who 'gave away' his company's rights or union's rights is accepted as an adequate explanation of collisions or events in the plant. That these 'rights' have historic foundations and continuities, and that they experience discontinuities too and have often to be

[39] For a predominantly organisational analysis, see Chandler (1978), chap. V. pp. 63–82.

renegotiated, reasserted and reestablished, is overlooked. I have argued that this question is embedded in a technological and organisational matrix. The entire structure of bargaining, once dismantled, will show the dynamics of power. Otherwise technology would have been irrelevant to the question of bargaining. As a Federation official in Bombay well-versed in bargaining and adjudication blithely exclaimed, 'After all what has new technology got to do with wages and other demands on work conditions?'[40]

We have also seen that the question of work satisfaction touches only the exterior of the issue of power in the work place. The thrust in a cooperative framework of bargaining has been that both managers and union leaders are intent upon securing work satisfaction, irrespectve of technological change, and they know that if work satisfaction reigns, the question of loss of power or deunionisation becomes irrelevant. It is true that work satisfaction removes the thorny problem of alienation and the 'feelings of dissatisfaction' would be less likely to provoke plant-level conflicts.[41] Yet, the issue of work satisfaction and industrial trends in a plant or industry cannot be simply reduced to the social psychology of job and class. For work satisfaction also depends upon the dynamics of power, and the elementary structure of industrial relations makes and unmakes to a large extent the question of satisfaction, dissatisfaction and rebelliousness. Robert Blauner makes an interesting comment. It was not without reason that when 'in 1880, that famous pioneer of survey research, Karl Marx, drew up a questionnaire consisting of 101 items, 25,000 copies of which were sent to various workers' societies and socialist circles,' this long schedule was 'composed entirely of questions of *objective fact* relating to size of the plant, working conditions, wages, hours, strikes and trade unions'. It may appear strange that 'in contrast with present day surveys (there) is a lack of questions concerning the *feelings* of the workers about their work, employers, and place in society,'

---

[40] Comment made by Madan Phadnis during an interview on 15 March 1991. Phadnis is the Vice President of the All India Newspaper Employees Federation, a CPI(M) and CITU leader in Bombay and the legal consultant to the Federation.

[41] Indeed, Reinhard Bendix and Seymour Martin Lipset have argued that 'the Marxian theory of why men under capitalism would revolt was based on an assumption of what prompts men to be satisfied or dissatisfied with their work.' See Bendix and Lipset, 'Karl Marx's Theory of Social Classes,' in Bendix and Lipset (1957), p. 32 ff.

(Blauner, 1967: 473). Yet it should not appear strange, and Marx was aware of the framing of the schedule, for work satisfaction is a structural product of industrial relations in modern society, the very structure that can give birth to the tendency towards deunionisation. Indeed, in a labour regime permeated with corporatism and a neofordist ethos, we can witness the simultaneous invoking of work satisfaction, of marginalisation of the union, and of the collective worker in the work process and in the plant.

It is not that all these facts (like boom in the newspaper industry, upward wage revision, marginalisation of unions at the plant level, abortive strikes, spread of new technology and a growing irrelevance of old concepts regarding wages) were not noted through the decade of the eighties. But these events were taking place at a time when the state of labour studies in India had not yet considered the *labour process* as the central concept and the union movement also remained indifferent to the issues emanating from the labour process, at least at the official level. One could say that the developments in the newspaper industry, and particularly industrial relations data, had been in search of a theory. We cannot explain the developments, particularly the conflicts, by taking recourse to the business cycle explanation simply, nor can we depend on a political (party-political) explanation of conflict waves. Along with these two explanations, there is another plausible explanation: changes in the forms of the institutionalisation of conflict (bargaining structure), in class capacities (in terms of union membership and other organisational resources), in the overall distribution of power in the industry, and in the technological mode provoke conflicts. Conflicts arise, furthermore, as they are needed by the management to restructure the industry in the wake of the adoption of new technology. A strategy of securing consent is thus inevitably accompanied by a strategy of provoking conflicts as well. All these remain to be theorised.

We can argue then, that collision/cooperation and subsequent marginalisation (in other words, deunionisation) is a dependent variable, determined by changes in the state of the industry or the economy, in the level of technology and changes in the bargaining structure, in the political position of labour in general and in the plant in particular. A substantial change in any of the factors may induce change in the levels of cooperation/conflict and change in the status of the collective worker. As one perceptive observer noted:

Industrial conflict reflects a dialectical process. The interplay of the determinants of conflict is constantly changing; the relative weight of these determinants is constantly changing. It is conflict itself that shapes and reshapes the factors at play at any given historical conjuncture (Franzosi, 1989: 478–79).

A great amount of political study remains to be done on the question of the structural origins of deunionisation. Labour studies in India will have to be extended to cover the entire industrial scenario in the country in order to understand the political nature of deunionisation.

7

Labour Process and the Labour Market

I started with the beginning of the 1980s—the Palekar Award, wage revision, modernisation, unionisation and the subsequent demobilisation of labour in the newspaper industry. I shall end with the beginning of the nineties. The whole industry has, meanwhile, been restructured; labour has been defeated everywhere on a worldwide front; new technology has been introduced; and the restructuration of economies, industries, and division of labour remain an ongoing, but at the same time an accomplished, reality. Demobilisation of labour in the graphics industry took place not only in India but internationally as well. In fact, demobilisation will be a misleading word here. What happened simply was that the union structure got outmoded in the wake of the introduction of new technology. Again, this took place not only within the country, but internationally too. The All India Newspaper Employees' Federation, which had been dominated by communist leadership, had grown up as member of the Standing Committee of Trade Unions of the Graphics Industry which had its headquarters in Berlin, the capital of the former German Democratic Republic. On 10 September 1991, in its last conference, the Standing Committee decided to wind up its activities and close down the organisation. With the fall of socialist countries, from where the Standing Committee had been deriving its strength and providing inspiration to the national federations, influencing their arguments and outlook, a whole era of unionism in the printing industry came to an end.[1]

[1] AINEF circular no. 39/91, 29 October 1991.

It is not that new technology, the political offensive of capital and restructuration affected only the unions having allegiance to the erstwhile Eastern bloc. Trade unions in the West also suffered. Recession hit the printing industry hard. The International Graphics Federation had to appeal to graphics workers outside Britain not to seek employment there as a deep recession had affected the British graphics industry, rendering over 7,500 members of the National Graphics Association unemployed.[2] The *Times* strike in London had ended in defeat. The Fifteenth Congress of the International Graphics Federation had to remind itself that:

as we approach the year 2000 there has never been a greater need for trade union solidarity and cooperation. No one should be more aware than workers in the graphics and media trade unions of the way in which developments in communications technology has created a 'shrinking' world. Just as this technology can be used for the rapid dissemination of news and useful information, it can also be used as the foundation for the spread of ideas and policies which are detrimental to the interests of working people and their families.

Many 'global' companies seek to impose their policies of exploitation and anti-trade unionism around the world. Many others follow their example. Under the banner of 'greater flexibility of labour' employers are attacking the conditions of employment of workers throughout the world. Even in countries where these conditions are low, the employers will always seek to drive them down still further . . . .

The last decade has shown that trade unions in the so-called developed world are not immune to this problem.

In Europe we are seeing the opposition by many employers and governments to the very idea of introducing a framework of fundamental workers' rights. This 'Social Charter' should be the basis of workers' rights everywhere, not only in Europe. But no one will give us these rights. We must be prepared to fight for them.[3]

Thus, newspaper workers everywhere had to raise the question of

[2] Cited in Circular no. 38/91, 29 October 1991.
[3] Ibid.

an inviolable social charter, after the industry had drastically changed under the impact of new technology, and management rights had been re-established and reasserted beyond challenge. We have seen the faint beginning of this demand for a social charter in the arguments of the Federation before the Bachawat Wage Board. But we have also seen that this call for a social charter tragically *followed* and not *preceded* the enactment of the process of deunionisation in the wake of the introduction of new technology. The unions had been rendered immobile. How strong could such a demand be in a situation marked by a loss of power?

Thus, it is not enough to say that the introduction of new technology is an ensemble of social relations; indeed, it is an ensemble of power relations. Management rights, the crumbling of the old union structure, the emergence of a social charter containing new demands, the demobilisation of workers and the process of accumulation of knowledge of the technology—we have seen that all these issues tell upon the power structure. And it is power that decides what, how far and on what terms the technology can be introduced and implemented. Thus, the issue of labour process can hardly be studied apart from a study of the interaction between division of labour and power.

As we analyse the reasons behind the introduction of microelectronics based technology in the Indian newspaper industry, the relation between the internationalisation of the economy and the microelectronics based technological revolution at once becomes apparent. Even the internationalisation of labour-controlling politics and methods (in short, the internationalisation of the politics of labour regime) is a clearly visible tendency today.[4] In discussing the labour process as the critical issue in the history of unionisation of newspaper workers in India, I have thus emphasised upon the politics of it. The various references to the politics of production, power and the division of labour, deunionisation, and so on, have to be seen in this light.

The history of the discussion on the labour process in recent

---

[4] Surprisingly, Manuel Castell's highly analytical essay on high technology and international division of labour omits labour from a discussion of a typology of the countries belonging to the developing world in the context of the technological divison of labour. See Castell (1989). I am indebted to Laurids Lauridsen for bringing to my notice the need to include labour in such a discussion and the context of new industralisation. See Lauridsen (1991).

times has taken many twists and turns. What started as a theoretical contribution by Braverman towards expanding some suggestions of Marx on the process of labour soon developed into a vast corpus of works. From the notion of deskilling that showed how the worker's subjectivity was killed in the process of production, to the idea of plant level studies that would show how the labour process actually objectifies class relations not merely in a factory, but in production in general—the historiography on the labour process has traversed a long way.[5] Plant based studies and studies on the shopfloor behaviour of workers have led to more attention to the factor of technology in the labour process. As managerial science has advanced in recent decades, technology has come to be seen as a managerial tool, technology itself a control mechanism and labour process studies have often boiled down to labour-control studies. Institutions, methods, bargaining mode and structure, the structure of industrial relations, and so on, have been increasingly studied as a part of labour process studies. Increasingly, again, the whole network of labour control devices (both within the plant and in the polity as a whole) has become the focus of study of what many have termed labour regimes.

It is not that politics was kept out. Labour process studies went much beyond Braverman. The idea of the diminishing subjectivity of labour has been increasingly contested. As I have shown, the whole range of analyses of fordism, neofordism, paternalism, state regulationism, and so on, have brought back the question of the relationship between power and division of labour, so ably expressed by Burawoy through the term 'politics of production,' in his discussions on the labour process. I have situated this study on the newspaper workers in this emerging discussion on the politics of production. But the added argument has been that the study of the labour process is not primarily a question of choosing between the subjectivity and objectivity of labour, but of analysing the elementary structures of the process, and the arrangement of various blocs which make up the totality of the process; it is, further, a

[5] The uncertain course labour process studies have traversed can be seen from a large number of works in recent times. An idea of the shifts in emphasis can be had from well-known works like Harry Braverman (1974); Zimbalist (1979); Brecher and The Work Relations Group (1978); Gorz (1976); Noble (1986); Burawoy, (1979); idem (1985); Edwards (1979); Montgomery (1979); Nichols and Beyon (1977); Elger (1979); Thompson (1983).

question of showing how labour responds to technology and to various institutions of the labour market. Indeed, unionised labour itself acts as an elementary part in the formation of the process. But this subjectivity, needless to add, has functioned within the given structure of capital-labour relations globally as well as within the nation.

This brings us to the question of the labour market. Ideologically and politically, labour process studies and labour market studies have remained contraposed in the historiography of labour. Labour market studies involving institutions of the market have often neglected the centrality of the labour process. But, more importantly—and this is of more relevance to us—studies of the labour process have neglected the whole range of institutional concerns affecting the market. Issues like the way in which wages are determined, the mobility of labour, factors affecting the tightness of the labour market, the structures of control and hierarchy within enterprises, the organisation and behaviour of institutions like trade unions—these are areas which, though exogenous, may enrich labour process studies. Our own discussion on the impact of new technology on the printing industry has shown how institutions like wage boards, trade unions and research organisations deeply affected the labour process in the newspaper industry. Apparently, these can be termed institutions of the labour market, but they are political in nature and show how non-economic elements play a role, besides the economic ones, in shaping the labour process. Could we then follow the 'post-institutionalist school' which includes Dunlop and Ross, among others, and say that we have to be closer to market analysis while paying considerable attention to the growth of unionisation and collective bargaining in our study of the impact of technology upon labour?[6]

My plea for including labour market questions does not amount to the acceptance of the labour market as the central issue in labour studies. But precisely to enrich the whole field of the *politics of production* as the key area in labour process studies, market institutions have to be seriously analysed. We have seen in the course of our findings how skill and knowledge of new technology was disseminated through institutions, how enquiry committees acted as legitimising agencies of new technology, how

---

[6] See, in this connection, Rodgers (1991).

wage institutions speeded up the process of technological introduction, how methods of state arbitration or adjudication presided over a period of change, how laws regulated defence by workers. In short, this study has explored the role of institutions in influencing the labour process. The implicit basis of such an approach throughout this study has been the relevance of labour market issues to the central question of the making of the labour process.

Institutional issues like the nature of employment contracts, the formal and informal rules concerning hiring of workers, length of the working day, nature of control over their work, extent of protection and security, organisation and representation of labour and of employers, the process of wage fixing, training and skill institutions, the organisation of jobs within firms like occupational hierarchics, the prevalence of corporate culture, the conventional standards of life and the conventional ideas of the standards of life—all these are crucial issues to institutional economics in the field of labour market researches (Rodgers, 1991: 8–9). But these are of great political relevance as well, as they bear upon the power structure and matrix and help in deciding the location of power in the process of labour.

I have shown earlier how the union in the *Statesman* attempted to keep control over the pace of modernisation by appearing to co-sponsor modernisation in the plant. One expression of this was the piloting of the training programme. I have also cited another example where a similar beginning towards skill generation and diffusion was made by the owners through the setting up of a research organisation and a research survey bulletin. From the institutional point of view, these have been systems of labour management—ways in which a labour force with new skills has been created and, it is important to add, with almost no cost whatsoever! Objectively then, the whole wage board quibbling over *producer wage* and *social wage*, ways to develop skills and kill old skills, the role of force, the threat of force or persuasion by the State and employers, the institutions for promoting a 'corporate culture,' the subtly subversive role of participatory mechanisms for workers in demobilising the workers, other industrial relations mechanisms for controlling workers' demands or managing concessions in ways which are consistent with high rates of accumulation and growth, instruments of flexibility and redeployment and other such issues should be seen not merely as factors affecting productivity, profitability, investment and technological upgradation, but political instruments determining power relations in a factory too. I started with a reference to the need for studying labour against the perspective of overdetermination of the twin processes: the labour process and the valorisation process. Now the whole question can be clarified further. It is politics and externalities like the institutions of the labour market which act as political agents for effecting this overdetermination. All crucial questions (like the ideology of labour and the regime of labour) are materialised through these institutions. It is a study of these institutions from such a perspective of overdetermination of the twin processes that has long been in order.[7]

Yet labour process studies can hardly remain only institutionalist studies. As one is often led to exasperation at the deluge of studies on division of labour and to comment, *but where is labour in it*, the question of subjectivity of labour still remains unaddressed in most of the studies on the labour process. And one has to keep reminding oneself that a study of labour market institutions does not diminish the centrality of the subjectivity of labour. Indeed, labour market institutions are an integral part of the regime of labour, and the struggling subjectivity of labour will continue to occupy our attention in any study of the labour regime. *Politics of Production*, then, signifies this subjectivity, concretely and historically situated in these institutions and modes and even beyond these!

I shall end with ideology. The subjectivity of labour brings in the question of ideology and class consciousness. There has been an overreaction, so to say, to the idealisation of 'class consciousness' done by Lukacs. The result was that workers were discussed without their class-consciousness being taken note of. Once again, labour process studies can be accused of neglect. Initially, analyses were attempted to dissect the consciousness of workers working and living in a fordist regime. But, then, typologies of labour regimes were constructed one after another without a parallel examination of the metamorphosis of working men's consciousness. In post-colonial countries, some attempts have been made to examine the ideological state of workers and their world of consciousness. But labour process studies are yet to accomplish or

[7] For the particularity of politics, see Deyo, 'State and Labor: Modes of Political Exclusion in East Asian Development' in Deyo (1987); see also Rodgers (1986).

reconstruct such a world in totality. These studies are yet fragmentary—stressing on the community origin of a section of workers, or on the labour aristocracy of public sector employees, or on the state of female proletarians in a paternalistic labour regime.

Indeed, the question of ideology can be envinced in the phenomenon of rigid institutionalism too in the world of the labour market. I have shown how the various notions of fair wage, social justice, the natural boundaries of managerial and workers' rights and the inevitability of mechanisation affected institutionalisation. The march of technology has to proceed here obviously under the overarching umbrella of the ideology and institutions of social welfarism. With the need for flexibility in the process of labour being increasingly felt by the bosses in the wake of new technology, there is the possibility that the ideology of social welfarism will be similarly affected by newer ideologies of dynamism, productivity, plant based cooperative functioning and corporatism. Even in the discussion of labour productivity, the question of what level to measure it—whether at the level of a particular operation, machine, product, factor, company or society—is an intensely ideological-political one. Indeed, the maintenance of certain institutions, challenging them and contesting their essentiality, by both capital and labour, will become more and more a political-ideological question. It is likely that, with the growing need for flexibility, capital will put less emphasis on technical change and more on the material reorganisation of labour. As new ways of publishing newspapers, and integrating various editions in one publication become crucial to flexible specialisation strategy, and as the demand becomes saturated with the markets becoming increasingly fragmented, flexible relationships as a strategy for managing labour will become more crucial. Seen in this context, the entire story of deunionisation is the story of an attack by capital on labour with the help of such a strategy. We have seen that where demobilisation has come through attrition, flexibility is the bitter dose imparted. Where the accommodation of cooperative relationships and hierarchy was achieved, there too flexibility came on the basis of the stabilisation of certain institutionalised relationships. As industrial relations in most newspapers in south India show, the unions, as if almost without knowing it, became a willing partner in creating such flexibility. Large sections of workers in smaller centres of big publishing giants remained non-unionised. The unions remained unperturbed. Though today the minimum wage is often granted as per the wage board recommendations, wage flexibility prevails in the form of uncertain or undetermined bonus or allowances. The rate of unionisation has slowed down. Of greater importance is however internal numerical flexibility, as no one is immediately sacked and no one is assured of gainful employment, with vacancies often remaining unfilled. In multi-edition, multi-publication concerns, even work organisation and assignments tend to be flexible. In sum, flexibility along with statist emphasis on technology has posed an ideological political challenge to collective labour in the production process.[8]

Burawoy comments in his introductory remarks in *The Politics of Production*:

> In the following chapters, I argue that the lurches which have plagued the history of Marxism—lurches between a voluntarism in which anything seems possible and a determinism in which nothing seems possible, between a naive workerism and bleak prognostications—can be brought into line with reality if we expand our understanding of production beyond its purely economic content and explicitly include politics (Burawoy, 1985: 7).

This politics denotes ideology too, though Burawoy unfortunately does not seem to have attached much importance to it (1985: 171–73). And ideology reinforces the question of subjectivity. It is true that subjectivity raises the question of so many images of the working class and so many images of the labour process held by the working class. Thus it is not an aggregated reality but a structured reality when we refer to the subjectivity of the worker in the labour process. A study of the structured world of workers' consciousness will, I am sure, enrich labour process studies, the pivot of which remains the politics of production. We know that the attitude of the official communist movement towards unionism, the state of labour studies in India and the general mood of anti-capitalist struggles at certain junctures have had a profound impact on workers' consciousness and their subjectivity. This theme remains to be studied further and analysed so that we can understand how

[8] Though the literature on flexibility is fast increasing, still Piore and Sabel remains the must. See Piore and Sabel (1984); Hirst and Zeitlin (1991); see also Islam (1989).

new technology and workers' subjectivity remain in an unequal relationship, how labour organisations becomes antiquated, and how technology as a disciplining process thus becomes successful.

Braverman had perhaps been aware of the criticisms regarding his alleged neglect of the subjectivity of workers in his discussions on the capitalist project of controlling the labour process. And he wrote:

> The displacement of labour as the subjective element of the process, and its subordination as an objective element in a productive process now conducted by the management, is an ideal realized by capital only within definite limits, and unevenly among industries (1974: 172).

We all know by now that this was a weak attempt at explaining away a critical error in conceptualising the labour process. I have shown how labour's own consciousness becomes a crucial issue in determining the victory of technology over labour, in rendering labour's own institutions (like the official trade unions) ineffective and antiquated, and how labour's own struggles influence the pace and form of the process of valorisation. It is labour struggles that connect the two vital processes of production: the process of valorisation and the process of labour.

This then has been the polemical context of this book as well as the context of the concluding observations—the need to speak out against the emergence of perspectives that conjure away the working class, perspectives that construct labour history only on the 'swan songs of artisans' engaged in their battle to defend their skills against the encroachment of capital, perspectives that remove labour from studies on the division of labour and, finally, perspectives that abound with prophecies of work degradation, and with the vanishing away of labour as a conscious agency in the modern production process altogether.

It is only that the working class has refused to be part of such a perspective. And, ironically, it is still the managers of capital who recognise that.

Bibliography

BOOKS AND PERIODICALS

All India Newspaper Employees' Federation (AINEF). 1986a. *Silver Jubilee Conference Souvenir*. Calcutta.
——————. 1986b. *Twenty Five Years of Glorious Struggles*. New Delhi.
Annable, James E. Jr. 1984. *The Price of Industrial Labor*. Massachusetts: Lexington Books.
Bakke, E. Wright, Clark Kerr and Charles Anrod. 1960. *Unions, Management and the Public*. New York: Harcourt Brace.
Bamber, Greg J. and Russell Lansbury (eds.). 1989. *New Technology—International Perspectives on Human Resources and Industrial Relations*. London: Unwin Hyman.
Banerjee, Partha Sarathi. 1988. 'Computerizing a Newspaper Organization: Issues in Labour Process and Externalities,' unpublished paper, National Seminar on Technology, Productivity and Industrial Relations, Shri Ram Centre for Industrial Relations and Human Resources. New Delhi, 23–25 March.
Baroda Productivity Council. n.d. *Some Glimpses of EKS*. Baroda: EKS Division of Baroda Productivity Council.
Bendix, Reinhard and S.K. Lipset (eds.). 1957. *Class, Status and Power—Social Stratification in Comparative Perspective*. London: Routledge and Kegan Paul.
Benson, Leslie. 1978. *Proletarians and Parties*. London: Tavistock.
Bhattacharya, Brojen. 1988. 'Heroic Struggle of Patrika—Jugantar Employees, 1946–48' in *Indian Press Since Independence*. New Delhi: IFWJ.
Blauner, Robert. 1957. 'Work Satisfaction and Industrial Trends in Modern Society,' in Reinhard Bendix and Seymour Martin Lipset (eds.), *Class, Status and Power: Social Stratification in Comparative Perspective*. London: Routledge and Kegan Paul.
Braverman, Harry. 1974. *Labour and Monopoly Capital: The Degradation of Work in the Twentieth Century*. New York: Monthly Review Press.
Brecher, Jeremy and The Work Relations Group. 1978. 'Uncovering the Hidden History of the American Workplace,' *Review of Radical Political Economics*, Vol. 10, No. 4, Winter.
Burawoy, Michael. 1978. 'Towards a Marxist Theory of the Labour Process—Braverman and Beyond,' *Politics and Society*, Vol. 8, Nos. 3–4.

Burawoy, Michael. 1979. *Manufacturing Consent—Changes in the Labour Process Under Monopoly Capitalism*. Chicago: University of Chicago Press.
—————. 1985. *The Politics of Production—Factory Regimes Under Capitalism and Socialism*. London: Verso.
Burawoy, Michael and Theda Skocpol. 1982. *Marxist Enquiries—Studies of Labor, Class and States*. Chicago: Chicago University Press.
Castell, Manuel. 1989. 'High Technology and the New International Division of Labour,' *Labour and Society*, Vol. 14.
Chakraborty, Rathin (ed.). 1984. *Gana Andolan O Sangbadpatra*. (in Bengali). Calcutta: Lokmat Prakashani.
Chandler, Margaret K. 1978. *Management Rights and Union Interests*. Connecticut: Greenwood Press.
Chatterjee, Rakhahari. 1980. *Unions, Politics and the State—A Study of Indian Labour Politics*. Delhi: South Asian Publishers.
Clegg, Hugh A. 1979. *The Changing System of Industrial Relations in Great Britain*. Oxford: Blackwell.
Craig, James. 1978. *Phototypesetting: A Design Manual*. London: Pitman Publishing.
Crouch, Colin and Allessandro Pizzorno (eds.). 1978. *The Resurgence of Class Conflict in Western Europe Since 1968*, 2 vols. London: MacMillan.
Dasgupta, Jayanta. 1985. 'Two Struggles in Newspapers,' *In the Wake of Marx*, Vol. 1, No. 3.
Datta, Satyabrata. 1990. *Capital Accumulation and Workers' Struggle in Indian Industrialisation—The Case of Tata Iron and Steel Company, 1910–1970*. Calcutta: K. P. Bagchi.
Deyo, Frederick C. 1987. *The Political Economy of New Asian Industrialism*. Ithaca: Cornell University Press.
—————. 1989a. *Beneath the Miracle—Labor Subordination in New Asian Industrialism*. Berkeley: University of California Press.
—————. 1989b. 'Labour Systems, Production Structures and Export-Manufacturing: The East Asian NICs, *South East Asian Journal of Social Science*, Vol. 17, No. 2.
Dijk, Meine Pieter Van, and Henrik Secher Marcussen (eds.). 1990. *Industrialization in the Third World—The Need for Alternative Strategies*. London: Frank Cass.
Dizard, Wilson P. Jr. 1982. *The Coming Information Age*. London: Longman.
Dobb, M. 1956. *Wages*. Cambridge: Cambridge Unviersity Press.
Dubois, Pierre. 1978. 'New Forms of Industrial Conflict,' in Colin Crouch and Allessandro Pizzorno (eds.), *The Resurgence of Class Conflict in Western Europe Since 1968*, Vol. 2. London: Macmillan.
Dunlop John T. 1957. 'The Task of Contemporary Wage Theory,' in George Taylor and Frank Pierson (eds.), *New Concepts in Wage Determination*. New York: McGraw Hill.
Edgren, Gus (ed.). 1989. *Restructuring, Employment and Industrial Relations— Adjustment Issues in Asian Industries*. Geneva: ILO.
Edwards, Richard. 1979. *Contested Terrain—The Transformation of the Workplace in the Twentieth Century*. New York: Basic Books.
Elger, T. 1979. 'Valorisation and Deskilling—A Critique of Braverman,' *Capital and Class*, No. 7, Spring.

Engels, Frederick. 1980. *Condition of the Working Class in England*. Moscow: Progress Publishers.

Etzioni, A. 1971a. *A Comparative Analysis of Complex Organizations*. New York: Free Press.

—————. 1971b. 'Two Approaches to Organizational Analysis—A Critique and a Suggestion,' in Jai Singh Ghorpade (ed.), *Assessment of Organizational Effectiveness*. California: Good Year Publication.

Evans, Christopher. 1979. *The Micro-Millennium*. New York: Washinghton Square Press Pocket Books.

Franzosi, Roberto. 1989. 'Strike Data in Search of a Theory: The Italian Case in the Post War Period,' *Politics and Society*, 17, No. 4.

Ganguly, Mira and **Bangendu Ganguly**. 1983–84. 'Marxism and Political Enquiry,' *The Calcutta Journal of Political Studies*, Vol. 4, Nos. 1–2.

Griffin, T. 1984. 'Technological Change and Craft Control in the Newspaper Industry: An International Comparison,' *Cambridge Journal of Economics*, Vol. 8, No. 1: 41–62.

Gill, Colin. 1985. *Work, Unemployment and the New Technology*. Cambridge: Polity Press.

Goodrich, Carter L. 1975. *The Frontier of Control*. London: Pluto Press (reprint).

Gorz, A. (ed.). 1976. *Division of Labour—The Labour Process and Class Struggle in Modern Capitalism*. New York: Harvester Press.

Gouldner, Alvin W. 1976. *The Dialectic of Ideology and Technology—The Origins, Grammar and Future of Ideology*. London: MacMillan.

Grieco, Joseph M. 1984. *Between Dependency and Autonomy—India's Experience with the International Computer Industry*. Berkeley: University of California Press.

Hirst, Paul and **Jonathan Zeitlin**. 1991. 'Flexible Specialisation Versus Post Fordism: Theory, Evidence and Policy Implications,' *Economy and Society*, Vol. 2, No. 1, February.

Hyman, R. 1973. 'Workers, Management and Strikes,' in David Wein (ed.), *Men and Work in Modern Britain*. London: Fontana.

—————. 1978. 'Occupational Structure, Collective Organization and Industrial Militancy,' in Colin Crouch and Allessandro Pizzorn (eds.), *Resurgence of Class Conflict in Western Europe since 1968*, Vol. 2. London: Macmillan.

Hyman, R., and **W. Streeck** (eds.). 1988. *New Technology and Industrial Relations*. Oxford: Basil Blackwell.

Islam, Iyanatul. 1989. 'Industrial Restructuring and Industrial Relations in ASEAN: A Firm Level Chronicle,' in Gus Edgren (ed.), *Restructuring, Employment and Industrial Relations—Adjustment Issues in Asian Countries*. Geneva: ILO.

Jacobi, Oho (ed.). 1986. *Technological Change, Rationalization and Industrial Relations*. New York: St. Martin's Press.

Kapur, K.L. 1986. *Pitfalls of Automation*. Silver Jubilee Conference Brochure, Calcutta.

Katz, Barbara Goody and **Almarin Phillips**. 1982. 'The Computer Industry,' in Richard Nelson (ed.), *Government and Technical Progress—A Cross Industry Analysis*. New York: Pergamon Press.

Kerr, Clark. 1977. *Labor Markets and Wage Determination*. Berkeley: University of California Press.

Kinter and Sicherman. 1975. *Technology and International Politics*. Massachusetts: Lexington Books.

Kluger, Richard. 1986. *The Paper: The Life and Death of the New York Herald Tribune*. New York: Alfred A. Knopf.

Lauridsen, Laurids. 1991. 'New Technologies, Flexibilization and Changing Capital–Labour Relations—The East Asian NICS; with special reference to Taiwan and South Korea,' unpublished paper presented at the Workshop on Aspects of Adoption of Microelectronics-based Technologies in India, Calcutta.

Lipset, Seymour Martin, M. Trow and J. Coleman. 1956. *Union Democracy: The Internal Politics of the International Typographical Union*. Glencoe: Free Press.

Mallett, Serge. 1975. *The New Working Class*. Nottingham: Spokesman Books.

Mamkoottam, Kuriakose. 1982. *Trade Unionism: Myth and Reality—Unionism in the Tata Iron and Steel Company*. Delhi: Oxford University Press.

Manwarning, T. 1981. 'The Trade Union Response to New Technology,' *Industrial Relations Journal*.

Marglin, Stephen. 1974. 'What Do Bosses Do? The Origins and Function of Hierarchy in Capitalist Production,' *Review of Radical Political Economics*, Vol. 6, Summer 1974 and Spring 1975.

Marx, Karl. 1976. *Capital*. Vol. 1. Harmondsworth: Penguin.

—————. 1987. *Economic Manuscripts of 1857–58, Marx–Engels Collected Works*, Vol. 29. Moscow: Progress Publishers.

McGregor, Douglas. 1960. *The Human Side of Enterprise*. New York: McGraw Hill.

Michels, Robert. 1962. *Political Parties*. New York: Free Press.

Mill, John Stuart. 1909. *Principles of Political Economy*. London: Longmans.

Mitchell, Daniel. 1972. 'Union Wage Policies: The Ross–Dunlop Debate Reopened,' *Industrial Relations*, Vol. 11, February.

—————. 1980. *Unions, Wages and Inflation*. Washington: Brookings Institution.

Montgomery, David. 1979. *Workers' Control in America—Studies in the History of Work, Technology and Labor Struggles*. New York: Cambridge University Press.

Mukhopadhyay, Vivekananda. 1984. 'Sangbadpatra, Byakti Swadhinata O Ganatantra,' in Rathin Chakraborty (ed.), *Gana Andolan O Sangbadpatra*. Calcutta: Lokmat Prakashani.

Mumford, E. 1973. Computer Programmers and System Analysts,' in David Weir (ed.), *Men and Work in Modern Britain*. London: Fontana.

Nair, A.V.G. 1984. *The Significance of the Settlement on the Use of Computers in the Banking Industry*. Cochin: AIBEA.

Nari, A.V. 1984. *The Revolutionary Significance of the Settlement on the Use of Computers in the Banking Industry*. Cochin: AIBEA.

National Confederation of Newspapers and News Agency Employees' Organizations (NCNNAEO). 1983. *Modernization in Newspapers—A Critical Study*. New Delhi: NCNNAEO.

Nelson, Richard (ed.). 1982. *Government and Technical Progress: A Cross Industry Analysis*. New York: Pergamon Press.

Nichols, Theo and Hue Beynon. 1977. *Living with Capitalism: Class Relations and the Modern Factory*. London: Routledge and Kegan Paul.

Noble, David F. 1977. *America by Design—Science, Technology and the Rise of Corporate Capitalism*. New York; Alfred Knopf.
—————. 1984. *Forces of Production—A Social History of Industrial Automation*. New York: Alfred Knopf.
Ostrovsky, N. 1977. *Holography and its Applications*. Moscow: Mir Publishers.
Phadnis, Madan. 1986. *Declaration of the All India Newspaper Employees Federation*. Silver Jubilee Conference Brochure, Calcutta: AINEF.
Pigou, A.C. 1933. *The Economics of Welfare*. London: Macmillan.
Piore, Michael J. and **Charles Sabel.** 1984. *The Second Industrial Divide—Possibilities for Prosperity*. New York: Basic Books.
Portes, Alejandro and **John Walton.** 1981. *Labour, Class and the International System*. New York: Academic Press.
Punekar, S.D. and **R. Varickayil** (eds.). 1990. *Labour Movement in India, Documents: 1891–1917*. New Delhi: ICHR.
Rada, Juan. 1980. *The Impact of Micro-electronics—a Tentative Appraisal of Information Technology*. Geneva: ILO.
Ramaswamy, E.A. 1984. *Power and Justice—The State in Industrial Relations*. Delhi: Oxford University Press.
Regalia, Ida. 1986. 'Centralisation or Decentralisation? An Analysis of Organisational Changes in the Italian Trade Union Movement at a Time of Crisis, in Oho Jacobi (ed.), *Technological Change, Rationalisation and Industrial Relations*. New York: St Martin's Press.
Research Institute for Newspaper Development. 1980–89. *RIND Survey*. Madras.
Rodgers, Gerry. 1986. 'Labour Markets, Labour Processes and Economic Development,' *Labour and Society*, Vol. 11, No. 2, May.
—————. 1990. *Labour Institutions and Economic Development*. Discussion Paper No. 41/1991. Geneva: International Institute for Labour Studies.
Ross, Arthur. 1960. 'What is Responsible Wage Policy?' in E. Wright Bakke, Clark Kerr and Charles Arnod (eds.), *Unions, Management and the Public*. New York: Harcourt Brace.
—————. 1968. 'The Trade Union as a Wage Fixing Institution,' in Richard Lester (ed.). *Labour: Readings on Major Issues*. New York: Random House.
Rowan, Richard. (ed.). 1973. *Collective Bargaining: Survival in the 1970s*. Philadelphia: University of Pennsylvania.
Rueschemeyer, Dietrich. 1983. 'Professional Autonomy and the Social Control of Experts,' in R. Dingwall and P.H. Lewis (eds.), *The Sociology of the Professions*. London: Macmillan.
—————. 1986. *Power and the Division of Labour*. Cambridge: Polity Press.
Sammadar, R. 1990. *New Technology in Indian Newspaper Industry*, Occasional Paper No. 121, Calcutta: Centre for Studies in Social Sciences.
Schreiber, Jean-Louis Seivan. 1974. *The Power to Inform—Media: The Information Business*. New York: McGraw Hill.
Segal, William and **Peter Philips.** 1988. 'Production Process Work Organisation and Labour Relations in the Post-War California Food Processing Industry,' *Review of Radical Political Economics*, Vol. 20, Nos. 2 and 3, Summer and Fall.
Simon, Herbert. 1957. 'Authority,' in Conrad Arensberg, et al. (eds.), *Research in Industrial Human Relations*. New York: Harper.

Smith, Anthony. 1980. *Goodbye Gutenberg*. Oxford: Oxford University Press.

Southall Roger (ed.). 1988. *Trade Unions and the New Industrialisation of the Third World*. London: Zed.

Statesman Employees' Union. 1982. *A Working Paper on the Press Tycoons: The Modernizing Onslaught on Newspaper Employees*. Calcutta.

Stryker, Robin. 1990. 'A Tale of Two Agencies: Class, Political, Institutional and Organizational Factors Affecting State Reliance on Social Science,' *Politics and Society*, Vol. 18, No. 1.

Thompson, P. 1983. *The Nature of Work: An Introduction to Debates on the Labour Process*. London: Macmillan.

Timashkova, O.K. 1981. *Scandanavian Social Democracy Today*. Moscow: Progress Publishers.

Toffler, Alvin. 1980. *The Third Wave*. Toronto: Bantam Books.

Touraine, Alan. 1965. *Workers' Attitude to Technical Change*. Paris: OECD.

Williams, Herbert Lee. 1978. *Newspaper Organization and Management*. Iowa: Iowa State University Press.

Wootton, Barbara. 1955. *The Social Foundations of Wage Policy*. London: Allen and Unwin.

Wortman, Max S. Jr. (ed.). 1970. *Critical Issues in Labor*. London: Collier Max Millan.

Wright, Erik Olin and Joachin Singlemann. 1982. 'Proletarianization in the Changing American Class Structure,' in Michael Burawoy and Theda Skocpol (eds.), *Marxist Inquiries: Studies of Labor, Class and States*, Chicago: Chicago University Press.

Zeitlin, Jonathan. 1973. 'Craft Control and the Division of Labour: Engineers and Compositors in Britain, 1890–1930,' *Cambridge Journal of Economics*, 1973; 263–74.

—————. 1990. 'The Triumph of Adversarial Bargaining: Industrial Relations in British Engineering, 1880–1939,' *Politics and Society*, Vol. 18, No. 3.

Zimbalist, Andres (ed.). 1979. *Case Studies on the Labor Process*. New York: Monthly Review Press.

REPORTS

Additional Material, Fresh Material, and New Material as Submissions to Wage Board, 3 vols., 1987.

Affidavit Filed by S.G. Franswah before the Supreme Court on Administration, Accounts etc., in Andhra Prabha Pvt. Ltd., Hyderabad, 1990.

Chart on New and Old Systems of Work in the Newspaper Industry and the Required Work-Force, Submitted to Wage Board, 1988.

Circulars of All India Newspaper Employees' Federation, 1981–90.

Dilsukh Ram Committee Report on Job Description, Evaluation, Upgradation, etc., Submitted to Bachawat Wage Board, 1989.

Indian Newspaper Society Submissions to Wage Board, Vol. 2, 1985.

Memorandum on Advantages and Disadvantages of New Technology Submitted to Wage Board, 1987.

Memorandum of Settlement in Ananda Bazar Patrika, Ltd., 1989.

Memorandum of Settlement in Times of India, Bombay, 1989.

Memorandum of Settlement in Printers (Mysore) Ltd., 1990.

Note on Clubbing of Establishments for the Purpose of Wage Fixation Submitted to Wage Board, 1988.

Palekar Tribunals Recommendations for Working Journalists and Non-Journalist Newspaper Employees, 1980.

Questionnaire Sent by Expert Committee for Newspaper Employees, 1990.

Reply to Supplementary Memorandum of INS to Wage Board, 1986.

Report of the All India Federation of Master Printers, 1983.

Report of the Conference of National Confederation of Newspaper and News Agency Employees Organisations, Nagpur, 1985.

Report of the Expert Group on Pension Scheme for Journalists as Well as Non-Journalist Employees of the Newspaper Establishments, (1989).

Report of the Fact Finding Committee on Newspaper Economics, 1975.

Second Press Commission Report, 1981.

Submissions of All India Newspaper Employees Federation Before the Bachawat Wage Board, Vols. I–III, 1986–87.

Supplementary Memoranda in Reply to Wage Board Questionnaire, Vols. I–II, n.d.

Surrejoinder in Reply to Employers' Memoranda to Wage Board, Vols. I–II, 1986.

Index

Tarun Bharat, 20
Tata Press, 69
tax planning, 67–68
technology, new, agreements, 194, 195; labour process and wage settlement, 159–67; and power at work place, 238–41
telecommunication development, 58. 59
Telegraph, 45, 73
Thantri Trust, 78
Thompson Press, 68, 71
Tilak, 12
Time, 73
Times, London, 37, 202
Times of India, 22, 25, 67, 112, 171; new technology and deunionisation in, 233; selling price of, 136; strike in, 14, 235–36; takeover by Dalmia–Jain group, 83–84
Times of India and Allied Publications Employees Unionisation, 234–36
Tiwari, N.D., 146
Toffler, Alvin, 58, 61
Touraine, Alan, 153
trade unions, 108, 109, 114–15, 138, 139, 191, 231–32; in Bombay, 12; movements, 129–30; wage boards and, 104
Trade Unions of Graphics Industry, 242
Trade Unions of the Graphics (Printing) Industry in Asian and Oceanic Countries, 19
Trow, N., 16, 114

uniform scale, of wages, 140–41
United States, 58
urbanisation, and magazine boom, 71
Uttar Banga Sambad, labour relations in, 103–104

valorisation process, 161, 164, 168, 187, 248
Vernacular press, 69, 70, 75, 88
Vietnam War, 57
visual display terminal (VDT), 36, 39–42, 46, 61, 155–56, 170, 222
Vivian Leigh Commission Report, 83, 84

wage, agreements, in non-newspaper industry, 97–99; boards, 114, 178; determination and related issues, 116–25, 139; employment tradeoff, 192–93; revision issue, 12, 68, 90, 105, 111, 124, 138, 141, 147, 156, 190; settlements, 90ff., 159–60, 166, 231, 232
Watergate scandal, 55, 57
West Bengal newspaper employees, 194
West Bengal Newspaper Employees' Federation (WBNEF), 20, 204, 210
wire services, 40
Wootton, Barbara, 130
word processing, 39–40
work (working), flow, 34–42; conditions, 181; hazards, 218; satisfaction, 173, 227, 228, 239, 240
Working Journalists Act, 21, 131
Working Journalists and Other Newspaper Employees (Conditions of Service) and Miscellaneous Provision Act, 1955, 178
Working Paper, 207; of *Statesman*, 172

Xerox Corporation, 54, 59

Yugadharma, 20

Zeitlin, Jonathan, 197